SCIENCE AS SOCIAL KNOWLEDGE

Science as Social Knowledge

*Values and Objectivity in
Scientific Inquiry*

HELEN E. LONGINO

PRINCETON UNIVERSITY PRESS
PRINCETON, NEW JERSEY

Library of Congress Cataloging-in-Publication Data

Longino, Helen E.
Science as social knowledge : values and objectivity in
scientific inquiry / Helen E. Longino.
p.   cm.
Bibliography: p.
Includes index.
ISBN 0-691-07342-2 (alk. paper)
ISBN 0-691-02051-5 (pbk.)
1. Philosophy—Methodology.   2. Science—Methodology.
3. Women's studies—Methodology.   I. Title.
HM24.L79   1990
301'.01—dc20   89-34623

This book has been composed in Linotron Sabon

Princeton University Press books are printed on
acid-free paper, and meet the guidelines for permanence
and durability of the Committee on
Production Guidelines for Book Longevity of the
Council on Library Resources

Printed in the United States of America by
Princeton University Press,
Princeton, New Jersey

10 9 8 7 6 5 4 3 2 1
(Pbk.) 10 9 8 7 6 5 4 3 2 1

This book is dedicated to
my mother
Helen O'Brien Longino
and to the memory of
my father
James Charles Longino, Jr.

CONTENTS

THIS book provides an account of scientific inquiry within which to make sense of scientific debates that have social and normative dimensions. I was first moved to undertake the project by the critiques of science and of particular scientific research projects that feminists in the sciences began to develop in the late 1970s. I began the book in frustration and with conviction—frustration that traditional philosophy of science had so little to say about the relation between social values and scientific inquiry and conviction that philosophical analysis was an invaluable tool for understanding that relation. Initially I conceived the volume as a philosophical critique of the idea of a value-free science. In the course of writing it and discussing its contents with friends and colleagues my ambitions changed quite radically. In particular, I abandoned a negative goal—rejecting the idea of value-free science—for a positive one—developing an analysis of scientific knowledge that reconciles the objectivity of science with its social and cultural construction. If no project of political transformation in the twentieth century can do without science, then neither can we do without a better philosophical understanding of scientific inquiry than is currently available.

As the book has been long in the making, so there are many individuals and institutions to thank for their assistance along the way. John Dupre, Anne Fausto-Sterling, Evelyn Fox Keller, and Elisabeth Lloyd read through the penultimate draft of the manuscript and made numerous invaluable suggestions for revisions. Many other friends and colleagues read portions of the book in earlier versions or discussed some of the ideas with me. They, of course, cannot be held responsible for any remaining errors or other infelicities. I have benefited particularly from conversations or correspondence with Nancy Cartwright, Jane Martin, Peter Taylor, Donna Haraway, Paul Schulman, Marjorie Grene, Gail Hornstein, Sharon Traweek, Catharine Stimpson, Merriley Borrell, Barbara Rosenblum, Sylvan Schweber, Joan Straumanis, Richard Grandy, Elizabeth Potter, Eric Holtzman, Diane Paul, Richard Lewontin, Evelyn Hammonds, Jane Braaten, Michèle Farrell, Marc Breedlove, Leon Wofsy, Nancy Hartsock, Sandra Harding, Kathryn Addelson, and Caroline Whitbeck. I am also grateful to my students Joanne Stewart, Yaakov Garb, Christine Halverson, Shannon Parrish, and Irene Rocca for their careful reading and helpful comments. The book is the better for the advice of all these people.

I am fortunate in having had excellent technical assistance. Eda Regan of the Mills College Library kept me informed of relevant periodical literature as it arrived and guided me patiently through several computer data base searches. Shannon Parrish turned my rough drawings for the figures in Chapter Seven into elegant products of computer graphics programs. Crissi Leibenson deserves special thanks for her help in typing the bibliography. Finally, I am grateful for Catherine Thatcher's skillful and thorough editing of the manuscript.

Several grants gave me the time to do the research for the book. An Interdisciplinary Incentive Award from the Ethics and Values in Science and Technology Program at the National Science Foundation (Grant No. OSS 8018095) gave me the opportunity to work with biologist Ruth Doell at San Francisco State University in 1981/1982 and to begin the project. Several years later a grant from the foundation's Visiting Professorships for Women Program (Grant No. RII 8504061) enabled me to spend the 1984/1985 academic year at the University of California at Berkeley doing the research for Chapters Seven and Chapter Eight. I was fortunate in being able to spend the Fall semester of 1984 at the Wellesley Center for Research on Women under the auspices of a grant to the center from the Mellon Foundation. Participation in the Mellon Seminar organized by Peggy McIntosh stimulated my thinking about the idea of a feminist science. The Mellon Foundation's grant for faculty development to Mills College enabled me to reduce my teaching load in the Fall of 1983 and thus to keep working on the project. The views expressed here are mine alone and do not necessarily reflect the views either of the National Science Foundation or the Mellon Foundation.

There are a number of people without whom this book would never have been begun, let alone completed. My mother and sisters have given me steadfast support and encouragement over the years. Bill Wilson offered compassionate wisdom. Ruth Doell was a generous tutor in biology. Together we embarked on a stimulating collaboration that continues to be fruitful. I am grateful for her friendship and instruction. Elizabeth V. Spelman read portions of the book at different stages and made many useful suggestions. More important is the friendship that is nurtured by doing philosophy together. Finally, Valerie Miner's sense of style and intolerance for long sentences made these chapters more readable. Her critical intelligence and wit sustained me through many drafts of the book.

SOME of the chapters are based on previously published materials. Portions of Chapter Two and Chapter Three were first published as "Evidence and Hypothesis," in *Philosophy of Science* 46, no. 1 (March 1979):35-56. Portions of Chapter Two and Chapter Four were first published as "Scientific Objectivity and the Logics of Scientific Inquiry," in *Inquiry: Interdisciplinary Journal of Philosophy and Social Science* 26 (March 1983):85-106. Portions of Chapter Five were published as "Beyond 'Bad Science': Skeptical Reflections on the Value Freedom of Scientific Inquiry," in *Science, Technology, and Human Values* 8, no. 1 (Winter 1983):7-17. Portions of Chapter Six are based on "Body, Bias and Behavior: A Comparative Analysis of Reasoning in Two Areas of Biological Science," written with Ruth Doell and published in *Signs: Journal of Women in Culture and Society* 9, no. 2 (Winter 1983):206-227. The first part of Chapter Nine is drawn from "Can There Be a Feminist Science?" published in *Hypatia: Journal of Feminist Philosophy* 2, no. 3 (Fall 1987):51-64. I am grateful to the editors of the journals for permission to use this material. I am, in addition, grateful to MIT Press for permission to use Figure 11 from Gerald Edelman and Vernon Mountcastle, *The Mindful Brain* (Cambridge, MA: Mit Press, 1978) p. 75, which appears as Figure 5 in Chapter Seven.

SCIENCE AS SOCIAL KNOWLEDGE

CHAPTER ONE

Introduction: Good Science, Bad Science

How do we judge the claims of science? The news media regularly report the latest hot item from the scientific journals. Scientific ideas and their proponents seem to command belief simply through the newsworthiness accorded them. Others, however, with less access to "the public mind," caution against any temptation to accept uncritically the pronouncements from the lab (or its public relations office). While these critics do not speak as one, recent academic commentary from various vantage points has highlighted the role of social and political interests in the making of scientific knowledge. Historians and social scientists have increasingly directed attention to so-called external factors in the development of knowledge. Their investigations include historical studies of the relation between theory and ideology—for example, Darwinian evolutionary theory and nineteenth-century capitalism, nineteenth-century craniometry and racism and sexism, and sociological studies detailing the connections between research and the interests of those conducting or supporting the research and of the role of science in policy making. Activists charge that political bias has shaped certain contemporary research programs—from studies affirming a genetic basis for group differences in intelligence to the prevalence of various forms of reductionism in the life sciences. How should these demonstrations and allegations of the interaction of science and social values affect our conception of scientific knowledge?

The links that historians, social scientists, and scientists themselves have demonstrated between the study of nature on the one hand and social values and ideology on the other raise pressing questions about such traditional philosophical topics as rationality, objectivity, and the nature of knowledge. The new awareness, however, of the relations between science and society has not yet had much impact in the philosophy of science. This book is an attempt to rectify this neglect by developing an account of scientific reasoning and knowledge that enables us to make sense of scientific debates that involve social ideology and values as well as the more stereotypically scientific issues of evidence and logic. My aim is to show *how* social values play a role in scientific research by analyzing aspects of scientific reasoning. I propose to do this by engaging in a philosophical analysis of certain features of evidential relations and by applying that analysis to certain areas of contemporary scientific research. In this chapter I shall map some of the debates within which this project is located.

CONSTITUTIVE AND CONTEXTUAL VALUES

It is, of course, nonsense to assert the value-freedom of natural science. Scientific practice is governed by norms and values generated from an understanding of the goals of scientific inquiry. If we take the goal of scientific activity to be the production of explanations of the natural world, then these governing values and constraints are generated from an understanding of what counts as a good explanation, for example, the satisfaction of such criteria as truth, accuracy, simplicity, predictability, and breadth. These criteria are not always equally satisfiable and, as I shall suggest, are appropriate to different conceptions of what counts as a good explanation. Nevertheless, they clearly constitute values by which to judge competing explanations and from which norms and constraints governing scientific practice in particular fields (for example, the requirement for repeatability of experiments) can be generated.

Independence from these sorts of values, of course, is not what is meant by those debating the value freedom of science. The question is, rather, the extent to which science is free of personal, social, and cultural values, that is, independent of group or individual subjective preferences regarding what ought to be (or regarding what, among the things that are, is best). For the sake of clarity I will call the values generated from an understanding of the goals of science *constitutive* values to indicate that they are the source of the rules determining what constitutes acceptable scientific practice or scientific method. The personal, social, and cultural values, those group or individual preferences about what ought to be, I will call *contextual* values to indicate that they belong to the social and cultural environment in which science is done.[1] The traditional interpretation of the value freedom of modern natural science amounts to a claim that its constitutive and contextual features are clearly distinct from and independent of one another. Can this distinction, as commonly conceived, be maintained?

The issue of the independence of science and values (or constitutive and contextual values) can be reformulated as two questions. One question concerns the relevance of scientific theories (and methods) to contextual values: To what extent do or should scientific theories

---

[1] I introduce this distinction in Longino (1983).

shape moral and social values? The other concerns the impact of contextual values upon scientific theories and methods: To what extent do social and moral values shape scientific theories? The first, then, has to do with the autonomy of questions of personal, social, and cultural values from the revelations, discoveries, and inventions of scientific inquiry. Does, for instance, the assertion that a certain form of behavior (for example, aggressive war) is an adaptation, sculpted into human nature by the chisel of natural selection, have any relevance to ethical judgments? This question and its cognates have been much discussed in the contemporary uproar about sociobiology. I shall pursue the question of the relevance of scientific theory to moral and political values as a consequence, instead, of the second question. This question concerns the autonomy of the content and practices of the sciences from personal, social, and cultural preferences regarding what ought to be and what, among the things that are, is best. I will argue not only that scientific practices and content on the one hand and social needs and values on the other are in dynamic interaction but that the logical and cognitive structures of scientific inquiry require such interaction.

When we ask whether the content of science is free from contextual values we are asking about the integrity and autonomy of scientific inquiry. These concepts can be understood both morally and logically or epistemologically. Thus scientists sometimes become defensive when asked to comment on the relation between science and values because they think their moral integrity is being challenged. Or they dismiss cases of value influence as "bad" science, practiced only by the corrupt or inept. But what does the attribution of epistemological integrity and autonomy to scientific inquiry mean in the first place?

Autonomy and integrity are separable attributes, and I shall consider them in sequence. In its most extreme form the attribution of *autonomy* is a claim that scientific inquiry proceeds undisturbed and unaffected by the values and interests of its social and cultural context, that it is propelled instead by its own internally generated momentum. In one sense this seems clearly false.

The dependence of most current science on corporate and/or government funding makes the conduct of science highly vulnerable to its funding sources. The questions to which the methods of scientific inquiry will be applied are at least partly a function of the values of its supporting context. That the questions also bear a logical relationship to prior research does not rule out their social determination. Consider, for instance, the commercialization of genetic engineering. The techniques of isolating and recombining selected bits of DNA molecules to effect the production of desired substances depend critically on the discovery of the structure of the DNA molecule in the 1950s and on the work that has been done since correlating segments of that molecule with phenotypic expressions of genetic information. There is a great deal of concern now that the commercial possibilities involved in the bacterial production of antibodies, growth and other hormones, et cetera, will incline biomedical research even further toward the search for cures of disease and away from the search for understanding of the causes of disease. This provides a simple and clear example of the interaction of internal and external factors in the development of inquiry. Studies of funding patterns and research pursued in other areas of inquiry reveal similar interactions.

This kind of palpable influence exerted by the social and cultural context on the directions of scientific development has led many observer-critics of science to reject the value freedom of science. Defenders of the idea that science is value-free can argue, however, that cases such as these show that science is not autonomous in the extreme sense but can also point out that the alleged science/value interactions are superficial ones. These sorts of considerations, the defender might continue, go nowhere towards showing that the internal, real practice of science is affected by contextual values. The thesis that the internal practices of science—observation and experiment, theory construction, inference—are not influenced by contextual values is what I call the thesis of the *integrity* of science. Contemporary criticisms of research in the biology of behavior and cognition pose a more severe challenge to the thesis of integrity, for they address not just how the context influences the questions thought worth asking but the answers given to those questions.

Societies in which one race or sex (or one race-sex combination, for example, white males) is dominant generally distribute their resources disproportionately, the greater share of benefits going to the dominant group. This distribution is usually justified on the basis of presumed inherent differences between the dominant and subordinated groups. Aristotle told us how women and slaves were inferior to free-born Athenian males. George Gilder and Michael Levin tell us how women are unsuited to the rigors of public life. Theories about the genetic basis of racial differences in I.Q. test performance and theories about the hormonal basis of gender differences are not propounded and contested in a vacuum. They are debated in a context informed about social inequality but divided about its nature and legitimacy.

To the extent that research on the biological basis of various socially significant differences is taken seriously as science, it is presumed to offer accurate and "unbiased" descriptions of what is the case—descriptions or theories that are not themselves in any part a product of cultural values or assumptions. This is what the thesis of the integrity of science claims and what the critics of this research deny. An account of evidence and reasoning in science ought, among other things, to give us a standard by which we can ascertain the degree to which these currently contested theories of cognition and behavior are or could be developed and supported independently of cultural values. This demand, it seems to me, encompasses two of the most pressing questions a contemporary methodologist of science must address—the questions of whether and to what extent a value-free or autonomous science is methodologically possible. These questions challenge traditional conceptions of rationality and objectivity. Answers to these questions would help us to assess the real relevance to cultural ideals and social policy of research with apparent social consequences. They would also prompt us to reexamine the ideas of "good science" and "bad science" and the assumption that value-laden or ideologically informed science is always bad science.

Debates about Science and Social Values

While most philosophers of science have ignored these questions, other theorists have either explicitly or by implication filled the void left by our silence. Several positions on the relation between science and values can be distinguished. One approach argues that to the extent that contextual values can be shown to influence reasoning, they are shown to have produced bad reasoning. This is the approach most scientists seem, by implication, to favor and to which many philosophers are committed in virtue of their analyses of reasoning and validation in the sciences. Another approach, the social constructionist tendency in sociology and history of science, argues that the processes by which scientific knowledge is built are social and hence ideological and interest-laden. A third, characteristic of many scientists who oppose some particular theory such as human sociobiology because of its social implications, tries to have it both ways. These critics state that science is value-laden and inevitably reflects the values of scientists and their society. Simultaneously they wish to claim that some specific (objectionable) scientific claim is also incorrect. To set my own inquiry in perspective, I shall briefly sketch out these approaches.

A recent article by Robert Richardson exemplifies the first form of response.[2] Richardson is sympathetic to the criticisms of science as

[2] Richardson (1984).

value-laden and attempts, in his article, to articulate the proper role of "ideology critique" in the sciences. He is one of the very few philosophers of science to have addressed these questions and to have brought them to the attention of the professional philosophical community. While his attention is a welcome exception to the rule, ironically the particular analysis he develops ultimately supports the view that social values are associated with bad science.[3]

The specific target of Richardson's argument is the supposition that demonstrating the ideological bias of a scientific explanation is sufficient reason to reject it. Some of the early rejections of human sociobiology as racist and sexist are examples of this supposition in practice. Richardson argues instead that to reject a theory or hypothesis one must show that it is false or not warranted. Showing that it is ideologically incorrect is not sufficient. To make his point he reviews a number of cases—some notorious, others less so—in which racist, individualist, or sexist ideology plays a role. In each instance he elegantly demonstrates that the offending hypotheses are inadequately warranted. The role of ideology in these cases is to blind the proponents of the hypotheses to the fact that their warrants are inadequate. The role of ideology critique is to explain why their proponents cling to inadequately warranted hypotheses. Thus, Richardson seems to be saying that, properly followed, the methods of inquiry sanctioned by the constitutive values of science weed out the influence of subjective preferences. This thesis can be called the thesis of the integrity of science.

One striking feature of Richardson's examples is that the hypotheses in question are unwarranted with respect to the field or discipline or theory within which they are propounded: they violate or ignore methodological constraints accepted by workers in the field, including the individuals whose work he is criticizing. For instance, claims by the sociobiologists Richard Dawkins and John Maynard Smith that phenomena such as certain forms of sexual or parental behavior or the apparent self-limitations on animal violence represent adaptations or "evolutionarily stable strategies" fail to demonstrate that there was variation from which the alleged adaptation could have been selected. But a trait is an adaptation or "evolutionarily stable strategy" only if there was such variation. The analyses of the particular cases are compelling for each case, but Richardson seems to assume that all cases will be like the ones he discusses. His analysis will not, however, apply

---

[3] Richardson does distinguish between value-laden and value-loaded science and states that all science is value-laden. He does not, however, explain what value-laden science might be in distinction from value-loaded science. Thus, his analysis invites being indiscriminately applied to all cases of contextual values in the sciences.

to those cases where the warrants themselves—that is, the methodological procedures or framing assumptions accepted within a field—are ideologically driven or value-laden. Moreover, the implication of Richardson's essay is that "ideology critique" has no role to play in discussions of "good science." But the scientist who is trying to do different science and to escape the ideology perceived in her or his field wishes to dissect its role in theories, not in order to show them wrong but to find the places where an alternative set of values might yield a different set of hypotheses. Richardson is persuasive about the particular examples he analyzes but does not support the claim that all cases of ideologically laden science are analogous to those.

The social constructionist approach urges us to abandon our obsession with truth and representation. The phrase "social constructionist" is used to refer to analytic programs in history and sociology of science that take scientific theories and hypotheses to be products of their political, economic, and cultural milieu. These programs employ a wide range of epistemological views, but their proponents are unanimous in rejecting the idea that science is objective or that it gives us an unbiased view of the real world. Social constructionism comes in two forms. The more modest form of the social constructionist thesis holds only that social interests influence the choice of research areas and problems. This is consistent with Richardson's view of the relation of science and values. Thus, defenders of the value neutrality of science can respond to the modest form of the thesis by pointing out that while such examples as the influence of governmental funding and commercial applicability on research show that science is not autonomous they do not have a bearing on the thesis of the integrity of science. Such defenders can invoke the distinction between discovery and justification and argue that as long as values are shown only to influence the discovery process, they have not been shown to undermine claims to objectivity in the justification process. And if values have influenced individuals' justification procedures, then so much the worse for those individuals. The objectivity of science, conceived as a set of rules and procedures for distinguishing true from false accounts of nature, is not undermined by arguments establishing modest forms of social constructionism.

The so-called "strong program in sociology of science" associated with the University of Edinburgh scholars Barry Barnes and David Bloor holds that social interests are more deeply involved in scientific practice.[4] The strong program questions not merely the autonomy but

---

[4] See, for example, the essays in Hubbard and Lowe, eds. (1979); Hubbard, Henifin, and Fried, eds. (1979); Ann Arbor Science for the People Collective (1977).

the epistemological integrity of science. Barnes and Bloor have argued that social interests determine the *acceptance* of hypotheses in the sciences. They argue (1) that there is no transcendent or context independent criterion of rational justification that renders some beliefs (hypotheses) more credible than others and (2) that the explanation why a given set of beliefs is found in a given context depends on features of the context and not on intrinsic properties of the beliefs. Bloor extends Durkheim's thesis that "the classification of things reproduces the classification of men" to the sciences. Other social constructionists argue similarly that all outcomes in the sciences are negotiated and that social interests are involved in the negotiation of technical outcomes, such as the description of experimental results, as much as of political outcomes, such as who will head a research group.[5]

Feminist scholars, too, have rejected the idea of the value neutrality of the sciences. Donna Haraway, in a series of studies of twentieth-century primatology, has concentrated on the ways socio-political-economic ideology constructs the subject matter of that discipline. She shows how the basic concepts and forms of knowledge are subtly transformed in response to changing political agenda. For Haraway science is a series of political discourses and must be read as such. Scientist turned historian Evelyn Fox Keller has argued that the language of mainstream science is permeated by an ideology of domination created in the very processes of personal psychological development and individuation characteristic of modern European and North American societies.[6]

Proponents of the integrity of science thesis can respond to the strong form of the social constructionist program in either of two ways, depending on what kind of argument is used. To the extent that the argument rests on case histories, they can respond (1) that it fails to show that all science is interest-shaped or value-laden and (2) that the cases on which it rests are instances of "bad science," just the sort of thing that scientific methods, properly followed, are designed to eliminate. To the extent that the argument rests on philosophical arguments, it is only as strong as those arguments. For example, many social constructionists cite Kuhn's *Structure of Scientific Revolutions* as the philosophical basis of their work.[7] Kuhn's views, however, have been subjected to searching philosophical criticism. In neither case does the demonstration of social influence require the proponents of value-free science to alter their views.

[5] Haraway (1981).
[6] Barnes and Bloor (1982); Bloor (1982); and Barnes and Edge, eds. (1982).
[7] See, for example, Knorr-Cetina and Mulkay, eds. (1983), pp. 1–18.

Finally, some critiques of research programs with racist or sexist implications seem to combine the assumptions of a Richardsonian and a social constructionist approach.[8] They argue that racist or sexist research is the inevitable product of a scientific community that excludes women of any background and members, male and female, of certain ethnic or racial groups. Citing Kuhn, they argue that all observation is theory-laden and that, hence, the observations of a racist or sexist scientific community will be laden with racism and sexism. At the same time these critics tackle particular research programs, such as the I.Q. research or human sociobiology, and show that these programs are methodologically flawed. Politically and polemically this approach can seem attractive as it suggests that if we want good—that is, methodologically respectable—research, we should put an end to exclusionary practices in science education and hiring. To eliminate the bad science more quickly, we should even engage in affirmative action to change the racial and sexual composition of the scientific work force.

Philosophically, however, this attempt to have it both ways is unsatisfactory. As Donna Haraway observed in a review of several collections of essays on sociobiology and hereditarianism, to simultaneously adopt an analysis of observation in science as theory- or paradigm-determined while asserting the incontrovertible existence of any fact is to embrace paradox.[9] Underlying her critique is the idea that if observation is theory-determined, then we can have no confidence that what appears to be a fact in the context of one theory will remain so in the next. Indeed, if sexist and racist science is bad science that ignores the facts or fails to treat them properly, this implies that there is a good or better methodology that will steer us away from biased conclusions. On the other hand, if sexist science is science as usual, then the best methodology in the world will not prevent us from attaining those conclusions unless we change paradigms. Is the scientific critic faced with a choice between critiquing methodologically incompetent science (but saying nothing more general about the relation between science and society) and critiquing science in general (but saying nothing in particular about politically pernicious science)? I will argue that this is a false dilemma. To see that this is so, however, requires a certain amount of philosophical groundwork.

The view that science is a social product is at least as old as Marxism. Marxists argued that the knowledge and culture of a society were ultimately determined by the relations of production. Part of what is at issue here is how to make good on that claim. According to Marx-

---

[8] The work of both Haraway and Keller is discussed in Chapter Nine.
[9] See the introduction to Barnes and Edge, eds. (1982), pp. 1–12.

ists, the knowledge and culture of a class society reflect the interests of its ruling class. A more objective and transformative knowledge can only be found or produced through another perspective—for Marxists, the perspective of wage laborers, or the proletariat. Feminist theorists have given this view a new form.[10] Knowledge in a male dominant society reflects the experience and interests of men. A more objective and transformative knowledge is therefore to be found in the perspective of women. Both forms of standpoint theory share the same weakness. Since neither wage laborers nor women share a common perspective, it becomes necessary to identify a subclass within each of those classes whose perspective does form an appropriate standpoint. However, the theory one is attempting to vindicate by a standpoint methodology is required to identify this subclass, thus making the procedure circular.

Are there criteria or standards of truth and rationality that can be articulated independently of social and political interests? I will argue that there are standards of rational acceptability that are independent of particular interests and values but that satisfaction of these standards by a theory or hypothesis does not guarantee that the theory or hypothesis in question is value- or interest-free. This argument involves a point similar to a different sort of feminist (and Marxist) claim. Feminist theorists have drawn our attention to the pervasiveness of interdependence in human societies—at its most obvious this claim is simply the observation that the public activities of production, commerce, and governance require the material support provided in the domestic realm to those carrying out those public activities. Individuals do not act alone but require others both for the execution and for the significance of their actions. Similarly, I will argue, the development of knowledge is a necessarily social rather than individual activity, and it is the social character of scientific knowledge that both protects it from and renders it vulnerable to social and political interests and values. The argument that develops this thesis is, therefore, simultaneously an account of what it means to say that science is socially constructed.

The Argument Ahead

This book is not an attempt to mediate between conflicting views about the relation between science and values but to explore some of the philosophical questions about scientific inquiry that such views

[10] See Hartsock (1983) and Jaggar (1985) for two different ways of developing feminist standpoint theory.

provoke. The investigation of scientific knowledge that forms the first section of the book aims to clarify the notion of the value freedom of scientific inquiry and to show that the ideal of value neutrality places unrealistic constraints on science as we know it. While my study is based on logical analysis of reasoning and of scientific inquiry, and so escapes the contingency of empirical studies, it is actual reasoning and actual inquiry that is analyzed. Philosophers are notorious for developing rigorous elaborations and analyses of formal models that are never realized in practice. My study does not rely on logical formalism, staying closer, therefore, to the texture of inference in both scientific and nonscientific reasoning.

In Chapter Two I explore some of the consequences of understanding scientific reasoning as a practice rather than as the disembodied application of a set of rules. I also set out my dissatisfactions with the views of scientific reasoning and knowledge that underpin current accounts of the relation between science and contextual values. In the following chapter I argue that evidential reasoning—both everyday and scientific—is context dependent. I resolve some of the resulting puzzles about objectivity in Chapter Four, where I develop an understanding of scientific inquiry as a set of necessarily social rather than individual practices. The result is a picture of scientific inquiry as a group endeavor in which models and theories are adopted/legitimated through critical processes involving the dynamic interplay of observational and experimental data and background assumptions. Since contextually located background assumptions play a role in confirmation as well as in discovery, scientific inquiry is, thus, at least in principle, permeable by values and interests superficially external to it.

Chapters Five through Eight illustrate the ways in which social and cultural values can and do influence the development of scientific knowledge. One significant test of philosophical analyses is the degree of illumination they afford of the (relatively) more concrete phenomena to which they are ultimately referred. The analyses of the first section enable us to understand a variety of the interactions between scientific inquiry and sociocultural values occurring in contemporary science.

Chapter Five develops a typology of ways in which values and interests perceived as external to or different from scientific ones can nevertheless play a significant part in shaping scientific knowledge and practice. I also use some recent scholarship on the development of early modern physics to demonstrate the possibility of convergence of contextual and constitutive values. This is followed by two sets of in-depth comparative studies of research on the biological bases of alleged sex differences in temperament, behavior, and cognition. Because of the potential social effects of research supporting claims that there is such a biological basis, whether genetic or physiological, this is a notoriously charged area. As noted above, it has drawn criticism of a variety of kinds—from dismissal either as prejudiced, or as "bad science," or analysis as the expression of ideology in paradigm-governed science.

While a case for the value ladenness of scientific inquiry might better be made by investigating an area much further removed from political controversy, this study was initially motivated by the desire to make a contribution to understanding this very area. The philosophical analysis of evidence, background assumptions, objectivity, et cetera, enables me to pull this work apart enough to distinguish the different levels at which ideology operates and to distinguish the different kinds of interest that interact with and in the research. One chapter in this series (Chapter Six) focusses on the logical structure and evidential base of several research programs on sex differences. In this chapter I compare the different roles gender ideologies play in structuring evidential relations. A second chapter (Seven) brings out the background assumptions informing much research on the role of fetal hormones in the development of sex-differentiated adult behaviors by a detailed comparison of this work with an alternative research program in neurophysiology. This comparison focusses on the different roles assigned to the brain in behavior. Both of these chapters distinguish different kinds of values and interests that operate in the description and interpretation of data as well as the different levels at which they operate. A third chapter (Eight) explores the relation of this biological research to assumptions underlying certain of our culture's ideals and values. These include not only the gender ideology underlying ideals of personhood but concepts of human agency and responsibility. It concludes by comparing how the different theories of scientific knowledge discussed in earlier chapters of the book would analyze these relations.

The final two chapters return to the consideration of general questions stimulated by the logical analysis and its application in the case studies. In his book *Between Science and Values* historian of science Loren Graham addressed the relevance of twentieth-century scientific theory to human cultural and personal values.[11] He was studying both the ways in which key ideas from relativity theory, quantum theory, ethology, and other fields had shaped thinking in the larger social and cultural contexts of science and the degree to which ideas from those

---

[11] Loren Graham (1981).

theories really do have consequences for traditional values. My study has approached these questions from a different direction, asking how those contexts shape the theories developed within them. The demonstration that general methodological constraints are inadequate to the task of ruling values out of scientific inquiry and that in specific and quite disparate areas of inquiry their role in shaping scientific knowledge can be clearly delineated suggests several questions. To what degree is scientific research an impartial arbiter of questions about human nature and about our relation to the rest of the natural world? What, if any, is the proper role of values in research programs? In Chapter Nine, I suggest an interpretation of feminist science as an example of any politically sensitive science and discuss the views of four other thinkers concerned with the relations between science and politics. Why has the idea of a value-free science persisted? And have any of the values and ideologies shaping scientific knowledge become encoded in the metascientific epistemological debates? The concluding chapter draws out the implications of the preceding analyses for these issues.

The prospect of a value-laden science is, for many, the prospect of a science whose results are continually in contestation. For others it is the more frightening prospect of a science continually at the mercy of dominant interests, a science that, under the guise of neutrality, helps create a world to serve those interests. The specters of Lysenkoism in the first half of the century and of creationism today are powerful incentives to support the goal of value-free science. They cannot be ignored in any responsible argument that science is not value-neutral. My argument does not require us to give Lamarckism or creationism equal time in the classroom. As I indicated, I will pursue general implications of understanding science as value-laden in the last section of this book. In the next several chapters I lay the philosophical groundwork for that discussion by examining concepts of evidence, reasoning, and objectivity. In this examination I will show what a value-free science might be, why it cannot be, and how we can avoid the paradoxes inherent in more traditional accounts by treating scientific knowledge as social knowledge.

CHAPTER TWO

Methodology, Goals, and Practices

IN Plato's dialogue, the *Meno*, Socrates and Meno, pursuing the question whether virtue can be taught or learned, stumble into the paradox of inquiry: What is it to inquire or to investigate things? Either one knows or one does not know something. If one knows it, there is no point to investigating it, and if one does not already know it, then one has no way of knowing if one's inquiry has led one to the truth. The development of the sciences since 500 B.C. seems to have put the lie to this sophisticated verbal trick, and yet can one be forgiven for wondering, How is it done? How do we move from the naive (though puzzling) perception of the world to theories of the detail and specificity of subatomic particle physics or molecular biology? This is both a historical and an individual question—about the history of science and about the development of knowledge and understanding in the individual. It is in part a psychological question—What about the human mind or brain impels and enables us to develop theories and explanations of the natural world?—and in part a philosophical question—If we do know, how do we know? What justifies us in claiming that our theories count as knowledge, and if they are knowledge, what are they knowledge of? These questions form the traditional task of the logic and methodology of the sciences.

As most college students still learn, the rest of the Platonic dialogues offer answers to these questions. In the *Meno*, for instance, Socrates argues that the acquisition of knowledge is a sort of remembering. The appreciation of necessary (geometrical) truths shown by Meno's untutored slave is the recollection of knowledge possessed by the soul when it was in a purer state. That knowledge lost and then regained is the knowledge of forms—nonmaterial entities that constitute true reality (patterns or ideas such as goodness and triangularity). The character and interrelationships of these forms are the proper subject of systematic inquiry. One knows that one's inquiry has led to truth because one recognizes objects of which the soul has past experience.

It is common now to view this solution to the paradox of inquiry as a flawed account of a priori knowledge. Western epistemology has developed many alternatives to the Platonic metaphysics and epistemology. The approach of philosophers to scientific methodology has nevertheless remained in important ways Platonic. We have focused on scientific theories as sets of propositions (or sentences or statements) expressing a variety of different kinds of claims and have set ourselves the task of analyzing their meanings, truth conditions, and logical interrelations. This has been an extremely fruitful enterprise, particularly when applied to the task of exhibiting the logical structure of specific scientific theories, like special relativity, or various quantum theories, or evolutionary theory. In our fascination with individual theories it is easy to lose sight of the fact that scientific inquiry is a collaborative human activity and consequently to approach the methodology of inquiry with tools for the analysis of theories. Theories, however, are the outcome of inquiry and not the process itself. As an activity scientific inquiry has certain goals, realization or nonrealization of which determine its success and the criteria by which to measure success. As a human activity it is also socially organized in certain ways that affect both goals and criteria of success. Finally, it develops within historical social and political contexts with which it is in dynamic interaction. The character of this interaction is the subject of this book.

INQUIRY: GOALS AND PRACTICES

Marjorie Grene, in *The Knower and the Known*, argued that the paradox of inquiry is solved by paying proper attention to the practical, or active, character of inquiry and to what Michael Polanyi called tacit knowing.[1] In a more recent article she argues once again that we must understand scientific inquiry as a human activity and endorses the application of Alasdair MacIntyre's concept of practices to the sciences.[2] I follow Grene in thinking of inquiry as an activity in which we engage as human beings and in believing that this overall approach enables one to think about the sciences and their place in human life more realistically than does reducing them to their products. MacIntyre's discussion of practices provides a good starting point for thinking about the methodology of inquiry, although I shall argue that at least in the case of scientific inquiry, his account must be significantly modified.

In his book *After Virtue* MacIntyre explicitly includes the sciences in the category of practices. A practice he defined as "any coherent and complex form of socially established cooperative human activity through which goods internal to that form of activity are realized in

[1] Grene (1966).
[2] Grene (1985).

the course of trying to achieve those standards of excellence which are appropriate to, and partly definitive of, that form of activity."[3] This definition expresses a conceptual linkage similar to the one above between goals ("internal goods") and criteria ("standards of excellence"). MacIntyre distinguishes internal from external goods. External goods seem to be the extrinsic or incidental rewards to be gained from engaging in a practice, as fame or wealth are external goods to be gained from engaging in the practice of science. The external goods associated with a particular activity can be attained through pursuit of other activities. Internal goods associated with a particular practice bear a noncontingent relation to that activity. They can only be specified in terms of that activity and, says MacIntyre, "they can only be identified and recognized by the experience of participating in the practice in question."[4]

MacIntyre develops the concept of internal goods through a discussion of portrait painting, distinguishing two kinds of such goods: excellence of the product of an activity and "the good of a certain kind of life." Excellence of the product is further analyzed as excellence in performance and excellence in each individual product, that is, each individual portrait. In our thinking about scientific inquiry we can recognize similar distinctions: the elegance of a scientist's argument and the ingenuity of a scientist's experiment in contrast to excellences of the resultant theory itself. The excellences of the theory can consist in, among other things, the internal cohesion of parts of the theory and in its relation to that aspect of the natural world of which it is a theory. The standards by which excellence is judged provide nonarbitrary and nonsubjective criteria to which individual taste and preference are subordinated.

I have been deliberately nonspecific about what in particular would constitute the excellences of a theory or other product of natural science inquiry. The value of MacIntyre's vocabulary of practices and their goals is that we can use this language to reformulate the question in new terms: What are the goals of scientific activity, realization of which determine the success of that activity and criteria by which to measure success? It is clear that in asking this question about scientific inquiry we are asking not just about external goods that might motivate any given individual in her/his practice and that could be attained by other means but about those internal goods that can only be achieved through the practice of science.

[3] MacIntyre (1981) p. 175.
[4] Ibid., p. 175.

There are at least three reasons to remain noncommittal regarding the specific internal goods of scientific inquiry. Scientific inquiry is unlike portrait painting in two very important ways: it is social and it is complex, consisting of many activities carried out by different persons. This point will be developed more fully in a later chapter. For the moment it is sufficient to notice that individuals and groups of individuals participate in scientific inquiry at very different levels and in different ways. Their perceptions of "the standards of excellence appropriate to" such inquiry may differ according to the character of their engagement. The technician, research associate, "principal investigator"; the experimenter and the mathematical modeller; the group of researchers pursuing a common research program; members of the scientific subfield and those outside the subfield who expect to use or rely on the results produced within it, may all understand their own practice differently. Knowledge, which one might also propose as one of the internal goods of science, is not the private domain of any of these individuals or communities practicing science. We must either accept that different conceptions of knowledge could develop in the context of different practices or suppose that there is some subset of practices belonging to all knowledge-productive practices. In the latter case the specification of internal goods and standards of excellence is not the exclusive privilege of those participating in a given identifiable practice. In the former, a unified knowledge or conception of knowledge gives way to multiplicity. I shall eventually argue that something like both of these is true. To the extent that MacIntyre's discussion of practices, however, suggests that the sciences can be identified with a single form of activity from which a single and coherent set of internal goods can be derived it is misleading.

A second reason to eschew a quick identification of the goals and goods of inquiry is common to scientific inquiry and to portrait painting. The precise excellences of theory (or painting) and the standards by which they are judged are to some extent a function of the historical and cultural context in which any given theory is developed and thus cannot be articulated independently of such context. Thirdly, in *this* historical period thinking about science is guided by at least two quite different conceptions of "good theory." MacIntyre's discussion of practices and their goods helps us to see that a "good theory," however understood, is only one among several goods internal to the practice of science. And this in turn enables us to see that the idea of "good theory" itself might hide several different possible goods. Modern philosophical work on scientific methodology has, in fact, been guided by quite different conceptions of what a good theory is or does.

Logical Positivists versus Wholists on Scientific Method

A methodology describes and analyzes methods for reaching a specific goal. This statement hides an ambiguity between prescription and description. One can describe the methods actually used by some specific group or individual to attain a specified goal or one can prescribe the methods one ought to use, the methods that will enable their users to attain specific goals. Defenders of given philosophical accounts of scientific methodology are not always clear or forthcoming as to how their accounts are to be understood or assessed. In reflecting on competing philosophical accounts it is useful to keep the distinction between prescriptive and descriptive functions in mind since they can fail as one but succeed as the other.

To illustrate the difference let me use a favorite stalking-horse of philosophers of science. Astrology seems to have as goals the prediction of future events or trends in a person's life and the analysis of individual character and temperament. It is possible to describe the methods used by astrologers to attain these goals. Such description would include details about the construction of horoscopic charts, about celestial observation, especially of those objects thought to exert the most influence on terrestrial phenomena, about the methods of calculating the interaction of those objects, and so on. Behind all those fatuous advice books there lie precisely spelled-out procedures for producing the advice. If one starts, however, not with what the practitioners do but with the goals they seek to attain, and if one asks not *how does S go about* attaining this goal but *what is the best way to go about* attaining it, that is, prediction of future events and analysis of character, it's unlikely that the answer will include any of the items listed above.

This distinction between prescription and description is also expressed in the artificial intelligence community's distinction between performance mode and simulation mode. In performance mode the AI researcher is interested in the best way to perform a certain task—for example, solving differential equations, developing proofs of logical theorems, finding the winning chess move. This corresponds to the prescriptive aspect of methodology, except that the programmer prescribes to a computing machine. In simulation mode the AI researcher is interested in modelling the behavior of humans performing a given task—for example, solving differential equations, developing proofs of logical theorems, finding the winning chess move—regardless of the behavior's success or efficiency or lack thereof. This corresponds to the descriptive aspect of methodology. The computer scientist Joseph Weizenbaum has remarked that the line between performance mode and simulation mode is somewhat fuzzy and often blurred by AI researchers.[5] Philosophers of science have engaged in a comparable blurring of prescription and description in the methodology of science.

In the following pages I will briefly review the two principal accounts of scientific knowledge that have underlain discussions of the relations between science and values. These are the accounts offered by logical positivists and empiricists on one side and the accounts offered by more historically oriented challengers of that approach on the other. Both accounts have attracted significant multidisciplinary followings. Because issues of logic and of fact are involved in their disagreements, the line between prescription and description is crucial to disentangling them.

At the height of the debates within philosophy of science about these two approaches the discussion centered on the nature of theory reduction. This was really a debate about the relations that historically successive theories in the same domain have to one another, or about scientific change. While most philosophers of science today would, I think, regard the positivists as having lost the debate about scientific change, no comparably sweeping and detailed philosophical view has replaced it. Furthermore, the assumption of one or the other of these two approaches in discussions of science and values or science and ideology has proceeded without the benefit of the criticisms of both approaches developed in the philosophy of science. And while neither approach offers a completely satisfactory account of scientific knowledge, each offers important, if partial, insights into its nature. For these reasons I think it is worth treading this ground yet again. I shall do so briefly and I shall concentrate on the explicit and implicit analyses of evidential relations, since the treatment of them lies at the heart of epistemology for the sciences. Although I shall discuss the work of C. G. Hempel and of Thomas Kuhn specifically, my review will be selective and fairly schematized. My intention here is not thoroughly to explicate and interpret their particular views as they have evolved over the years but to discuss those aspects of their work that have provided the poles around which much of the debates about the roles of values and ideology in the sciences cluster. In addition to discussing the approaches of Hempel and Kuhn I shall briefly discuss a contemporary movement that carries on some of the traditions of positivism, scientific realism.

[5] Weizenbaum (1976).

Logical Positivism

Logical positivist philosophy of science was radical empiricist epistemology applied to science. Epistemology is prescriptive in the sense that it lays down rules for what is to count as knowledge and what is to count as meaningful discourse. In the version of empiricism developed by the positivists that which is meaningful (statements, sentences, et cetera) is that whose content is experiential or observational in nature. That which is knowledge is that whose content is true and experienced or derived from known experiential (observational or basic) statements in a rule-governed way. These sketchily presented fundamental notions were given elaborate formal expression in the writings of philosophers like Rudolph Carnap, Carl Hempel, and Karl Popper (though the latter would not call himself a positivist).

The assumption in positivists' writings is not only that they are prescribing the correct methods for acquiring knowledge but that they are at the same time describing how science is done. For example, it is a consequence of their accounts of concept formation and theory confirmation that scientific knowledge develops in a cumulative fashion. According to the cumulative model, successive theories in a field differ only in accounting for a wider and wider range of phenomena and are consistent with earlier theories accounting for the same data. Their references to the history of science indicate that they believe cumulativity to characterize the actual development of science. Their writings include very little case study work to support their assumption of the congruity of prescription and description in their analyses. The assumption seems supported, instead, by something like the following argument. Since science has provided knowledge of the natural world, and since the natural sciences are empirical, that is, rely on observation and experiment, the logical positivist prescriptions must be just clearer and more formal expressions ("logical reconstructions") of what scientists do. Both premises require deeper exploration. One can ask in what sense the sciences have provided knowledge of the natural world. One can also ask whether the empirical nature of the natural sciences means that they rely exclusively on observation and experiment, as they would have to for the conclusion to follow. These questions acquire some urgency in light of the problems encountered by positivist attempts to analyze evidential relations, or what they called "confirmation." I shall discuss the most famous of these.

In his celebrated essay "Studies in the Logic of Confirmation,"[6] Hempel is engaged in a search for "general objective criteria determin-

---

[6] Hempel (1965), pp. 3–51.

ing whether . . . a hypothesis H may be said to be corroborated by a given body of evidence E."[7] His aim in the essay is to provide definitions of the concepts of confirmation and disconfirmation that characterize those relations in a purely formal way: the criteria of confirmation "should contain no reference to the specific subject matter of the hypothesis."[8] For Hempel one ought to be able to tell simply by looking at the logical forms of a hypothesis sentence and an evidence sentence whether the confirmation relation holds between them, just as one can tell simply by inspecting the logical forms of premise sentences and conclusion sentences whether the implication relation holds between them. The search, then, is for formal syntactic criteria of confirmation analogous to the formal criteria for the validity of deductive arguments.

The requirements developed by Hempel are met by his satisfaction criterion of confirmation. The relation of direct confirmation is characterized thus:

> An observation report B directly confirms H if B entails the development of H for the class of objects mentioned in B.[9]

And the relation of confirmation is as follows:

> An observation report B confirms a hypothesis H if H is entailed by a class of sentences each of which is directly confirmed by B.[10]

We need only concern ourselves with the notion of direct confirmation. As the development of a hypothesis H for some class C is what H would assert if there existed only those objects that are members of C, the development of the hypothesis '$(x)(Ax \rightarrow Bx)$' for a class a would be '$Aa \rightarrow Ba$.' All observation reports that entailed '$Aa \rightarrow Ba$', for example, '$-Aa$', 'Ba', '$Aa\&Ba$', '$-Aa\&Ba$', '$Aa\&Ba\&Ca$' would directly confirm '$(x)(Ax \rightarrow Bx)$.' For example, the hypothesis "all bodies falling from rest move at a uniformly accelerated rate" is confirmed by the observation report "this hammer, when released at time t, moved at a uniformly accelerated rate" because the development of "all bodies falling from rest move at a uniformly accelerated rate" for the class consisting of the hammer released at t entails the observation report by being identical with it.

This definition provides the syntactic, formal criterion for which Hempel was searching since we need only check to see that certain

7 Ibid., p. 6.
8 Ibid., p. 10.
9 Ibid., p. 37.
10 Ibid.

entailment relations hold in order to determine whether a given sentence confirms another. The question, however, is: Can this definition of the confirmation relation be the source of a description of the relation between evidence and hypothesis?

The situation seems from an epistemological point of view ideal: the justification of hypotheses becomes a very straightforward matter, and philosophers have only to solve the problem of induction in order to finish tidying the house of science. Reality, however, has a habit of eluding the ideal, in this instance no less than in others, for actual evidential relations in science are not captured by the analysis of confirmation. To see this one need only consider arguments Hempel himself has advanced in a different context. In the course of arguing against the inductivist view of the formulation of hypotheses, that is, the view that hypotheses are formulated, or developed, by being inferred inductively from observations, he remarks:

> Take a scientific theory such as the atomic theory of matter. The evidence on which it rests may be described in terms referring to directly observable phenomena, namely to certain macroscopic aspects of the various experimental and observational data which are relevant to the theory. On the other hand, the theory itself contains a large number of abstract, non-observational terms such as 'atom,' 'electron,' 'nucleus,' 'dissociation,' 'valence' and others, none of which figures in the description of the observational data.[11]

In other words, scientific hypotheses are about underlying processes involving such putative items as atoms, neutrinos, quarks, et cetera. The evidence for such statements is not described in statements about "observation reports" of individual atoms but in statements about cloud chambers, lines observed in spectrographic analysis, et cetera. Hempel takes this as showing that it is impossible to devise rules that would enable one to infer new hypotheses from observations, as the inductivists hoped. Such rules could be devised, if at all, only if the same predicates occurred in the hypotheses as occurred in the descriptions of observations. As this is patently not the case, such rules cannot be constructed.

The implications of this state of affairs are, however, equally devastating for Hempel's analysis of confirmation, if intended as a description of the evidential relation. The analysis he provides is of a formal, syntactic relation between sentences. This relation holds only between sentences containing the same predicates: the development of a hy-

[11] Ibid., p. 6.

pothesis for a class contains only those predicates occurring in the hypothesis, and as an observation report only confirms a hypothesis if it entails its development for the class of objects mentioned in the observation report, it too must contain at least one of the predicates occurring in the hypothesis.[12] That is, the confirmation relation as Hempel conceives it makes the same impossible demand upon science as does the inductivist conception. Hypotheses forming part of the atomic theory of matter are not evidentially supported by statements about atoms, by statements containing the same terms as occur in the hypothesis, but by statements containing quite different kinds of terms. The same is true for most, if not all, interesting scientific theories. Thus Hempel was right in claiming that one could not, from scrutiny of observations alone, develop in a rule-governed way hypotheses that would account for or explain the observations, but he was wrong in his implicit claim that one could, simply by scrutinizing a hypothesis once developed, determine in a rule-governed way the observation reports that would confirm the hypothesis.[13] As an account of evidential relations that could form the basis for an account of scientific reasoning, this analysis of confirmation won't do. Scientific reasoning somehow crosses the gulfs identified in Hempel's critique of an inductivist logic of discovery. The epistemological foundation offered by traditional positivism for the natural sciences is, therefore, inadequate.

Wholism

By contrast, a group of historically oriented philosophers of science, principally Norwood Russell Hanson, Thomas Kuhn, and Paul Feyerabend, seemed to reject the logical empiricist approach of Hempel in

[12] While an observation report may contain predicates not occurring in the hypothesis, only those occurring in both observation report and hypothesis are relevant to confirmation; compare ibid., pp. 37–38n. Because Hempel was an adherent to the theoretical term/observational term dichotomy, it is important to notice that his argument here depends not on that distinction but simply on the fact that hypotheses contain different descriptive (i.e., nonlogical) terms than the sentences describing potential evidence for them. Thus, a rejection of the empiricist version of the theoretical/observational distinction cannot save the analysis of confirmation.

[13] The use of "bridge principles" to leap over the gap between experimental/observational and theoretical language is subject to well-known objections and in this context seems highly ad hoc. Hempel has, in recent work, retreated from the position discussed here and adopted the Duhemian view that a test or experiment never conclusively confirms or disconfirms or falsifies a hypothesis but rather is relevant to the hypothesis in conjunction with certain assumptions. As Hempel discusses them in his *Philosophy of Natural Science* (1966), they are assumptions about the experimental instruments and measuring devices used to generate observations and data. I shall argue for the necessity of more interpretative assumptions in Chapter Three.

toto.[14] They were struck by the fact that the history of science repeatedly reveals that apparently inconsistent theories seem nevertheless adequately supported by the data they are intended to explain. Thus both the Ptolemaic and the Copernican theories, rival cosmologies, and medieval impetus theory and Newtonian physics, rival theories of motion, were attempting to explain and were evidentially supported by more or less the same data. This feature of successive scientific theories leads these philosophers to deny that the cumulative model of scientific growth is adequate to describe all scientific change.

These thinkers' critique of logical positivism did not focus directly on the relation between evidence and hypothesis but on the characterization of what serves as evidence. In the empiricist view the fundamental base of inquiry, the source of confirming or disconfirming instances, is a set of observations or observation statements that are established independently of any theory. According to empiricist principles of significance, their meaning, exhaustible in actual or potential experiences, was unproblematic and the meaning of all other descriptive terms or statements dependent on observation terms and statements. The historically oriented critics of the empiricists rejected the latter's fundamental assumption of the independence of observation (experience) from theory. Science did not show a linear progression from experience to theory accounting for experience but rather the periodic acceptance and abandonment of large-scale frameworks ("paradigms") within which science was done. To explain how such seemingly incompatible frameworks could be applied to roughly the same phenomena, such as celestial motions recorded or observable in the fifteenth through the seventeenth centuries, these scholars introduced the notions of theory-ladenness and incommensurability.

Theory ladenness was a concept used to describe both meaning and observation. To say that meanings are theory-laden is to say that the meanings of terms occurring in a theory are determined by the theory, with the consequence that the same word used in different theories has different meanings: "mass," for example, means something different in classical and relativistic mechanics. To say that observation is the-

[14] Compare Hanson (1958); Kuhn (1970a, 1970b); Feyerabend (1962, 1970a). Kuhn (1977b) has seemed to retreat from the strong version of the incommensurability thesis discussed here, urging that "incommensurable" does not mean "incomparable" but signals the absence of a common language in which to translate two different theories for purposes of comparison. Rough translations are now held to be possible. His remarks concerning the determination of common applications and of similarity relations suggest, however, that this retreat is more apparent than real. Moreover, it is the strong version of incommensurability that has had so much influence on contemporary studies of science.

ory-laden is to say that one sees and experiences the world in a way prescribed by one's theory (or theories). Confirming or disconfirming observations, on this view, cannot be specified independently of a theory but are themselves given content, at least in part, by theory and described in language whose meaning was dependent on the whole of a theory. This insistence that the elements of a theory, including its supporting data, can only be understood in the context of the whole has given rise to the designation "wholism" for this family of views.

The arguments of the wholists differed slightly. Feyerabend emphasized the theory dependence of meaning, while Kuhn and Hanson emphasized the theory dependence of observation, relying in part for support from gestalt experiments on vision. Regardless of emphasis, the consequence of theory ladenness is incommensurability: two (or more) opposing theories accounting for the same phenomena cannot be compared with each other and against "the facts" in any way that enables us to determine which is false and which, if any, true. Because observation and meaning are theory-laden, (1) there is no neutral or independent set of data that can serve as arbiter between the theories and (2) the theories are expressed in mutually untranslatable languages. The theories are incommensurable. One accepts or rejects a theory not because of rational deliberation about the evidential support of a theory but as one acquires or loses (religious) faith. To change one's theory (or paradigm) involves changing one's world view and hence one's world; to change one's theory is to change what one sees and, apparently, what there is to be seen. In adopting a new theory one adopts a way of seeing the world that confirms the theory. The neutrality and precision whose possibility is assumed in Hempel's analysis, the straightforward determination of confirming, disconfirming, or irrelevant observation reports are thus rejected for an account of theory choice much vaguer and seemingly more subjective. According to the accounts offered by Kuhn and Feyerabend, theory choice in science is no longer a uniquely pure expression of rationality and objectivity but is described as nonrational or irrational, and certainly not evidence-determined.

Many contemporary critics of science have appealed to this wholistic conception of theories in support of the claims that a particular research program or the sciences in general are inevitably infected by the values and ideologies of the societies that sponsor them, or cannot be a trustworthy guide to the natural world. Positivists, to the extent that they endorse the claims of the sciences to provide a value-free understanding of the natural world, are the philosophical villains. Certainly the historical work of the wholists decisively refutes the empiricists' claim that their prescriptions can also function as descriptions of scientific practice. It does not, however, refute the claim that those prescriptions provide the best methods for attaining the goals of scientific practice. To suppose it does, as some followers of wholists have done, is to confuse prescription and description just as the empiricists have. Many philosophers of science objected that scientific inquiry on this account became hopelessly subjective and knowledge relative. Indeed the models that the wholists proposed to replace the empiricist account have, however, been shown to be at best paradoxical.[15] The paradox lies in the supposition that two theories could be both mutually incommensurable and mutually inconsistent. It has been argued, for instance, that if we regard the meaning of a term occurring in one theory as changed when it occurs in some other theory, then we cannot say that any theories contradict one another: given two theories that appear to be incompatible, on this view, scientists asserting hypotheses associated with the two theories are using the common terms in different ways and hence could not be said to be inconsistent with one another. Just as theories could not be said to be contradictory, so they could not be said to be in agreement or consistent with one another.

The consequences of the wholist solution, then, undermine the presuppositions of the problem. If theories are really incommensurable, we cannot make the initial judgment that they offer incompatible explanations of the same phenomena, for we have no way to justify judgments of compatibility or incompatibility, difference or sameness. Such judgments require a common ground of intelligibility that incommensurability denies. Assimilating theory acceptance to gestalt switches, as Kuhn realizes, renders evidential considerations either useless or self-deceptive. Taken seriously, it also makes the fact that some theories do work better than others quite mysterious. Objections of paradoxicality and mystery can be met with the claim that there is no other way to account for the cases of theory change to be found in the history of science. I shall argue in the next chapter that we are not faced with quite such a Hobson's choice and that attention to the intellectual practices in which scientific inquiry partly consists, rather than solely to the products of such practices, produces an account that accommodates the dual requirements of mutual intelligibility and applicability to historical cases.

Scientific Realism: An Alternative?

In the last ten to fifteen years a new position has been developed as an alternative to both positivism and wholism, attracting a growing num-

[15] Compare in particular Shapere (1964) and Achinstein (1968), pp. 92–98.

ber of defenders among philosophers of science. This is the view dubbed "scientific realism," a term used to designate a number of related positions. These positions have in common a rejection of the instrumentalism that many positivists adopted as a way of preserving the value of scientific theorizing even while denying the literal meaningfulness of theoretical terms in science. They also reject the conventionalism of Quine and the relativism characteristic of wholism. Hilary Putnam, Richard Boyd, W. H. Newton-Smith, and Jarrett Leplin, among others, have all defended realist theses.[16] Put most crudely, realism is the claim that the theories of the "mature" sciences (for example, physics) are approximately true and that the more recent theories of such sciences approach truth more closely than earlier theories. In contrast to instrumentalism, which treats theories as calculating devices or prediction machines, realism holds that the theoretical claims of a science are to be interpreted literally. In contrast to wholism, realism maintains that the theoretical claims, literally interpreted, are (approximately) true and, by implication, that we can *know* that they are true.

The most common arguments for realism involve the principle of inference to the best explanation, a new version of the abductive or retroductive inference discussed by C. S. Pierce and N. R. Hanson. Inference to the best explanation was introduced to recent philosophy by Gilbert Harman.[17] When used in defence of scientific realism, explanatory power is invoked at three different levels. (1) An individual theory can be said to provide the best explanation of a certain set of data. According to the principle of inference to the best explanation, this is a good reason for believing that the theory is true. The explanatory superiority of the theory relative to alternatives constitutes empirical grounds for believing it in addition to more direct forms of empirical evidence, such as positive instances, survival of attempts at experimental disconfirmation, et cetera. (2) The philosophical thesis of scientific realism is said to provide the best or only explanation for the predictive success of current theories in the so-called mature sciences as well as for the increase in predictive success obtained in these sciences over time. To paraphrase Hilary Putnam, if our theories are not literally true, then it is impossible to understand how our theories enable us to intervene successfully in natural processes.[18] (3) Scientific realism is also said to provide the best or only explanation for the success of certain methodological principles. This methodological argument has

[16] Putnam (1978); Boyd (1973, 1984); Newton-Smith (1981); Leplin (1984).
[17] Harman (1965).
[18] Putnam (1978), p. 19.

been developed most extensively by Richard Boyd.[19] Boyd argues that the instrumental or observational reliability of scientific methods can best or only be explained by theoretical reliability. What this seems to mean is that the methods of science, application of which produces true observational statements or predictions, rely on theoretical considerations so heavily that their successful use is understandable only on the supposition that those theoretical considerations are also true.

The consequence of this form of scientific realism for an account of evidence is a broadening of the category *evidence* to include not just empirical data but the explanatory virtues of the theory with respect to that data. There is a quite general problem with this strategy that affects all three of the argument types listed above. Put most simply it is that explanatory arguments at best demonstrate the plausibility of their conclusions.[20] That the truth of some hypothesis h would explain some set of phenomena does not show that h is true but that h is plausible. The situation is not improved by calling h a best explanation. In the first place this licenses us to infer only that h is the most plausible. Such a comparison holds only among currently available alternatives and does not rule out the later emergence of a yet superior hypothesis incompatible with h. Secondly, the use of "best explanation" as a criterion of truth seems circular. For what are the criteria for comparative assessments of explanations? Surely h_1 is a better explanation of e than h_2, other things being equal, if h_1 is true and h_2 is not. If truth is among the criteria we use to determine explanatory superiority, then explanatory superiority cannot in turn be used as an independent criterion of truth. Finally, Harman argued that enumerative induction was an example of inference to the best explanation, in that a generalization such as "all A's are B's" is the best explanation of the truth of its instances, such as "this A is a B."[21] Contrary to Harman I would maintain that the strength explanatory arguments do have is parasitic on an implicit use of enumerative induction. If h is plausible because it would explain e, then it is even more plausible if conditions similar to those described by h have in the past successfully explained phenomena similar to e, and less plausible if conditions similar to h have never been directly verified.

Thus, that a particular hypothesis (or theory) h offers the best explanation of some set of data e is not in itself grounds for believing that h is true. As for the use of explanatory arguments to support the more

---

[19] See Boyd (1973, 1984).
[20] For an extended argument to this effect see Achinstein (1971), pp. 119–124.
[21] Harman (1968).

sweeping philosophical claims, Arthur Fine has observed that one cannot expect those skeptical of the validity of explanatory arguments at the "ground level" to have their doubts placated by their use at a higher or metalevel.[22] And, as a number of respondents, including Fine, Larry Laudan, and Bas van Fraassen, have pointed out, the arguments, in their details, rest on inaccurate portrayals of contemporary and past scientific inquiry. For example, regarding the second-level argument (that the predictive success of science mandates a scientific realism), Laudan presents a long list of theories that were eminently successful in their day but that we now regard as untrue.[23] Since truth cannot be an explanation for the success of these theories, we are certainly not compelled to believe that current successful theories are true. Against the third-level methodological argument (that is, the argument that scientists' successful use of certain methodological principles is only explicable on realist assumptions), Arthur Fine has argued that the realist assumes that the methodological principles in question always work, that is, that using them sanctions belief only in theories that we will not later reject.[24] To suppose this is so is to ignore the fact that the history of science, even the very recent history of science, is littered with failures. The methodological principles are not infallible and, therefore, their success does not require explanation.[25] Moreover, van Fraassen has proposed a nonrealist explanation for the putative success of a specific principle claimed by Richard Boyd to be explainable only on realist assumptions.[26] The realist's is, therefore, not the only explanation, and the realist is challenged to produce an argument that her/his explanation is indeed superior to the nonrealist's.

Explanatory power is, therefore, both too weak and too strong to serve in the manner required. It is too weak because as yet unconsidered alternative explanations are always possible, and the explanatory power of one hypothesis, therefore, cannot rule out the possible truth of those others. It is too strong because explanations, even those deemed best at the time, often turn out later to be false (or are later deemed to be false), and the explanatory power criterion would, therefore, license inferences to false hypotheses. The arguments for and against scientific realism have become increasingly subtle, and this discussion cannot hope to do them complete justice. What I do hope to

[22] Fine (1984).
[23] Laudan (1981).
[24] Fine (1984), pp. 87–88.
[25] Ibid., pp. 89–90.
[26] van Fraassen (1980).

have established is that the view that explanatory power constitutes in and of itself a form of evidence for the truth of hypotheses is not a satisfactory alternative to positivist or wholist conceptions of evidence and scientific reasoning.

Knowledge and Values

The tension between the logically oriented positivists and the historically oriented wholists has seemed the primary tension in contemporary Anglo-American philosophy of science. It has, as I've indicated, also been an epistemological pivot for discussions about values in the sciences. In this respect the realists just mentioned make common cause with the positivists. In neither account is there room for social values in scientific inquiry. Those who argue against the value neutrality of the sciences have found support in the wholist view. The wholists, however, have differed among themselves about the role of values. Contrary to some of his followers, Kuhn has argued for a primarily internalist conception of scientific inquiry according to which the values involved in the choice of theories are internal or epistemic values. Feyerabend has expressed a much more inclusive attitude, consistent with his rejection of general standards or canons of rationality. This difference is related to deep differences about the goals of scientific inquiry that are obscured by the debate about scientific change.

THE CONFLICTING GOALS OF INQUIRY

What, then, are the goals of scientific practice? Within the tradition I've been discussing there are two major conceptions discernable in a dichotomy that cuts across the division between positivists and wholists. According to one conception, the proper concern of science is the construction of comprehensive accounts of the natural world. This involves the piecemeal working out of puzzles, the gradual extension of a theory to more and more facts. Scientific inquiry, on this view, is the search for descriptions of the natural world that allow for the prediction and control of an increasing number of its aspects. Both Hempel and Kuhn seem to perceive the enterprise of science in this way. Hempel, for example, writes of the sciences as intimately connected with and responsible for various improvements in human life and, in one essay, describes the goal of scientific inquiry as "the attainment of an increasingly reliable, extensive, and theoretically systematized body of information about the world."[27] For Kuhn the struggles characteristic

[27] Hempel (1960), p. 60.

of "revolutionary science" are features of precursor or immature science. Mature science is characterized by consensus regarding basic assumptions and methods and consists in the working out of puzzles using the tools provided by that paradigm. The basic scientist "aims to elucidate the scientific tradition in which he was raised rather than to change it. . . . The puzzles on which he concentrates are just those which he believes can be both stated and solved within the existing scientific tradition."[28] They differ, of course, in their views of which analysis will bring out most perspicuously the logical features of the scientific enterprise and in their views of the scope of progressivity in science. But, with or without a paradigm, it is the gradual accretion of systematically related hypotheses, experiments, and observations, the extension of an explanatory idea or framework to a greater range of phenomena, that constitutes scientific growth or progress. Even though it is Kuhn's notion of revolutionary science that has captured the imagination of many, if not most, of his readers, Kuhn himself insists that the real work of science begins once a community has adopted a paradigm.

According to the other conception, which informs the work of both Popper and Feyerabend, the work of science is the discovery of truth about the natural world. Both of them are skeptical about the possibility of any methodical way of making judgments of truth. Both regard the consensus and expansionism that characterize Hempel's and Kuhn's models of scientific practice as imposing a stifling dogmatism that can only hinder scientific progress. Popper has been concerned with the problem of demarcating science from pseudoscience.[29] Since lots of pseudoscientific theories had explanatory power, he saw this not as a virtue but as a vice. The mark of a scientific theory or hypothesis was its refutability and only those tests of a theory counted that consisted of attempts to refute it. Theories that survived such tests could be provisionally accepted. Because finding confirming instances is so easy, confirmation must always be suspect. The point of scientific inquiry for Popper is not finding an account that works but the constant rejection of what has been falsified. Feyerabend rejects the refutability criterion and indeed any other methodological restriction. Knowledge ought to be our goal, and our best hope lies in the proliferation of novel ideas unhindered by epistemological prescriptions. We can never know in advance what procedures will enable us to discover

[28] Kuhn (1977a), p. 234.
[29] Popper (1959, 1963).

"deep-lying secrets of nature."[30] Even though progress may be measured only by the number of false ideas from which we free ourselves, clearly it is the goal of faithfully representing nature and not that of expanding explanatory paradigms or our technological dominion over nature that dictates this conception of progress. Again, these thinkers differ on the details of the logical analysis they provide: Popper, remaining true to some of the empiricist tenets, emphasizes the direct comparison of theory with experience, while Feyerabend urges the impossibility of such comparison, the proliferation of hypotheses, and the necessity of alternatives for the assessment of theories.[31]

The dichotomy in these approaches should be seen not so much as a contradiction to be resolved in favor of one or the other position, so much as reflective of a tension within science itself between its knowledge-extending mission and its critical mission. This tension is expressed both in scientists' self-accounting and in the public perception of and demands on science. Technological advance, for instance, requires explanatory growth—progress in the knowledge-extending mission of science, as genetic engineering is dependent on, for some in fact is, the expansion of microbiological theory and molecular biology. Accurate representation of the natural world, on the other hand, calls upon aspects of science's critical mission: testing, retesting, rejecting, and reformulating hypotheses. Recent discussions in evolutionary theory provide examples of both missions. Sociobiology is an attempt to extend the explanatory principles of Darwinian evolution to the social behavior of animals, including human animals.[32] The debate about punctuated equilibrium concerned the proposed rejection of Darwinian gradualism in favor of a view according to which species change took place in relatively sudden episodes during which many characteristics changed relatively simultaneously.[33]

Kuhn himself describes possible conflicts among the goals of science in a lecture "Objectivity, Value Judgment, and Theory Choice," written partly in response to critics of *The Structure of Scientific Revolutions*.[34] He argues that, according to his account, theory choice or acceptance is not a subjective matter, as those critics charged. It is guided, he says, by five criteria that he later in the lecture calls permanent val-

[30] Feyerabend (1975), p. 20.

[31] Hilary Putnam (1974) has noted a similar distinction in philosophical methodologists' conceptions of the aims of science.

[32] The classical statement is Wilson (1975).

[33] See Niles Eldredge and Stephen J. Gould (1972) and Stephen J. Gould and Niles Eldredge (1977).

[34] Thomas Kuhn (1977a), pp. 320–339.

ues in science. These are accuracy, scope, fruitfulness, consistency, and simplicity. The body of the essay details the inherent ambiguity of these criteria, the different weights that can be assigned them by different individuals, and the different interpretations they receive in different historical periods. Competing theories can satisfy these criteria to different degrees, which means the scientist's judgment depends on the weight she or he assigns them. Accuracy clearly is a virtue associated with the representational or critical mission of the sciences, while scope and fruitfulness are virtues associated with its explanatory or knowledge-extending mission.

According to the first, explanatory, view, natural phenomena recalcitrant to treatment within a given theoretical framework are viewed as problems—challenges to the explanatory and/or predictive power of the framework that will be met within the framework's terms. The methodology appropriate to such a conception is a problem-solving methodology. On the second view recalcitrant anomalies are seen as potential falsifications of a theory or hypothesis—a challenge to reject or reformulate central theses. According to this view, anomalies are to be sought by experiments, and the methodology appropriate is one of criticism. Most scientists and philosophers of science would deny the exclusivity of their concern with either explanation or truth. In the short run, and in our reflective thinking about science, we do best to keep them distinct.

This is particularly so as the sciences begin to address, begin to appear to have the capability to address, fundamental issues about human nature. Think, for instance, about experimental behavioral psychology. The original and guiding principle of this view is that variations in human behavior are dependent on variations in environment rather than intrinsic psychological or biological variations in human beings. Elaborating this principle for specific behavioral and environmental variables has been the task of much of academic psychology. This elaboration provides the theoretical foundation for behavior modification techniques (technology). But it is also possible to ask whether the original principle is true and to design experiments specifically to answer that question. Such experiments would be intended to discover possible counter-instances to rather than applications and developments of the original principle.

For instance, an experiment may be designed to discover what percentage of a given population will respond (under what conditions) in a given way to a given environmental stimulus. What percentage of male college students, for instance, will show changes in their tolerance of violence towards women upon being shown a certain kind of film?

The social psychological experiment designed to answer such a question assumes to some degree a behaviorist account of human action. The experiment will serve not only to answer its initiating question but to extend the behaviorist theory within which the question originates. By contrast an experiment may be designed to test the idea that behavior is dependent upon environmental stimuli. Will identical twins raised in different environments exhibit the same or different behavioral patterns of response to a given range of stimuli? The study designed to answer this question tests the behavioral principle that environmental stimuli are the primary determinants of behavior and, depending on the results of the study, it can be used to falsify or to confirm the broadly stated behaviorist claim.

If we fail to distinguish these two possible goals of scientific activity, these two conceptually different ways in which a theory or scientific result may be praiseworthy, we will see the experiments that extend the scope of the theory as tests with positive results and we will see what are either problems or limitations of a theory's scope as decisive falsifications.

My concern in this study is with a scientific practice perceived as having true or representative accounts of its subject matter as a primary goal or good. When we are troubled about the role of contextual values or value-laden assumptions in science, it is because we are thinking of scientific inquiry as an activity whose intended outcome is an accurate understanding of whatever structures and processes are being investigated. Such an understanding would then guide our behavior and attitudes towards these phenomena. If that understanding is itself conditioned by our or others' values, it cannot serve as a neutral and independent guide. In assessing particular research programs, however, it is important to keep in mind that both knowledge extension and truth can guide scientific inquiry and serve as fundamental, but not necessarily compatible, values determining its assessment. The same inquiry may be undertaken under the aegis of both goals and be assessed with respect to both. The point of drawing attention to this duality, if not multiplicity, of purpose is not to say that a scientist *either* seeks for truth *or* seeks to extend already accepted or established knowledge. A scientist's activity can be evaluated with respect to both goals. In some cases this will result in contrary assessments. And while we may raise the question of contextual values in relation to the sciences conceived under the goal of truth, if contextual values have played a role in a given inquiry, this is so regardless of the description under which that inquiry is to be assessed.

Thus, while a demonstration of the contextual value-ladenness of a particular research program may serve to disqualify it as a source of unvarnished truth about its subject matter, such demonstration may have little bearing on one's assessment of it as an example of scientific inquiry. This suggestion, however, anticipates the arguments of the next several chapters. In these I analyze several key features of the intellectual practices constituting inquiry. The account of scientific knowledge emerging from this analysis has points of convergence with both the empiricist and the wholist view. My aims are to show both how social and cultural values play a role in scientific inquiry and how broadening our conception of that inquiry from an individual to a social activity enables us to see that the sciences are not, nevertheless, hopelessly subjective.

CHAPTER THREE

Evidence and Hypothesis

IN THIS chapter I approach the subject of hypothesis acceptance through thinking about inference, that is, by thinking about the intellectual practice of reasoning. Rather than start by analyzing the structure or language of a theory, I begin by considering the activity that has theories as (one of) its outcomes and then consider the consequences of understanding that activity for our understanding of that outcome.

Reasoning consists in determining the logical relations that exist among sets of propositions. While we often caricature reasoning as a kind of linguistic calculation that moves through and produces sequences of logical implications, this seems only one expression (and a rare one) of a much more general ability that includes determining consistency, inconsistency, contradiction, implication, and so forth. Reasoning may result in a judgment or in the suspension or withholding of judgment. This distinguishes it from inferring, which consists in the inferrer's coming to a conclusion on the basis of a logical relation the conclusion (or a sentence expressing it) purportedly bears to some presumed bit of information and/or other beliefs. Inference is thus a sometime result of the activity of reasoning.

Presumably we make inferences, accept or reject hypotheses, or assess their relative acceptability on the basis of evidence. This is to say that evidence and evidential relations are at the heart of inference and reasoning about empirical matters. Perhaps not all of our beliefs have evidential support, but at least those adopted in rational, reflective moments either have evidential support or are thought by us to have evidential support (else, these being reflective moments, we wouldn't have adopted them). This seems simple enough, until we ask what it means to say of some real or imagined state of affairs that it is or would be evidence for some hypothesis.

PHILOSOPHICAL PRELIMINARIES

In attempting to answer this question it may be useful first to distinguish three kinds of relations with which one might be concerned in discussing evidential support:

(1) A relation between a sentence describing a state of affairs said to be evidence and a sentence, the hypothesis, for which the state of affairs is said to be evidence. An example would be the relations between the members of the pair "table A is plastic" and "all tables are plastic" and of the pair "table A is not plastic" and "not all tables are plastic." In the first pair the first sentence is a consequence of the second. In the second pair, the second sentence is a logical consequence of the first.

(2) A relation between a state of affairs said to be evidence and another state of affairs described by a hypothesis for which the former is said to be evidence. For example, this table's being made of wood might be said to be (part of the) evidence that all tables are wooden, or that some tables are wooden, that not all tables are plastic, that at least one tree has been destroyed, and so on. Similarly, a line of condensation in a cloud chamber might be said to be evidence for the passage of some type of particle through the apparatus. The first three evidential relations hold, if they hold, in virtue of class inclusion and exclusion relations, the fourth and fifth in virtue of presumed causal relations.

(3) A relation between a state of affairs said to be evidence and a statement or proposition, the hypothesis, for which the former is said to be evidence, as this table's being made of wood might be someone's evidence for the hypothesis that a tree was destroyed.

A goodly amount of philosophical discussion, for example Hempel's work on confirmation and commentary on it, has been directed toward the analysis of relations in the first category. One problem with thinking about evidential relations as relations between sentences is the restriction of examples, and consequently the analysis, to sentences related by logical relations such as entailment. As we saw in the previous chapter, this is too restrictive. The second and third categories are, however, the kind of relation being referred to in nonphilosophical discussion of evidence. Scientists, lawyers, persons engaged in reasoning, are concerned about objects, events, and states of affairs and what inferences can be made, or conclusions drawn, from them. Although relations in the third category may depend in some way on relations in the second category, ordinary talk makes little distinction between locutions belonging to the two: both "Smith's sudden disappearance is evidence that Smith is guilty" and "Smith's sudden disappearance is evidence for the hypothesis that Smith is guilty" reflect acceptable usage (and, to this ear, a distinction primarily of degrees of certainty). This study follows, for the most part, the nonphilosophers' usage: it is concerned with evidential relations as relations between an object, event, or state of affairs said to be evidence and that (for convenience, the hypothesis) for which it is said to be evidence. It is worth noting that the hypothesis, that for which there is or is said to be evidence, is not a sentence (as in 1 above) but a proposition or statement whose content can be expressed in different sentences of the same or different languages.

My concern with evidence in this chapter is primarily descriptive—that is, I am concerned not with what constitutes good evidence or with what makes one hypothesis better-supported than another but with what determines that something is or is taken to be evidence in the first place. My assumption in thus proceeding is that normative questions, questions concerning what criteria should govern our assessment of evidence, require as their basis a nonnormative analysis of the character of evidential relations. Even to talk about something being evidence independently of its being so taken by some person is to introduce an implicit assessment of its value. In order, therefore, to avoid (what would be at this stage) contamination by normative considerations I shall approach the description of evidential relations by considering what is involved in taking something to be evidence. Since it is we who, in our search for support of beliefs, hypotheses, theories, assign the status of evidence to objects and states of affairs, an analysis of the structure of this assignment will also be an analysis of evidential relations. The conceptual points concerning evidence will be illustrated by citing cases from the history of science. In addition I shall discuss the two standard approaches to evidential relations, some of whose problems were analyzed in the previous chapter and some more recent expressions of those approaches in light of the analysis developed here. This alternative analysis will put us in position to address the questions about scientific objectivity and scientific value neutrality that form the philosophical core of the discussion of biological politics. While my concern is an understanding of the role of evidence in scientific inquiry, I begin by discussing evidential relations in nonspecialized contexts.

Evidential Reasoning and Background Assumptions

Any singular state of affairs, such as the level of mercury in a glass tube, of itself, points nowhere. The same is true of a pair of states, such as the levels of mercury in the tube at successive times, or the levels of different mercury samples in two different tubes. States of affairs, that is, do not carry labels indicating that for which they are evidence or for which they can be taken as evidence. Any attempt to find some unique or direct relation between states of affairs and those hypotheses for which they are taken as evidence reveals, in fact, that there is no such relation and that anything that is the case or is imagined to be the case can be taken to be evidence that something else is the case. What determines whether or not someone will take some fact or alleged fact, x, as evidence for some hypothesis, h, is not a natural (for example, causal) relation between the state of affairs x and that described by h but are other beliefs that person has concerning the evidential connection between x and h.[1] To put it another way, states of affairs are taken as evidence in light of regularities discovered, believed, or assumed to hold. The evidential relations into which a given state of affairs can enter will thus be as varied as the beliefs about its relations with other states, or as the beliefs about the connections between a class of states to which it can be said to belong and other states (or classes of states). Some examples will make this clearer.

Consider someone, myself, coming to believe that an eight-year-old child has the measles, and suppose I base this belief on the fact that her stomach is covered with red spots. What explains why I come to believe she has the measles rather than that, say, the moon is blue, is some belief that I have about the relationship between having a red-spotted stomach and having the measles in light of which I take her red-spotted stomach to be evidence that the child has the measles. Ordinarily we might suppose that the relevant belief is that a red-spotted stomach is a symptom of the measles, but it is entirely possible that I should come to believe that she has the measles because a crystal ball reader told me that if this child's stomach appeared covered with spots on a given day she would have a disease called measles. We can even imagine the crystal ball reader going on to say that the disease is a systemic viral infection and that it can afflict the brain, without saying anything about any regular or symptomatic connection between red spots and measles. In both cases what is taken as evidence is the same: red spots on the child's stomach. What explains why it is taken as evidence differs: in the one case I believe that red spots are a symptom of measles and in the other, presuming that crystal ball readers are a reliable source of information, I believe what the reader told me. The alleged regularities in light of which the child's rash is taken as evidence of her having the measles are different: in the first case there is a regularity thought to hold between having the measles and having a red-spotted stomach, in the second there is a regularity thought to hold between the reader's predictions and what eventually happens.

---

[1] That is, it is not relations of the second type mentioned above but beliefs about relations of the second type that determine whether one takes some state of affairs to be evidence for some hypothesis, h.

The same state of affairs can also be taken as evidence for different hypotheses. Consider again this unfortunate child's red-spotted stomach. If one believes that red spots are a symptom of the measles, then one will take the presence of red spots as evidence that she has the measles. Suppose, however, that one believes not that stomach rashes are a symptom of the measles but that they are symptomatic of some gastric disorder. One will then take the red-spotted stomach as evidence that she has some gastric ailment. Once it is seen that the same state of affairs can be evidence for different hypotheses, depending upon what further beliefs are brought to bear upon the situation, it becomes clear that the same state of affairs can be taken as evidence for conflicting hypotheses. It is entirely possible, though perhaps improbable from our point of view, that someone will associate a red-spotted stomach with good health and good fortune and so take the red spots as evidence that she is in good health—a hypothesis not at all compatible with that attributing measles to her or that attributing a gastric disorder to her.

A quite different sort of example shows how different aspects of the same state of affairs can be taken as evidence for the same hypothesis, or, of course, for different hypotheses. Just as states of affairs do not stand in unique evidential relations with hypotheses, so, too, there is not a uniquely correct description for each object of description. A given item, event, or state of affairs can be correctly described in different ways depending on the points of view and interests of those describing it. For instance, "the gray hat" and "the hat on the banister" are descriptions that can be used to refer to the same hat. The consequences of emphasizing one aspect of the hat rather than another include the possibility of its receiving under one description an evidential assessment different from that received in a context in which some other aspect is emphasized. Suppose two men walk into a house and, upon seeing a gray hat on the banister, exclaim "Nick is here." It seems obvious that both have taken the presence of the gray hat on the banister as evidence that Nick is in the house. Suppose each is asked why he came to believe that Nick is in the house. One replies that Nick is the only person he knows with a hat just that shade of gray, the other that Nick always throws his hat on the banister in just that way. Thus it is not simply that both have taken the hat as evidence that Nick is present. More precisely, one has taken the presence of a gray hat, regardless of its location, as evidence that Nick is also present in light of his belief that Nick is the only person who owns a hat just that shade of gray, while the other has taken the hat's being on the banister, regardless of its color, as evidence that Nick is present in light of his belief that Nick always tosses his hat on the banister in just that way. It is the gray hat on the banister that is evidence of Nick's presence, yet were it to be on the hatrack or cocked at a different angle, though the same shade of gray, it would not be evidence for one, and were it a different shade of gray, though sitting on the banister in just that way, it would not be evidence for the other. Their differing (though not conflicting) beliefs lead each to pick a different aspect of the same state of affairs as evidentially relevant.

This example, too, can be suitably modified to show that different and possibly conflicting hypotheses can be thought to be supported by the same state of affairs. Suppose that one man, as before, believes that Nick is the only person with a hat just that shade of gray, but the other believes that James is the only person who tosses hats on the banister in just that way. The first, paying attention only to the color of the hat, will take it as evidence that Nick is in the house, but the second, paying attention only to the location of the hat, will take it as evidence that James, rather than Nick, is in the house.[2]

What these examples show is that how one determines evidential relevance, why one takes some state of affairs as evidence for one hypothesis rather than for another, depends on one's other beliefs, which we can call background beliefs or assumptions. Thus, a given state of affairs can be taken as evidence for the same hypothesis in light of differing background beliefs, and it can be taken as evidence for quite different and even conflicting hypotheses given appropriately conflicting background beliefs. Similarly, different aspects of one state of affairs can be taken as evidence for the same hypothesis in light of differing background beliefs, and they can serve as evidence for different and even conflicting hypotheses given appropriately conflicting background beliefs.

The function of background beliefs is analogous to the function of background conditions in causal interactions. In an atmosphere that contains oxygen if one rubs two dry sticks together a flame (or at least a spark sufficient to ignite combustible materials such as straw or paper) results. In most contexts (those in which it is not surprising that there should be oxygen in the atmosphere) we pick out the rubbing of the sticks as the cause of the spark. We acknowledge that if there were no oxygen in the atmosphere, nor any functional equivalent of oxygen,

---

[2] It might be claimed that color is more central as evidence than location in this example, as the grayness of the hat is more important to its being the hat that it is than is the location and spatial attitude of the hat at any given moment. The features of the hat are being used as evidence not that the hat is the hat that it is but that James, owner of the hat, is in the house. In this respect color and location are equally central as evidence.

the sticks' friction would not cause the spark, but we do not regard the presence of oxygen as a cause of the spark. The presence of the oxygen is rather an enabling condition of the causal interaction. So it is with evidence and background beliefs: a state of affairs will only be taken to be evidence that something else is the case in light of some background belief or assumption asserting a connection between the two. The background belief is an enabling condition of the reasoning process in much the same way that environmental and other conditions enable the occurrence of causal interactions. The two processes are, however, disanalogous in that, while the end result of a causal interaction is an event or occurrence distinct from its cause, in the case of reasoning from evidence the end result need not be belief in, or inference to, the hypothesis detached from beliefs concerning the state or states of affairs taken to be evidence for it. The end result is often the more modest but complex belief that the hypothesis in question is probable or plausible in light of that state or states of affairs.

Background beliefs are what some philosophers would call principles of inference, but they are not principles in the sense that they can be abstracted from the sequence of reason for believing and belief. The examples above show that background beliefs can vary even though the pair "reason for believing" and "belief" or the pair "evidence" and "hypothesis" is the same. Rather than principles abstracted from a sequence they are beliefs in light of which one takes some x to be evidence for some h and to which one would appeal in defending the claim that x is evidence for h. Background beliefs function as they do because they are beliefs or assumptions about connections (actual or presumed, correlational or causal) between particular kinds of states of affairs and other kinds (of states of affairs). A given evidential relation may be determined by just one background belief or by a set of assumptions of varying degrees of generality and complexity, but in the absence of any such beliefs no state of affairs will be taken as evidence of any other.[3]

---

[3] The beliefs or assumptions mentioned so far have been about relations between particular kinds of things, events, or states. Not all beliefs that function as background beliefs in inferring are of this apparently synthetic or empirical nature. There are some, such as the beliefs expressed by such formulae as "if all observed a's have been F, then (it is likely that) all a's are F" and "if a is analogous to b in that it possesses properties F, G, and H, which are possessed by b, then (it is likely that) a also possesses the property I which is possessed by b," that seem much more abstract and schematic. The impetus for talk of principles of inference may have come from considering these beliefs, which are like principles of nondeductive reasoning. Because these principles function as the more empirical background beliefs do in inferring—that is, they allow one to identify a certain state of affairs as evidence that something else is the case—it seems better to drop

Consideration of the examples also shows that there is no unique or intrinsic relation between states of affairs in virtue of which they possess evidential status. The connections or regularities that we believe to hold between states of affairs and in light of which evidential relations are assessed are connections or regularities from some point of view, which is always susceptible to change. As will be argued more fully below, it follows from the fact that taking some state of affairs, x, to be evidence for some h is a function of background assumptions and that x's actually being evidence for h is similarly a function of background assumptions. Evidential support of hypotheses is thus a relative matter: while in the context of one set of beliefs or assumptions x will be evidence for h, in the context of a different set x will be evidence not for h but for some hypothesis, h', or for no hypothesis at all.

The dependence of evidential assessments on background assumptions might be conceded for nonspecialized contexts but denied for scientific contexts. This is in fact a common way of distinguishing science from nonscience. It can be argued that precisely what distinguishes scientific reasoning from ordinary, everyday reasoning is that in scientific inquiry inferences relying on hidden background assumptions are disallowed. Whereas one is perhaps sloppy about evidence in everyday contexts, evidential relations in science are clear, fixed, and absolute, independent of further assumptions. Recent work in the history of science, however, has persuaded many that such an attitude is unjustifiable.

As an initial illustration consider what might be inferred from the (supposed) fact that day and night alternate at a steady rate. (I oversimplify the actual situation for illustrative purposes.) This fact considered by itself suggests nothing. In the light of a heliostatic cosmology however, it can be taken as evidence that the earth is spinning round its axis at a steady rate. In the light of a geostatic cosmology, the evidential relation is quite different: the steady alternation of day and night would be evidence that the sun is moving round the earth at a steady rate. In both cases it must also be assumed that exposure to the sun and daylight are causally related. Considering the hypotheses in question independently of the theories with which we might associate them, we find no immediate relation to states of affairs that could count as evidence for them: "the earth is spinning round its axis at a steady rate" implies no statements that could describe evidence for the claim independently of something like the heliostatic theory. Only in

the appellation *principle* (at least in this context). We are then left simply with a distinction between more and less abstract background beliefs.

light of the latter is the steady alternation of day and night evidence for the hypothesis. The point is that it's not a matter of not thinking of the appropriate evidence for the hypothesis but a matter of having any reason at all to think that there is a relation between the earth's spinning on its axis at a steady rate and the steady alternation of day and night. The evidential relevance of the latter (supposed) fact depends on the background assumptions operative in any given context.

This example shows both the dependence of evidential status on background beliefs and the resulting possibility that the same state of affairs can be taken as evidence for conflicting hypotheses. To the extent that no one is said to have actually made the inferences involved, it may be said to be fictitious. However, examples of the use of a given state of affairs as evidence for conflicting hypotheses abound in the past (and the present) history of scientific inquiry, particularly at those junctures of major theory change, when experiments and discoveries are subject to multiple interpretations. Two well-known instances are the Michelson-Morley interferometer experiments in the late nineteenth century and Priestley's experiments with mercury oxide in the late eighteenth century. A schematic discussion of these will have to suffice to show how the uses to which these experimental results were put exemplify the account of evidential relations defended here.

The Michelson-Morley experiments were carried out to measure the relative motion of the earth in the ether, this to be determined by the difference in the speed of light beams sent out at 90° angles to each other, this in turn to be determined by shifts in the interference fringe system displayed by the interferometer. The Michelson-Morley apparatus showed no experimentally significant displacement. Perhaps because this null result was influential in the eventual acceptance by the scientific community of Einstein's special theory of relativity, it is often regarded as the experimental proof of the theory. However, given the assumptions of nineteenth-century classical physics, it could equally well be, and was by some, viewed as decisive evidence for the Lorentz-Fitzgerald contraction hypothesis, the hypothesis that bodies moving at speeds close to the speed of light contract in length along the direction of their motion.

According to Einstein, once the notion of absolute space is abandoned, a "luminiferous ether" is superfluous. Thus, that no effect of the ether on the motion of light could be detected by means of the interferometer showed that there was no ether to affect it. In the context of the assumptions of relativity theory, then, the experimental results are taken as evidence that there is no ether. In the context of the classical physics, in which the ether played so crucial a role, it simply was not possible to take the experiment in that way. It was troubling, it indicated that the theory needed alteration, but it was not, in a logical, as opposed to psychological, sense, a crucial experiment between the classical and relativistic theories. That is, it could not be assessed independently of the governing assumptions of one or the other of the two points of view, and hence its evidential relevance was determined by these assumptions.[4]

The "discovery" of oxygen by Joseph Priestley and Antoine Lavoisier provides an illustration of the role of background beliefs in highlighting different aspects of a given state of affairs in such a way as to have it support conflicting hypotheses. Priestley formed a mercury calx (now, oxide of mercury) by heating the metal in atmospheric air. He then found that by concentrating sunlight on the calx in a test tube it would become mercury again (decalcinate). In addition the decomposing calx released air in which combustible objects burned more brightly and quickly than in atmospheric air, in which mice were more frisky, and which gave Priestley a slight "high" when he inhaled it.

Lavoisier performed the same manipulation of mercury following instructions provided by Priestley in his description of the experiment and got similar results. The two thus had the same experimental information but approached it with different background beliefs. Priestley was still working with the phlogiston theory, while Lavoisier had rejected it and the qualitative theory of elements of which it was a part. Priestley's argument that the gas was "dephlogisticated air" rested primarily on the livelier combustion occurring in it, which was taken as evidence that the air had been depleted of its phlogiston and hence absorbed it more quickly from burning objects. Lavoisier, however, believing that a specific proportion of the atmospheric air combined with metals in calcination, took the fact that Priestley's air was released in the course of decalcination, together with the fact that it had properties that distinguished it from ordinary air, as evidence that a wholly new gas had been isolated, one that must combine with others to constitute atmospheric air. After further experimentation revealed its acidifying properties, he came to call it "oxygen gas." In the context

---

[4] This discussion must be schematic as there is considerable disagreement concerning the role and necessity of background beliefs in the development and acceptance of the special theory of relativity, as well as disagreement as to just which assumptions must be made. Compare Zahar (1973) and the ensuing discussions by Feyerabend (1974), Miller (1974), and Schaffner (1974), as well as Alan Musgrave (1974). The account presented here is intended as a framework within which such disputes can take place.

For defenses of the contraction hypothesis from the charge of being ad hoc see Holton (1973), pp. 261–352, and Grünbaum (1963), especially pp. 386–397.

of their differing background beliefs and assumptions different aspects of the same state of affairs became evidentially significant.[5]

EVIDENTIAL REASONING AND THEORY ACCEPTANCE

I have discussed the dependence of evidential relations on background beliefs or assumptions and shown that given appropriately differing background beliefs the same state of affairs can be taken as evidence for different and conflicting hypotheses. The cases of the Michelson-Morley experiment and of the discovery of oxygen show that this dependence holds even for scientific experiments and the hypotheses they are alleged to support, that is, they show that experimental results can be taken as evidence for hypotheses only in the context of some set of background beliefs. Reflection on these cases and their outcomes raises a number of related questions. Can reasoning and inference be shielded from influence by social and individual values, interests, and subjective preferences? Upon what is the acceptance of the background beliefs operative in the contexts discussed based? What sorts of criteria are relevant to deciding between different or competing (sets of) background beliefs? It is clear that if the criterion is evidential support, there must be some further set of background beliefs in light of which whatever is taken as evidence is so taken. On the other hand, to require that acceptance of all hypotheses, theories, assumptions, or beliefs be evidentially based is to fall into an infinite regress. I shall approach these questions by first contrasting the analysis of evidence and inference developed here with the accounts discussed in the previous chapter and more recent variations on them.

The Positivist Tradition

The relation described by Hempel is a formal one. As detailed in Chapter Two, evidence, on that view, is described in observation reports whose relevance to the hypotheses they confirm is secured by their entailing instances of these hypotheses. What would count as evidence for a hypothesis is determined by the form of hypothesis sentences and evidence sentences, not by their content. This means that inference to a hypothesis is not mediated by possibly value-laden assumptions. The only background assumption that might be at work is the principle of enumerative induction and then only in those cases where a universally quantified hypothesis is the object of confirmation. The problem of criteria of acceptance of background assumptions reduces to the justi-

[5] For more details see Lavoisier (1952) and Conant (1957).

fication of deductive and inductive inference. It becomes a philosophical and not an empirical or scientific problem.

While this might seem an ideal answer to the problems posed by background assumptions, it will not do as an analysis of evidential relations in the sciences. As argued in the previous chapter, the sentences describing evidence for hypotheses and those expressing hypotheses are typically not related in the appropriate ways. It is true that some laws, for example Boyle's law relating the pressure, volume, and temperature of a gas and Galileo's law of free fall, are of this nature. Thus, some evidential reasoning can be accounted for as inductive generalization or as reliance on empirical generalizations. Boyle's law is a generalization of a finite set of observed correlations between measured properties of gasses. It is supported by those correlations in light of the principle of induction. We can use the observation of changes in one of these parameters as evidence for claims about changes in another in light of Boyle's law. A description of the evidential relation confined in its scope to empirical generalizations is, however, of limited utility.

One solution would simply be to restrict the hypotheses and theories proposable in scientific contexts to propositions expressing only relationships among observables. This was the course taken by Blaise Pascal in his work on aero- and hydrostatics.[6] It is also one of the reasons his name does not appear in short lists of the seventeenth-century founders of modern science. Pascal urged and followed a rigorously empiricist research program, which effectively prevented him from distinguishing atmospheric weight from atmospheric pressure.

A slightly more permissive solution is to try to accommodate the use of nonobservables by scientists. The logical positivists' criterion of significance was one attempt to do this: terms purportedly referring to nonobservable, theoretical entities are admissible in a theory only as long as it is possible to eliminate such terms in a "rational reconstruction" of the theory. There is an extensive literature documenting the failure of this proposal in its many forms.[7]

In one of the most ambitious recent contributions to the literature of scientific confirmation Clark Glymour has proposed what he calls the "bootstrap" strategy to overcome the problem of determining the evidential relevance of observation reports to hypotheses containing

[6] See "Preface to the Treaties on the Vacuum," "New Experiments Concerning the Vacuum," and Pascal's letters to Pere Noel and Le Pailleur in Pascal (1952). See also Pascal (1937), pp. 2–66, 91–112.

[7] For example, Maxwell (1962); Putnam (1975); Scriven (1958).

terms other than those in the reports.[8] The central idea of the bootstrap strategy is this: a hypothesis *h* is confirmed by using other hypotheses (from the theory *T* of which *h* is a part) to deduce instances of *h* from data obtained by established observational and experimental procedures. The idea is worked out in its greatest detail for those cases where an instance of *h* is a sentence assigning a particular value to some theoretical quantity, like pressure or temperature, but is generalizable to nonmathematical reasoning as well. A hypothesis *h* is said to be directly confirmed by evidence *e* relative to *T* if instances of *h* are deduced from *e* and a set of auxilliary hypotheses of *T* . An auxilliary hypothesis of *T* essential to the direct confirmation of *h* by *e* is indirectly confirmed relative to *T*.

Detailed discussions of possible and actual argumentation in four episodes in the history of science illustrate the deployment of the bootstrap strategy in scientific reasoning. Bootstrap confirmation is, in at least some cases, a better representation of actual reasoning. Glymour also argues that it is better able to give reason and coherence to many nostrums common among scientists, such as the preference for a variety of evidence, than some previous accounts. Although intended as a modification of the Hempelian model of confirmation that does not collapse into Kuhnian wholism, bootstrap confirmation does not solve the problems posed by the introduction of background assumptions (a.k.a. auxilliary hypotheses) as mediators of evidential relations.

For application of bootstrapping in its strict form a theory must be axiomatized or axiomatizable. That is, it must be developed at least well enough that auxiliary hypotheses are available for the bootstrap testing of other hypotheses.[9] The influence of values or subjective preferences could be ruled out on the simple inductive model because confirmation depended only on independently established observation reports. In the bootstrap model confirmation of a hypothesis *h* is relative to the auxiliary hypotheses used in deducing instances of *h* from observation reports. Thus, ruling out the influence of values or subjective preferences on the model depends on the degree to which the auxiliary hypotheses are themselves free of or confirmed in a manner that rules out such influence.

Regarding the confirmation of an auxiliary hypothesis, there are several possibilities. (1) All the hypotheses of a theory *T* may be confirmable in the sense that each is confirmed or confirmable relative to some

---

[8] Glymour (1980).

[9] As I understand it, auxiliary status is relative to particular tests in which a hypothesis is used for bootstrapping and is thus not an intrinsic or permanent character of some hypotheses as opposed to others.

subset of the hypotheses of T. Thus, the auxiliary hypotheses are confirmed relative to some subset of T. (2) All the hypotheses of T may be confirmable in the sense that those auxiliary hypotheses not themselves confirmed or confirmable relative to T are established independently of T, for example by being part of and confirmed relative to some other theory T'. (3) Some of the auxiliary hypotheses of T are neither confirmed relative to T nor established independently of T.

The third possibility, of course, offers no guarantee against influence by subjective preference. The first possibility can be subdivided into two subcases: (a) all the hypotheses are directly confirmed relative to T and (b) all the hypotheses of T are either directly or indirectly confirmed relative to T. Subcase (a) generates a strong criterion and subcase (b) a weak criterion for the admissibility of hypotheses. While the strong criterion would make contextual motivations for the adoption of some hypothesis irrelevant, it represents a state that is rarely, if ever, realized in practice. When a theory is being developed, the criterion for the inclusion of specific hypotheses or principles is not that they are directly confirmed relative to (other hypotheses of) the theory but that they are relevant to the explanation of the phenomena comprehended by the theory. In the terms of the current discussion we could say that we admit hypotheses if they are relevant to the confirmation of other hypotheses of the theory without requiring that they themselves be directly confirmed relative to the theory. To require direct confirmation of all hypotheses places constraints on the practice of science comparably unreasonable to those imposed by the older account of confirmation. In practice, then, the first possibility regarding the confirmation of auxiliary hypotheses must be interpreted as its second subcase, the weak criterion: some hypotheses are directly confirmed relative to the theory and others are not. The latter are indirectly confirmed. Since a value- or interest-laden hypothesis could be essential to the direct confirmation of another hypothesis, the weak criterion is not sufficient to block contextual values, interests, and subjective preferences from the assessment of evidential relevance and hence from hypothesis acceptance.[10]

Thus, a scientific methodology that guaranteed noninterference by evaluative concerns would have to restrict admissable theories to those satisfying the second set of possibilities. Is the rule or set of rules contained in this set adequate for the sciences we have? One major prob-

[10] I take this to be an implication of Glymour's remark that "virtually any hypothesis in a theory can be worked into a computation of almost any quantity"; Glymour (1980), p. 374.

lem with adopting this as a constraint on our theories is that procedures for independently establishing the requisite auxiliary hypotheses are often not available, if at all, until well after a theory has been developed and adopted. Such a constraint, like the strong version of the first possibility, would eliminate any science more sophisticated than Pascal's.[11]

Thus, an empiricism that grants independent meaningfulness to nonobservational statements and that acknowledges the logical gap between hypotheses and evidence statements has no a priori grounds for eliminating contextual values from scientific reasoning. The methodological constraints that might have eliminated value-laden auxiliary hypotheses or background assumptions are the very ones shown to be too restrictive for the analysis of evidential relations. Similar considerations can be applied to the possibility of distinguishing evidence *simpliciter* from what is taken as evidence. To insist on this possibility presupposes that we have a way, in the case of differing evidential assessments owing to different background assumptions, of deciding which assumption is correct and which false. This would have to involve appeal to evidence, and what is offered as evidence will in turn be so in light of further background assumptions. Thus the relativity of evidential relations is thorough: if a set of data e is taken to be evidence for hypothesis h in light of background assumption b, then we cannot with any finality determine whether it is correctly so taken by examining the evidential support for b, since whatever data e' is taken to be evidence for b is so in light of some further assumption b'. To maintain that there is a distinction between what is taken to be evidence and what is *really* evidence is to suppose that there is some nonempirical way to discover the truth or falsity of background assumptions. The bootstrap model does draw our attention to the discrete character of the auxiliary hypotheses or assumptions required to secure the evidential relevance of particular bits of data to particular hypotheses. Thus, even though observational and experimental data relevant to the direct confirmation of auxiliary hypotheses may not be available (either in fact or in principle), we are not precluded from inquiring as to what kinds of reasons *can* be offered in their support. That is, we may have reasons to accept a set of background assumptions that are short of reasons demonstrating the truth of those assumptions.

[11] This seems to be the substance of Feyerabend's complaints against methodology. See, for example, Feyerabend (1970a).

The Wholist Tradition

In the account of evidential relations emerging from the Wholist view there is no comparable problem about admitting certain types of theories. The denial of a theory-independent observation language and of theory-neutral observation, however, leads, as we saw above, to paradox. Charges of paradoxicality can be dismissed if there is no other way to account for the cases of theory change to be found in the history of science. If what seem to us to be the same states of affairs are taken as evidence for different and sometimes conflicting theories, then it must be that the meaning of terms used to describe those states of affairs have changed and that what is seen is different. The situation that prompts the paradoxical analysis, however, is not at all surprising in light of the analysis of evidential relations developed in this paper. If some state of affairs is evidence for a hypothesis only in light of some further background belief or assumption, then changes in background beliefs will result in changes in evidential status. Thus, it is not necessary to suppose that we must account for all cases of apparently conflicting theories supported by what seems to be the same body of evidence by saying that terms in the two theories have different meanings. Rather we can say that the relevant background beliefs have changed.

Kuhn's own examples are quite amenable to this kind of treatment. He says, for example, that an Aristotelian and a Galilean physicist looking at a swinging stone or pendulum *see* different things: the Aristotelian sees a body falling with difficulty, a case of constrained fall, while the Galilean sees oscillatory motion, a pendulum. The visual experience of each is incommensurable with that of the other to such a degree that if they were to begin talking about the stone they would be talking about different things. Clearly there is a profound difference between what the Galilean and the Aristotelian want to say about the swinging stone. Alas, Kuhn's attempt to explain and describe that difference leaves us finally unable to say that there is a difference since there is no common referent of their potential remarks.

Using the notion of background beliefs, however, a more satisfactory analysis of the situation is possible. The Aristotelian believes that the natural motion of all items (elements) in the sublunary sphere is in a straight line to their natural place. This belief about motion determines what features of the swinging stone are going to be important, and clearly what is important in the situation is that the stone (whose natural place is at the center of the earth) eventually comes to rest at a position which is as close to the center as it can get (given that it is constrained by the string or chain) and hence that the stone, swinging, is in a state of unnatural motion until it comes to rest at its final position.

The Galilean, in accounting for this same phenomenon, is operating with the impetus theory of motion that already had a theory of the oscillatory motion of vibratory strings. In the context of this theory, features other than those that strike the Aristotelian become important, in particular the repetitive and oscillatory character of the stone's motion. In this respect the motion of the stone is analogous to that of the vibrating string and is given an analogous explanation.

It is not, therefore, necessary to say that the Aristotelian and the Galilean are seeing different things. Rather we can say that they are seeing the same thing but attending to different aspects of it. It is true that the aspects singled out become the focus of explanation and can be used as evidence for the differing hypotheses about the motion of the swinging stone, but there is no need to suppose that the Galilean or the Aristotelian must fail to see aspects that interest the other, nor to suppose that there is no description of the situation that both could accept and that would then form the basis for discussion of differences.[12] To use the notion of background beliefs as opposed to gestalt-type notions for analysis of this example and similar ones shows also that it is not always the case, in theory change, that exactly the same body of evidence supports conflicting theories. In the pendulum case different features constitute evidence for different hypotheses, so they are not strictly speaking supported by the same evidence, even though the different features are features of what is identifiable as the same state of affairs.

Kuhn analyzes the discovery of oxygen by both Priestley and Lavoisier in similar fashion. Priestley and Lavoisier, when looking at the new substance, *saw* different things: Priestley saw dephlogisticated air and Lavoisier saw oxygen. But though he later repeated the experiment on his own, Lavoisier initially constructed his different account on the basis of Priestley's own "theory-laden" description of the experiment. Priestley's description, then, cannot have been as "theory-laden" as one would have to suppose on Kuhn's account, that is, he must have described his experiments in such a way that they could be viewed as having different evidential relevance to one with different background beliefs and information. Thus, in addition to eluding the philosophical difficulties attendant upon Kuhn's analysis the account of this case offered earlier in the chapter seems to accord better with the actual facts.

---

[12] I am relying in the above on Kuhn's own reading of the impetus theory's account of vibration. See Kuhn (1970a), p. 120.

Mary Hesse, in the essay "Theory and Observation," has recast one of Feyerabend's examples to make a parallel point about meaning.[13] Hesse rejects the idea that there is or could be a stable and theory-neutral observation language. Her argument depends neither on historical example nor on theories of perception but on remarks about learning the meaning and use of (and assigning these to) referring terms and predicates. Referring terms, she argues, are used to denote members of classes of similar things. The relation of similarity is not, however, transitive; therefore the application of such a term to a class of objects, in particular the specification of the class to which the term is applied, eventually and inevitably involves some loss of information. As the stock of referring terms and the generalizations into which they enter grows, conflicts arise among the generalizations. These conflicts are resolved by reclassifying objects, that is, changing the meanings of terms in order to preserve consistency among generalizations or to preserve the applicability of a generalization. Thus, Hesse concludes, as does W.V.O. Quine on the basis of similar considerations, that no predicates are immune to revision, no predicates can be part of a stable and theory-neutral observation language.

Hesse goes on to argue that the theory ladenness of observation terms does not, however, support theses of radical theory incommensurability. In any given case two proponents of different theories will find areas of intersection between their theories, aspects of experience in which they are inclined to use terms in the same way. Their theories overlap here, and if they are talking about phenomena both within and outside of their area of common experience, it's quite possible that they will make predictions that coincide in the common area but diverge in the area beyond. Feyerabend's example is "fall." While there is a range of experiences about which an Aristotelian and a follower of Anaximenes will agree in their use of "fall," there is also a range of possible experiences (which neither in fact had) about which they would fail to agree. As long as their discourse remains within the boundaries of their common experience, however, they cannot know that they are using terms in different ways. On the other hand, the overlap is the basis that enables them to communicate, to know, for instance, when each is signifying negation and when agreement. Thus, Hesse argues, it enables them ultimately to discover that regarding some area outside the overlap they do disagree and to reconstruct from their common language whether their disagreement lies in the theories they hold, in the meanings they have assigned to terms occurring in

[13] Hesse (1980), pp. 63–110, especially pp. 95–99.

those theories, or both. As was established above, however, theory ladenness does not account for all cases of conflicting evidential assessment. I would add to this list, therefore, the background assumptions in light of which they assess the evidential relevance of their common experience.

Several useful lessons can be gleaned from Hesse's discussion. One emerges from her particular way of arguing against the existence of a theory-neutral observation language. Suppose some term o occurs in the description of data used as evidence for some hypothesis h belonging to theory T. The theory with which o is laden, and with respect to which the use of o is not neutral, may not be T but some other theory. It does not follow from the theory ladenness of meaning, therefore, that observations cannot be used as independent tests of theories but only that they cannot be so used in connection with theories presupposed by the descriptions of those observations. Secondly, her discussion is a good reminder that even when proponents of incompatible theories agree on the description of what they are observing, it doesn't follow that we can label their description as theory-neutral. Their theories may in that one instance coincide with each other but could well conflict with a third when it is brought to bear on the same phenomena. The thesis of theory ladenness, as Hesse reworks it, therefore, does not imply that incompatible theories are incommensurable or that incompatible hypotheses belong to incommensurable theories. A theory-laden description of a set of observations is not the only description that can be given of that set, and the theory with which the description is laden may not be the theory in whose support that set of observations is cited.

Summary

The model of evidential relations that I have defended has points of resemblance with both the positivist and the wholist accounts. Like the positivist account, it presupposes that data can be specified independently of the hypotheses and theories for which the data have evidential relevance. This is not to deny that some data (or evidence) may only be conceived or sought in the context of investigating some hypothesis, but it is to insist that the description of data cannot presuppose the truth of the hypothesis for which they serve as evidence. The model also resembles Kuhn's in that some third, distinct, element is appealed to as providing the context in which the assessment of the evidential relevance of experiments and observed (or alleged) states of affairs takes place. The character of this further element differs. In this analysis, while background beliefs determine what states of affairs count as evidence for a hypothesis, all three of these elements—state of affairs, hypothesis, background beliefs—are independently specifiable. For Kuhn, however, the further element, the paradigm, so determines the context of assessment that one's perception of the world changes with the theories one adopts in such a way that one sees it as confirming the theory. This creates a bond between evidence and hypothesis impossible to break and even destroys, ultimately, the concept of evidence as something to which one can appeal in defending a hypothesis. The limitations on incommensurability on which Hesse insists restore meaningfulness to the concept of evidence, although evidential relations must be understood relative to some context of assumptions.

EVIDENTIAL REASONING AND RATIONALITY

Kuhn's and Feyerabend's examination of historical cases led them to say that theory choice is not determined by evidence, since there is no theory-independent way to describe the evidence, that is, there is no set of neutral and stable evidence statements to which one can appeal in deciding between two conflicting theories. To the charge that on this account science is irrational Kuhn responds by claiming that insofar as theory choice is determined by values, in particular such internal values as simplicity or greater problem-solving ability, it is not irrational. Feyerabend, on the other hand, has embraced and encouraged irrationality: Galileo was irrational to accept Copernicanism because it was less strongly supported by the available evidence than the Ptolemaic theory, but Galileo was right: flying in the face of evidence made him a better, more creative scientist, therefore it's better to be irrational. To adhere to theories just because they are evidentially supported hinders scientific progress.

Whatever one may think of these strictures, it seems clear that what leads both Feyerabend and Kuhn to their respective assessments of rationality in science is not just historical cases but an implicit acceptance of the formal, positivist (Hempelian) conception of evidence.[14] Because the relationship of evidence to hypothesis, in the Kuhn and Feyerabend accounts, is not direct and unequivocal, because neither states of affairs nor hypotheses stand in unique relationships with each other, hypothesis acceptance is thought not to be based on evidence and hence to be, to that extent, irrational. For both, the positivist analysis is a

[14] One could respond to Feyerabend, for instance, that Galileo did not fly in the face of evidence but that he chose (in light of other theoretical commitments) which data to take seriously and which to ignore.

description of an ideally rational procedure to which science, for better or for worse, fails to measure up. Many of their followers in the sociology of science seem to have absorbed the same attitude.[15]

So to regard the formal positivist analysis is to assume that a procedure such as it describes is possible, but just not the way things are, for one reason or another. And in fact the arguments against positivist forms of empiricism presented by both Kuhn and Feyerabend rely heavily on historical example and, in Kuhn's case, on a psychological hypothesis about perception. The account of evidential relations defended in this chapter, while it may have implications for psychology and while it suggests a new approach to the analysis of historical cases, rests on considerations of a logical character. Thus, the positivist account is not even an ideal and must be rejected not because the vagaries of human psychology prevent us from realizing it but because it involves a radical misconception of the way in which hypotheses and evidence are related to one another. In that account hypotheses and evidence are abstracted from their dynamic context of inquiry, of observation and reasoning, and treated as elements in a static, unchanging construction, as museum pieces.

In this chapter I have argued that the relation between hypotheses and evidence is determined by background assumptions operative in the context in which data are being assessed. Before going on to the questions of values, subjectivity, and objectivity that such an account clearly provokes, let me summarize the main features and additional advantages of this account.

However we end up characterizing observational data, *they* are what serve as evidence for hypotheses (and theories). Data—even as represented in descriptions of observations and experimental results—do not on their own, however, indicate that for which they can serve as evidence. Hypotheses, on the other hand, are or consist of statements whose content always exceeds that of the statements describing the observational data. There is, thus, a logical gap between data and hypotheses. In some cases, as noted above, they are related as instance or instances of generalization. Even instances, however, are *evidence* for the truth or plausibility of their generalizations only in light of some version of the principle of enumerative induction.[16] As was also

[15] See, for example, the introductions to two collections of essays in the sociology of science: Barnes and Edge, eds. (1982), pp. 1–12; and Knorr-Cetina and Michael Mulkay, eds. (1983), pp. 1–17.

[16] The empiricist account of confirmation can, then, be seen as a limiting case describing the relation of hypotheses *h* and evidence *e* when *e* is assigned evidential relevance to *h* by the principle of simple induction. The abstractness of the principle of induction

noted above, in the interesting cases of scientific reasoning, for example, that concerning the characterization of and relations among subatomic particles, hypotheses contain (as essential components) expressions not occurring in the description of the observations and
experimental results serving as evidence for them. But causal hypotheses, too, contain expressions ("cause," "influence") that do not occur
in the statements of correlation that serve for evidence for them. In
these cases reliance upon background beliefs or assumptions that assert relations (of causality or other forms of interrelation) between
these different classes of phenomena is much more apparent than it is
in cases of (relatively) simple inductive or probabilistic reasoning.

Background beliefs or assumptions, then, are expressed in statements that are required in order to demonstrate the evidential import
of a set of data to a hypothesis. As such, they both facilitate and constrain reasoning from one category of phenomena to another. Although I shall use these terms interchangeably, it is appropriate to
speak of beliefs when these statements are more or less explicitly
adopted as tenets and of assumptions when their necessity to a bit of
evidential reasoning is not explicitly acknowledged. Relativizing evidential import to background assumptions thus involves abandoning
the attempt to specify the relation between evidence and hypotheses by
means of syntactic criteria and seeing this relation as involving substantive assumptions instead. Evidential relations are not autonomous
or eternal truths but are necessarily constituted in the context in which
evidence is assessed. I've considered above some cases in which different background assumptions facilitated varying interpretations of the
same experimental data. In later chapters devoted more specifically to
the discussion of particular scientific research projects I shall look
more closely at the ways in which both the immediate context of research and its social environment interact in the interpretation and assessment of data.

If rationality is, at least in part, the acceptance or rejection of beliefs
on the basis of evidence, then theory and hypothesis choice is, when
based on evidence, rational. Rationality, however, is not the infallible
road to truth or away from error that it is often claimed to be. Both
the Aristotelian and the Galilean are being rational when they defend
their respective accounts of the swinging stone. What explains why it
serves as evidence for different hypotheses is not that the two see it

(cf. n3), it should be noted, does not make it a formal or syntactic principle. As has been
noted since Hume, it involves a substantive claim about the persistence of regularities in
the natural world. And a Popperian falsificationist would urge that we cease to rely on
it.

differently and in ways determined by those hypotheses in question but that they hold different background assumptions in light of which its evidential relevance is differently assessed. Once it is accepted that the evidential relation is always determined by background assumptions, then it is easy to see that there could be a neutral description of a given state of affairs, that is, one agreed to by both parties to a dispute, and no agreement on the hypotheses for which it is taken as evidence. It is also easy to see that both parties are being perfectly rational. It is rational to take some state of affairs as evidence for a hypothesis in light of background assumptions one accepts. It would be irrational to assess evidential relations in a manner inconsistent with such background assumptions and antirational or nonrational to accept or reject hypotheses with no regard for evidence.

CONCLUSION

This approach to evidence solves a number of problems. Substantive background assumptions can bridge the gap between hypotheses and evidence that the formal ties of the positivist analysis cannot. Thus, the fact that conflicting hypotheses and theories have seemed to be supported by the same state of affairs can be explained by appealing to the different background beliefs in light of which the state is assigned evidential relevance to one or another hypothesis. The appeal to incommensurability, with its attendant logical difficulties, becomes unnecessary. Background assumptions may not always be explicit, but they are articulable.

Besides offering a solution to these logical problems the analysis has two additional strengths. In focussing discussion on the relation between evidence and hypotheses rather than on that between evidence and theories it can be used to examine the structure of reasoning in current and ongoing research projects that may not yet have developed a system of explanation comprehensive enough to be called a theory. A great deal of contemporary biological research is of this nature and is still structured by background assumptions that mediate inferences between data and hypotheses. Thus, the contextual analysis can be used to compare inference and argument in the formation of theories as well as in the defense of finished theories.

Its second strength consists in its ability to accommodate the interests of the different communities that have a stake in any given scientific research program. In particular, it is sensitive to the demands that nonspecialists who look to scientific inquiry for an account of the natural world (ought to) pose to any seriously proposed hypothesis: What is the evidence? And why is this data evidence for this hypothesis? In other words, Why should I believe (or accept) this?[17] However incommensurability is understood, it implies the meaninglessness of this question asked by one who is not part of the community advancing a particular theory or hypothesis. The formal requirements of data and a rationale for assigning to the data evidential relevance to the hypothesis proposed at least provides a framework within which externally (and internally) generated questions of belief and justification make sense.

While this approach solves some problems, it generates others. In particular, by relativizing what counts as evidence to background beliefs or assumptions, hypothesis acceptance on the basis of evidence is also thus relativized. This invites the question: How can science so described come close to meeting the ideal of objectivity? The intrusion of subjective preference into evidential relations can, it seems, only be blocked by some absolute, nonrelative means of determining which hypotheses are supported and which not. If background beliefs mediate the relation between hypotheses and their evidence, then if any states of affairs are evidentially relevant to them, that is, to the background beliefs, this relevance can itself only be ascertained in light of further background beliefs. In the light of this argument the promise of external or theory-independent standards of evaluation seems to vanish. In the absence of that clear and distinct perception of the truth of assumptions and fundamental propositions posited by Descartes and other rationalists, the choice of background assumptions is as relative as the determination of evidential relations. Without some absolute and nonarbitrary means of determining acceptable or correct background assumptions there seems no way to block the influence of subjective preference. The next chapter, therefore, addresses the problem of objectivity posed by a contextualist analysis of evidence.

[17] For a defense of antispecialization see Maxwell (1980).

CHAPTER FOUR

Values and Objectivity

OBJECTIVITY is a characteristic ascribed variously to beliefs, individuals, theories, observations, and methods of inquiry. It is generally thought to involve the willingness to let our beliefs be determined by "the facts" or by some impartial and nonarbitrary criteria rather than by our wishes as to how things ought to be. A specification of the precise nature of such involvement is a function of what it is that is said to be objective. In this chapter I will review some common ideas about objectivity and argue that the objectivity of science is secured by the social character of inquiry. This chapter is a first step, therefore, towards socializing cognition.

Some part of the popular reverence for science has its origin in the belief that scientific inquiry, unlike other modes of inquiry, is by its very nature objective. In the modern mythology, the replacement of a mode of comprehension that simply projects human needs and values into the cosmos by a mode that views nature at a distance and dispassionately "puts nature to the question," in the words of Francis Bacon, is seen as a major accomplishment of the maturing human intellect.[1] The development of this second mode of approaching the natural world is identified, according to this view, with the development of science and the scientific method. Science is thought to provide us with a view of the world that is objective in two seemingly quite different senses of that term. In one sense objectivity is bound up with questions about the truth and referential character of scientific theories, that is, with issues of scientific realism. In this sense to attribute objectivity to science is to claim that the view provided by science is an accurate description of the facts of the natural world as they are; it is a correct view of the objects to be found in the world and of their relations with each other. In the second sense objectivity has to do with modes of inquiry. In this sense to attribute objectivity to science is to claim that the view provided by science is one achieved by reliance upon nonarbitrary and nonsubjective criteria for developing, accepting, and rejecting the hypotheses and theories that make up the view. The reliance

---

[1] This mythology originates with the founders of modern science—compare Isaac Newton's "Rules of Reasoning in Philosophy" in Newton (1953), pp. 3–5—and has come to be the standard view.

upon and use of such criteria as well as the criteria themselves are what is called scientific method. Common wisdom has it that if science is objective in the first sense it is because it is objective in the second.

At least two things can be intended by the ascription of objectivity to scientific method. Often scientists speak of the objectivity of data. By this they seem to mean that the information upon which their theories and hypotheses rest has been obtained in such a way as to justify their reliance upon it. This involves the assumption or assurance that experiments have been properly performed and that quantitative data have not been skewed by any faults in the design of survey instruments or by systematic but uncharacteristic eccentricities in the behavior of the sample studied. If a given set of data has been objectively obtained in this sense, one is thereby licensed to believe that it provides a reliable view of the world in the first of the two senses of objectivity distinguished above. In light of the problem of theory ladenness discussed in Chapter Three, this kind of objectivity must be qualified. What can be reliable is the relation of measurements one to another within a particular dimension or kind of scale—for example, the relation between what we label as the pressure and temperature of a gas. Here what is reliable is a certain covariance in the measurements obtained by the use of certain instruments. That pressure and temperature are real properties of real entities or that their measurements provide us an unmediated view of the natural world as it is does not follow from their covariance. Thus, scientists' concern for the objectivity of data does not have implications for the philosophical view known as scientific realism and discussed in Chapter Two. While objective, that is, reliable, measurement is indeed one crucial aspect of objective scientific method,[2] it is not the only dimension in which questions about the objectivity of methods can arise. In ascribing (or denying) objectivity to a method we can also be concerned about the extent to which it provides means of assessing hypotheses and theories in an unbiased and unprejudiced manner.

In this chapter I will explore more deeply the nature of this second mode of scientific objectivity and its connection with the logic of discourse in the natural sciences. As we saw above, logical positivists have relied upon formal logic and a priori epistemological requirements as keys to developing the logical analysis of science, while their historically minded wholist critics have insisted upon the primacy of scientific practice as revealed by study of the history of science. According to the

[2] It has become a subject of increased concern lately in light of several alleged incidents of data faking. Compare Broad (1981).

former view, science does indeed appear to be, by its very nature, free of subjective preference, whereas according to the latter view, subjectivity plays a major role in theory development and theory choice. Witnesses to the debate seem to be faced with a choice between two unacceptable alternatives: a logical analysis that is historically unsatisfactory and a historical analysis that is logically unsatisfactory. This kind of dilemma suggests a debate whose participants talk past one another rather than addressing common issues. Certainly part of the problem consists in attempts to develop a comprehensive account of science on the basis either of normative logical constraints or of empirical historical considerations. My analysis makes no pretense to totality or completion. It suggests, rather, a framework to be filled-in and developed both by epistemologists whose task is to develop criteria and standards of knowledge, truth, and rational belief and by historians and sociologists whose task is to make visible those historical and institutional features of the practice of science that affect its content. The extended case study in chapters Six through Eight shows how it can be applied to the analysis of a particular research program. To make way for this interdisciplinary framework, I begin by briefly reviewing the treatment of objectivity and subjectivity in the competing analyses of the logic of science.

OBJECTIVITY, SUBJECTIVITY, AND INDIVIDUALISM

The positivist analysis of confirmation guaranteed the objectivity of science by tying the acceptance of hypotheses and theories to a public world over whose description there can be no disagreement. Positivists allow for a subjective, nonempirical element in scientific inquiry by distinguishing between a context of discovery and a context of justification.[3] The context of discovery for a given hypothesis is constituted by the circumstances surrounding its initial formulation—its origin in dreams, guesses, and other aspects of the mental and emotional life of the individual scientist. Two things should be noted here. First, these nonempirical elements are understood to be features of an individual's psychology. They are treated as randomizing factors that promote novelty rather than as beliefs or attitudes that are systematically related to the culture, social structure, or socioeconomic interests of the context within which an individual scientist works. Secondly, in the context of justification these generative factors are disregarded, and the hypothesis is considered only in relation to its observable conse-

---

[3] Hempel (1966), pp. 3–18, and Popper (1962), pp. 42–59.

quences, which determine its acceptability. This distinction enables positivists to acknowledge the play of subjective factors in the initial development of hypotheses and theories while guaranteeing that their acceptance remains untainted, determined not by subjective preferences but by observed reality. The subjective elements that taint its origins are purged from scientific inquiry by the methods characteristic of the context of justification: controlled experiments, rigorous deductions, et cetera. When one is urged to be objective or "scientific," it is this reliance on an established and commonly accepted reality that is being recommended. The logical positivist model of confirmation simply makes the standard view of scientific practice more systematic and logically rigorous.

As long as one takes the positivist analysis as providing a model to which any inquiry must conform in order to be objective and rational, then to the degree that actual science departs from the model it fails to be objective and rational. As noted above with respect to evidence and inference, both the historians and philosophers who have attacked the old model and those who have defended it have at times taken this position. The only disagreement with respect to objectivity, then, seems to be over the question of whether actual, historical science does or does not realize the epistemological ideal of objectivity. Defenders of the old model have argued that science ("good science") does realize the ideal. Readers of Kuhn and Feyerabend take their arguments to show that science is not objective, that objectivity has been fetishized by traditionalists. These authors themselves have somewhat more subtle approaches. While Kuhn has emphasized the role of such subjective factors as personality, education, and group commitments in theory choice, he also denies that his is a totally subjectivist view. As noted earlier, he suggests that values such as relative simplicity and relative problem-solving ability can and do function as nonarbitrary criteria in theory acceptance. Such values can be understood as internal to inquiry, especially by those to whom scientific inquiry just is problem solving.[4] Feyerabend, on the other hand, has rejected the relevance to science of canons of rationality or of general criteria of theory acceptance and defends a positive role for subjectivity in science.[5]

The shortcomings of these models as accounts of evidence were discussed in the preceding chapters. How can the contextualist analysis of evidence, with its consequent denial of any logically guaranteed in-

[4] Laudan (1977) does articulate criteria for what counts as progress. These are not necessarily criteria or standards for truth.
[5] Feyerabend (1975).

dependence from contextual values, be accommodated within a perspective that demands or presupposes the objectivity of scientific inquiry?

As a first step in answering this question it is important to distinguish between objectivity as a characteristic of scientific method and objectivity as a characteristic of individual scientific practitioners or of their attitudes and practices. The standard accounts of scientific method tend to conflate the two, resulting in highly individualistic accounts of knowledge. Both philosophical accounts assume that method, the process by which knowledge is produced, is the application of rules to data. The positivist or traditional empiricist account of objectivity attributes objectivity to the practitioner to the extent that she or he has followed the method. Scientific method, on this view, is something that *can* be practiced by a single individual: sense organs and the capacity to reason are all that are required for conducting controlled experiments or practicing rigorous deduction. For Kuhn and for the contextualist account sketched above rationality and deference to observational data are not sufficient to guarantee the objectivity of individuals. For Kuhn this is because these intellectual activities are carried out in the context of a paradigm assented to by the scientific community. But, although Kuhn emphasizes the communitarian nature of the sciences, the theory of meaning he developed to account for the puzzling aspects of scientific change that first drew his attention reduces that community to a solipsistic monad incapable of recognizing and communicating with other monads/communities. Kuhn's account is, thus, as individualist as the empiricist one. The contextualist account makes the exercise of reason and the interpretation of data similarly dependent on a context of assumptions. Why is it not subject to the same problems?

OBJECTIVITY, CRITICISM, AND SOCIAL KNOWLEDGE

Two shifts of perspective make it possible to see how scientific method or scientific knowledge is objective even in the contextualist account. One shift is to return to the idea of science as practice. The analysis of evidential relations outlined above was achieved by thinking about science as something that is done, that involves some form of activity on the part of someone, the scientist. Because we think the goal of the scientist's practice is knowledge, it is tempting to follow tradition and seek solutions in abstract or universal rules. Refocussing on science as practice makes possible the second shift, which involves regarding scientific method as something practiced not primarily by individuals but by social groups.

The social nature of scientific practice has long been recognized. In her essay "Perception, Interpretation and the Sciences" Marjorie Grene discusses three aspects of the social character of science.[6] One she sees as the existence of the scientific disciplines as "social enterprises," the individual members of which are dependent on one another for the conditions (ideas, instruments, et cetera) under which they practice. Another related aspect is that initiation into scientific inquiry requires education. One does not simply declare oneself a biologist but learns the traditions, questions, mathematical and observational techniques, "the sense of what to do next," from someone who has herself or himself been through a comparable initiation and then practiced. One "enters into a world" and learns how to live in that world from those who already live there. Finally, as the practitioners of the sciences all together constitute a network of communities embedded in a society, the sciences are also among a society's activities and depend for their survival on that society's valuing what they do. Much of the following can be read as an elaboration of these three points, particularly as regards the outcome, or product, of scientific practices, namely scientific knowledge. What I wish particularly to stress is that the objectivity of scientific inquiry is a consequence of this inquiry's being a social, and not an individual, enterprise.

The application of scientific method, that is, of any subset of the collection of means of supporting scientific theory on the basis of experiential data, requires by its nature the participation of two or more individuals. Even brief reflection on the actual conditions of scientific practice shows that this is so. Scientific knowledge is, after all, the product of many individuals working in (acknowledged or unacknowledged) concert. As noted earlier, scientific inquiry is complex in that it consists of different kinds of activities. It consists not just in producing theories but also in (producing) concrete interactions with, as well as models—mechanical, electrical, and mathematical—of, natural processes. These activities are carried out by different individuals, and in this era of "big science" a single complex experiment may be broken into parts, each of which will be charged to a different individual or group of individuals. The integration and transformation of these activities into a coherent understanding of a given phenomenon are a matter of social negotiations.

One might argue that this is at least in principle the activity of a

[6] Grene (1985).

single individual. But, even if we were to imagine such group efforts as individual efforts, scientific knowledge is not produced by collecting the products of such imagined individuals into one whole. It is instead produced through a process of critical emendation and modification of those individual products by the rest of the scientific community. Experiments get repeated with variations by individuals other than their originators, hypotheses and theories are critically examined, restated, and reformulated before becoming an accepted part of the scientific canon. What are known as scientific breakthroughs build, whether this is acknowledged or not, on previous work and rest on a tradition of understandings, even when the effect of the breakthrough will be to undermine those understandings.[7]

The social character of scientific knowledge is made especially apparent by the organization of late twentieth-century science, in which the production of knowledge is crucially determined by the gatekeeping of peer review. Peer review determines what research gets funded and what research gets published in the journals, that is, what gets to count as knowledge. Recent concern over the breakdown of peer review and over fraudulent research simply supports the point. The most startling study of peer review suggested that scientific papers in at least one discipline were accepted on the basis of the institutional affiliation of the authors rather than the intrinsic worth of the paper.[8] Commentary on the paper suggested that this decision procedure might be more widespread. Presumably the reviewers using the rule assume that someone would not get a job at X institution if that person were not a top-notch investigator, and so her/his experiments must be well-done and the reasoning correct. Apart from the errors in that assumption, both the reviewer and the critic of peer review treat what is a social process as an individual process. The function of peer review is not just to check that the data seem right and the conclusions well-reasoned but to bring to bear another point of view on the phenomena, whose expression might lead the original author(s) to revise the way they

---

[7] James Watson's account of the discovery of the molecular structure of DNA, read in conjunction with the story of Rosalind Franklin's contributions to that discovery in Sayre (1975), provides a vivid example of this interdependence. See Watson (1968). Participant accounts of recent developments in one or another science usually offer good illustrations of this point. Weinberg (1977) and Feinberg (1978) account for the mid-1970s states of cosmology and microphysics, respectively. Each presents what can be called the current canon in its field, making clear the dependence of its production upon the activity and interaction of many individual researchers.

[8] See Peters and Ceci (1982, 1985) and the associated commentary. For additional discussion of peer review see Glazer (1988); Goleman (1987); Cole and Cole (1977); Cole, Cole, and Simons (1981).

think about and present their observations and conclusions. To put this another way, it is to make sure that, among other things, the authors have interpreted the data in a way that is free of their subjective preferences.

The concern over the breakdown of peer review, while directed at a genuine problem, is also exaggerated partly because of an individualist conception of knowledge construction. Peer review prior to publication is not the only filter to which results are subjected. The critical treatment *after* publication is crucial to the refining of new ideas and techniques. While institutional bias may also operate in the postpublication reception of an idea, other factors, such as the attempt to repeat an experiment or to reconcile incompatible claims, can eventually compensate for such misplaced deference. Publication in a journal does not make an idea or result a brick in the edifice of knowledge. Its absorption is a much more complex process, involving such things as subsequent citation, use and modification by others, et cetera. Experimental data and hypotheses are transformed through the conflict and integration of a variety of points of view into what is ultimately accepted as scientific knowledge.[9]

What is called scientific knowledge, then, is produced by a community (ultimately the community of all scientific practitioners) and transcends the contributions of any individual or even of any subcommunity within the larger community.[10] Once propositions, theses, and hypotheses are developed, what will become scientific knowledge is produced collectively through the clashing and meshing of a variety of points of view. The relevance of these features of the sociology of science to objectivity will be apparent shortly.

The social character of hypothesis acceptance underscores the publicity of science. This publicity has both social and logical dimensions. We are accustomed to thinking of science as a public possession or property in that it is produced for the most part by public resources— either through direct funding of research or through financial support of the education of scientists. The social processes described under-

---

[9] In what I take to be a similar vein, Bruno Latour (1987) claims that in science a statement made by an individual becomes a fact only as a consequence of what others do with the statement. Latour, however, emphasizes the agonistic as opposed to the cooperative dimension of social relations in the sciences.

[10] The precise extension of "scientific community" is here left unspecified. If it includes those interested in and affected by scientific inquiry, then it is much broader than the class of those professionally engaged in scientific research. For a discussion of these issues and some consequences of our current restricted understanding of the scientific community see Addelson (1983).

score another aspect of its publicity; it is itself a public resource—a common fund of assertions presumably established to a point beyond question. It thereby constitutes a body of putative truths that can be appealed to in defense or criticism of other claims.

From a logical point of view the publicity of science includes several crucial elements. First, theoretical assertions, hypotheses, and background assumptions are all in principle public in the sense of being generally available to and comprehensible to anyone with the appropriate background, education, and interest. Second, the states of affairs to which theoretical explanations are pegged (in evidential and explanatory relationships) are public in the sense that they are intersubjectively ascertainable. As noted in the previous chapter, this does not require a commitment to a set of theory-free, eternally acceptable observation statements but merely a commitment to the possibility that two or more persons can agree about the descriptions of objects, events, and states of affairs that enter into evidential relationships. Both features are consequences of the facts (1) that we have a common language which we use to describe our experience and within which we reason and (2) that the objects of experience which we describe and about which we reason are purported to exist independently of our seeing and thinking about them.[11]

These two aspects of the logical publicity of science make criticism of scientific hypotheses and theories possible in a way that is not possible, for instance, for descriptions of mystical experience or expressions of feeling or emotion. First, a common language for the description of experience means that we can understand each other, which means in turn that we can accept or reject hypotheses, formulate and respond to objections to them. Second, the presupposition of objects existing independently of our perception of them imposes an acceptance of constraints on what can be said or reasonably believed about them. Such acceptance implies the relevance of reports and judgments other than our own to what we say or believe. There is no way, by contrast, to acquire the authority sufficient to criticize the description of a mystical experience or the expression of a particular feeling or emotion save by having the experience or emotion in question, and these are not had in the requisite sense by more than one person. By contrast, the logical publicity of scientific understanding and subject matter, by contrast, makes them and hence the authority to criticize

[11] One might say that the language game of science presupposes the independent existence of objects of experience. Contemporary arguments about scientific realism can be understood as arguments about (1) the nature of this presupposition and (2) what categories of objects it covers.

their articulation accessible to all.[12] It should be said that these constitute necessary but not sufficient conditions for the possibility of criticism, a point I shall return to later. It is the possibility of intersubjective
criticism, at any rate, that permits objectivity in spite of the context
dependence of evidential reasoning. Before developing this idea further
let me outline some of the kinds of criticism to be found in scientific
discourse.

There are a number of ways to criticize a hypothesis. For the sake of
convenience we can divide these into evidential and conceptual criticism to reflect the distinction between criticism proceeding on the basis
of experimental and observational concerns and that proceeding on
the basis of theoretical and metatheoretical concerns.[13] Evidential criticism is familiar enough: John Maddox, editor of *Nature*, criticizing
Jacques Benveniste's experiments with highly diluted antibody solutions suggesting that immune responses could be triggered in the absence of even one molecule of the appropriate antibody;[14] Richard Lewontin analyzing the statistical data alleged to favor Jensen's
hypothesis of the genetic basis of I.Q.;[15] Stephen Gould criticizing the
experiments of David Barash purporting to demonstrate punitive responses by male mountain bluebirds to putative adultery on the part
of their female mates.[16] Such criticism questions the degree to which a
given hypothesis is supported by the evidence adduced for it, questions
the accuracy, extent, and conditions of performance of the experi-

---

[12] To avoid possible confusion about the point being made here, I wish to emphasize
that I am contrasting the descriptive statements of science with expressions of emotion.
Descriptions of emotion and other subjective states may be as objective as other kinds
of description, if the conditions for objectivity can be satisfied. Objectivity as it is being
discussed here involves the absence (or control) of subjective *preference* and is not necessarily divorced from our beliefs about our subjective states. Locke (1968) discusses the
different ways in which privacy is properly and improperly attributed to subjective states
(pp. 5–12).

[13] The distinction between the different kinds of concerns relevant to the development
and evaluation of theories is discussed for different purposes and with significant differences in detail by Buchdahl in a discussion of criteria choice, by Laudan in a discussion
of the problems that give rise to the development of theory, and by Schaffner in a discussion of categories for comparative theory evaluation. A more complete categorization
of concerns and types of criticism than that offered here requires a more thorough study
of past and present scientific practice. See Gerd Buchdahl (1970); Larry Laudan (1977);
and Kenneth Schaffner (1974).

[14] Maddox, Randi, and Stewart (1988) and Benveniste's reply in Benveniste (1988).
The chapter "Laboratories" in Latour (1987) can be read as providing a series of examples of evidential criticism (pp. 63–100).

[15] Lewontin (1970, 1974).

[16] Gould (1980).

ments and observations serving as evidence, and questions their analysis and reporting.[17]

Conceptual criticism, on the other hand, often stigmatized as "metaphysical," has received less attention in a tradition of discourse dominated by empiricist ideals. At least three sorts can be distinguished. The first questions the conceptual soundness of a hypothesis—as Einstein criticized and rejected the discontinuities and uncertainties of the quantum theory;[18] as Kant criticized and rejected, among other things, the Newtonian hypotheses of absolute space and time, a criticism that contributed to the development of field theory.[19] A second sort of criticism questions the consistency of a hypothesis with accepted theory—as traditionalists rejected the heliocentric theory because its consequences seemed inconsistent with the Aristotelian physics of motion still current in the fifteeth and sixteenth centuries;[20] as Millikan rejected Ehrenhaft's hypothesis of subelectrons on the basis not only of Millikan's own measurements but of his commitment to a particulate theory of electricity that implied the existence of an elementary electric charge.[21] A third sort questions the relevance of evidence presented in support of a hypothesis: relativity theorists could deny the relevance of the Michelson-Morley interferometer experiment to the Lorentz-Fitzgerald contraction hypothesis by denying the necessity of the ether;[22] Thelma Rowell and others have questioned the relevance of certain observations of animal populations to claims about dominance hierarchies within those populations by criticizing the assumptions of universal male dominance underlying claims of such relevance;[23] critics of hypotheses about the hazards of exposure to ionizing radiation direct their attention to the dose-response model with which results at high exposures are projected to conditions of low exposures.[24] Thus most of the debate centers not on the data but on the assumptions in light of which the data are interpreted. This last form of criticism, though related to evidential considerations, is grouped with the forms of conceptual criticism because it is concerned not with how accurately the data has been measured and reported but with the assumptions in light

[17] The latter two kinds of questions are concerned with the objectivity of data, a notion mentioned above.

[18] Bernstein (1973), pp. 137–177.

[19] Williams (1966), pp. 32–63. A somewhat different account is presented by Hesse (1965), pp. 170–180.

[20] Kuhn (1957), pp. 100–133, 185–192.

[21] Holton (1978).

[22] Jaffe (1960), pp. 95–103.

[23] Rowell (1974).

[24] See Longino (1987).

of which that data is taken to be evidence for a given hypothesis in the first place. Here it is not the material presented as evidence itself that is challenged but its relevance to a hypothesis.

All three of these types of criticism are central to the development of scientific knowledge and are included among the traditions of scientific discourse into which the novice is initiated. It is the third type of criticism, however, which amounts to questioning the background beliefs or assumptions in light of which states of affairs become evidence, that is crucial for the problem of objectivity. Objectivity in the sense under discussion requires a way to block the influence of subjective preference at the level of background beliefs. While the possibility of criticism does not totally eliminate subjective preference either from an individual's or from a community's practice of science, it does provide a means for checking its influence in the formation of "scientific knowledge." Thus, even though background assumptions may not be supported by the same kinds of data upon which they confer evidential relevance to some hypothesis, other kinds of support can be provided, or at least expected.[25] And in the course of responding to criticism or providing such support one may modify the background assumption in question. Or if the original proponent does not, someone else may do so as a way of entering into the discourse. Criticism is thereby transformative. In response to criticism, empirical support may be forthcoming (subject, of course, to the limitations developed above). At other times the support may be conceptual rather than empirical. Discussions of the nature of human judgment and cognition and whether they can be adequately modelled by computer programs, and of the relation of subjectively experienced psychological phenomena to brain processes, for instance, are essential to theoretical development in cognitive science and neuropsychology respectively. But these discussions involve issues that are metaphysical or conceptual in nature and that, far from being resolvable by empirical means, must be resolved (explicitly or implicitly) in order to generate questions answerable by such means. The contextual analysis of evidential relations shows the limits of purely empirical considerations in scientific inquiry. Where precisely these limits fall will differ in different fields and in different research programs.

As long as background beliefs can be articulated and subjected to criticism from the scientific community, they can be defended, modi-

---

[25] Conceptual criticism of this sort is a far cry from the criticism envisaged by Popper. For him metaphysical issues must be decided empirically, if at all. (And if they cannot be so tested, they lack significance.)

fied, or abandoned in response to such criticism. As long as this kind of response is possible, the incorporation of hypotheses into the canon of scientific knowledge can be independent of any individual's subjective preferences. Their incorporation is, instead, a function in part of the assessment of evidential support. And while the evidential relevance to hypotheses of observations and experiments is a function of background assumptions, the adoption of these assumptions is not arbitrary but is (or rather can be) subject to the kinds of controls just discussed. This solution incorporates as elements both the social character of the production of knowledge and the public accessibility of the material with which this knowledge is constructed.

Sociologically and historically, the molding of what counts as scientific knowledge is an activity requiring many participants. Even if one individual's work is regarded as absolutely authoritative over some period—as for instance, Aristotle's and later Newton's were—it is eventually challenged, questioned, and made to take the role of contributor rather than sole author—as Aristotle's and Newton's have been. From a logical point of view, if scientific knowledge were to be understood as the simple sum of finished products of individual activity, then not only would there be no way to block or mitigate the influence of subjective preference but scientific knowledge itself would be a potpourri of merrily inconsistent theories. Only if the products of inquiry are understood to be formed by the kind of critical discussion that is possible among a plurality of individuals about a commonly accessible phenomenon, can we see how they count as knowledge rather than opinion.

Objectivity, then, is a characteristic of a community's practice of science rather than of an individual's, and the practice of science is understood in a much broader sense than most discussions of the logic of scientific method suggest. These discussions see what is central to scientific method as being the complex of activities that constitute hypothesis testing through comparison with experiential data—in principle, if not always in reality, an activity of individuals. What I have argued here is that scientific method involves as an equally central aspect the subjection of hypotheses and the background assumptions in light of which they seem to be supported by data to varieties of conceptual criticism, which is a social rather than an individual activity.[26]

[26] This is really a distinction between the number of points of view (minds) required. Many individuals (sharing assumptions and points of view) may be involved in testing a hypothesis (and commonly are in contemporary experiments). And though this is much rarer, one individual may be able to criticize her or his own evidential reasoning and background assumptions from other points of view.

The respect in which science is objective, on this view, is one that it shares with other modes of inquiry, disciplines such as literary or art criticism and philosophy.[27] The feature that has often been appealed to as the source of the objectivity of science, that its hypotheses and theories are accepted or rejected on the basis of observational, experimental data, is a feature that makes scientific inquiry empirical. In the positivist account, for instance, it was the syntactically and deductively secured relation of hypotheses to a stable set of observational data that guaranteed the objectivity of scientific inquiry. But, as I've argued, most evidential relations in the sciences cannot be given this syntactic interpretation. In the contextual analysis of evidential relations, however, that a method is empirical in the above sense does not mean that it is also objective. A method that involved the appeal to observational or experimental data but included no controls on the kinds of background assumptions in light of which their relevance to hypotheses might be determined, or that permitted a weekly change of assumptions so that a hypothesis accepted in one week on the basis of some bit of evidence *e* would be rejected the next on the same basis, would hardly qualify as objective. Because the relation between hypotheses and evidence is mediated by background assumptions that themselves may not be subject to empirical confirmation or disconfirmation, and that may be infused with metaphysical or normative considerations, it would be a mistake to identify the objectivity of scientific methods with their empirical features alone. The process that can expose such assumptions is what makes possible, even if it cannot guarantee, independence from subjective bias, and hence objectivity. Thus, while rejecting the idea that observational data alone provide external standards of comparison and evaluation of theories, this account does not reject external standards altogether. The formal requirement of demonstrable evidential relevance constitutes a standard of rationality and acceptability independent of and external to any particular research program or scientific theory. The satisfaction of this standard by any program or theory, secured, as has been argued, by intersubjective criticism, is what constitutes its objectivity.

Scientific knowledge is, therefore, social knowledge. It is produced by processes that are intrinsically social, and once a theory, hypothesis, or set of data has been accepted by a community, it becomes a public resource. It is available to use in support of other theories and hypoth-

[27] This is not to deny the importance of distinguishing between different modes of understanding—for instance, between scientific, philosophical, and literary theories—but simply to deny that objectivity can serve as any kind of demarcation criterion.

eses and as a basis of action. Scientific knowledge is social both in the ways it is created and in the uses it serves.

OBJECTIVITY BY DEGREES

I have argued both that criticism from alternative points of view is required for objectivity and that the subjection of hypotheses and evidential reasoning to critical scrutiny is what limits the intrusion of individual subjective preference into scientific knowledge. Are these not two opposing forms of social interaction, one dialogic and the other monologic? Why does critical scrutiny not simply suppress those alternative points of view required to prevent premature allegiance to one perspective? How does this account of objectivity not collapse upon itself? The answer involves seeing dialogic and monologic as poles of a continuum. The maintenance of dialogue is itself a social process and can be more or less fully realized. Objectivity, therefore, turns out to be a matter of degree. A method of inquiry is objective to the degree that it permits *transformative* criticism. Its objectivity consists not just in the inclusion of intersubjective criticism but in the degree to which both its procedures and its results are responsive to the kinds of criticism described. I've argued that method must, therefore, be understood as a collection of social, rather than individual, processes, so the issue is the extent to which a scientific community maintains critical dialogue. Scientific communities will be objective to the degree that they satisfy four criteria necessary for achieving the transformative dimension of critical discourse: (1) there must be recognized avenues for the criticism of evidence, of methods, and of assumptions and reasoning; (2) there must exist shared standards that critics can invoke; (3) the community as a whole must be responsive to such criticism; (4) intellectual authority must be shared equally among qualified practitioners. Each of these criteria requires at least a brief gloss.

Recognized Avenues for Criticism.   The avenues for the presentation of criticism include such standard and public forums as journals, conferences, and so forth. Peer review is often pointed to as the standard avenue for such criticism, and indeed it is effective in preventing highly idiosyncratic values from shaping knowledge. At the same time its confidentiality and privacy make it the vehicle for the entrenchment of established views. This criterion also means that critical activities should receive equal or nearly equal weight to "original research" in career advancement. Effective criticism that advances understanding should be as valuable as original research that opens up new domains for understanding; pedestrian, routine criticism should be valued comparably to pedestrian and routine "original research."

Shared Standards.   In order for criticism to be relevant to a position it must appeal to something accepted by those who hold the position criticized. Similarly, alternative theories must be perceived to have some bearing on the concerns of a scientific community in order to obtain a hearing. This cannot occur at the whim of individuals but must be a function of public standards or criteria to which members of the scientific community are or feel themselves bound. These standards can include both substantive principles and epistemic, as well as social, values. Different subcommunities will subscribe to different but overlapping subsets of the standards associated with a given community. Among values the standards can include such elements as empirical adequacy, truth, generation of specifiable interactions with the natural or experienced world, the expansion of existing knowledge frameworks, consistency with accepted theories in other domains, comprehensiveness, reliability as a guide to action, relevance to or satisfaction of particular social needs. Only the first of these constitutes a necessary condition that any research program must meet or aspire to meet, and even this requirement may be temporarily waived and is subject to interpretation.

The list shares some elements with the list Thomas Kuhn presents in his essay "Objectivity, Values and Theory Choice,"[28] and like the items in his list they can be weighted differently in different scientific communities and they must be more precisely formulated to be applicable. For example, the requirement that theories have some capability to generate specifiable interactions with the natural or experienced world will be applied differently as the sorts of interactions desired in a community differ. The particular weighting and interpretation assigned these standards will vary in different social and historical contexts as a function of cognitive and social needs. Furthermore, they are not necessarily consistent. As I suggested in Chapter Two, the goals of truth or accurate representation and expansion of existing knowledge frameworks exist in some tension with each other.

Standards do not provide a deterministic theory of theory choice. Nevertheless, it is the existence of standards that makes the individual members of a scientific community responsible to something besides themselves. It is the open-ended and nonconsistent nature of these standards that allows for pluralism in the sciences and for the contin-

[28] Kuhn (1977a).

ued presence, however subdued, of minority voices. Implicit or explicit appeals to such standards as I've listed underwrite many of the critical arguments named above.

Community Response. This criterion requires that the beliefs of the scientific community as a whole and over time change in response to the critical discussion taking place within it. This responsiveness is measured by such public phenomena as the content of textbooks, the distribution of grants and awards, the flexibility of dominant world views. Satisfaction of this criterion does not require that individuals whose data and assumptions are criticized recant. Indeed, understanding is enhanced if they can defend their work against criticism.[29] What is required is that community members pay attention to the critical discussion taking place and that the assumptions that govern their group activities remain logically sensitive to it.

Equality of Intellectual Authority. This Habermasian criterion is intended to disqualify a community in which a set of assumptions dominates by virtue of the political power of its adherents.[30] An obvious example is the dominance of Lamarckism in the Soviet Union in the 1930s. While there were some good reasons to try experiments under the aegis of a Lamarckian viewpoint, the suppression of alternative points of view was a matter of politics rather than of logic or critical discussion. The bureaucratization of United States science in the twentieth century tends similarly to privilege certain points of view.[31] The exclusion, whether overt or more subtle, of women and members of certain racial minorities from scientific education and the scientific professions has also constituted a violation of this criterion. While assumptions about race and about sex are not imposed on scientists in the United States in the way assumptions about inheritability of acquired traits were in the Soviet Union, as I will demonstrate in the following chapters, assumptions about sex structure a number of research programs in biology and behavioral sciences. Other scholars have documented the role of racial assumptions in the sciences.[32] The long-standing devaluation of women's voices and those of members of

[29] Beatty (1985) makes a similar point.
[30] Invocation of this criterion confirms the kinship of this account of objectivity with the account of truth that Jürgen Habermas has developed as part of his theory of communicative competence. This relationship will be further discussed in Chapter Nine.
[31] See Levins and Lewontin (1985), pp. 197–252, for further discussion of this point.
[32] See Gould (1981); Lewontin, Rose, and Kamin (1984); Richardson (1984).

racial minorities means that such assumptions have been protected from critical scrutiny.

The above are criteria for assessing the objectivity of communities. The objectivity of individuals in this scheme consists in their participation in the collective give-and-take of critical discussion and not in some special relation (of detachment, hardheadedness) they may bear to their observations. Thus understood, objectivity is dependent upon the depth and scope of the transformative interrogation that occurs in any given scientific community. This communitywide process ensures (or can ensure) that the hypotheses ultimately accepted as supported by some set of data do not reflect a single individual's idiosyncratic assumptions about the natural world. To say that a theory or hypothesis was accepted on the basis of objective methods does not entitle us to say it is true but rather that it reflects the critically achieved consensus of the scientific community. In the absence of some form of privileged access to transempirical (unobservable) phenomena it's not clear we should hope for anything better.

The weight given to criticism in the formation of knowledge represents a social consensus regarding the appropriate balance between accurate representation and knowledge extension. Several conditions can limit the extent of criticism and hence diminish a scientific community's objectivity without resulting in a completely or intentionally closed society (for example, such as characterized Soviet science under Stalin or some areas of Nazi science).

First of all, if scientific inquiry is to have any effect on a society's ability to take advantage of natural processes for the improvement of the quality of its life, criticism of assumptions cannot go on indefinitely. From a logical point of view, of course, criticism of background assumptions, as of any general claim, can go on ad infinitum. The philosophical discussion of inductive reasoning is an example of such unending (though not useless) debate. The utility of scientific knowledge depends on the possibility of finding frameworks of inquiry that remain stable enough to permit systematic interactions with the natural world. When critical discussion becomes repetitive and fixed at a metalevel, or when criticism of one set of assumptions ceases to have or does not eventually develop a connection to an empirical research program, it loses its relevance to the construction of empirical knowledge. It is the intrinsic incapacity of so-called "creation science" to develop a fruitful research program based on its alleged alternative to evolutionary theory that is responsible for the lack of attention given to it by the contemporary United States scientific community. The appeal by its advocates to pluralistic philosophies of science seems misguided, if not disingenuous.

Secondly, these critical activities, however crucial to knowledge building, are de-emphasized in a context that rewards novelty and originality, whether of hypotheses or of experimental design. The commoditization of scientific knowledge—a result of the interaction of the requirements of career advancement and of the commercial value of data—diminishes the attention paid to the criticism of the acquisition, sorting, and assembling of data. It is a commonplace that in contemporary science papers reporting negative results do not get published.

In the third place, some assumptions are not perceived as such by any members of the community. When, for instance, background assumptions are shared by all members of a community, they acquire an invisibility that renders them unavailable for criticism. They do not become visible until individuals who do not share the community's assumptions can provide alternative explanations of the phenomena without those assumptions, as, for example, Einstein could provide an alternative explanation of the Michelson-Morley interferometer experiment. Until such alternatives are available, community assumptions are transparent to their adherents. In addition, the substantive principles determining standards of rationality within a research program or tradition are for the most part immune to criticism by means of those standards.

From all this it follows again that the greater the number of different points of view included in a given community, the more likely it is that its scientific practice will be objective, that is, that it will result in descriptions and explanations of natural processes that are more reliable in the sense of less characterized by idiosyncratic subjective preferences of community members than would otherwise be the case. The smaller the number, the less likely this will be.[33] Because points of view cannot simply be allowed expression but must have an impact on what is ultimately thought to be the case, such diversity is a necessary but not a sufficient condition for objectivity. Finally, these conditions reinforce the point that objectivity is a matter of degree. While the conditions for objectivity are at best imperfectly realized, they are the basis of an ideal by reference to which particular scientific communities can be evaluated. Ascertaining in greater detail the practices and institutional arrangements that facilitate or undermine objectivity in any particular era or current field, and thus the degree to which the ideal of objectivity

---

[33] This insistence on the variety of points of view required for objectivity is developed on a somewhat different basis for the social sciences by Sandra Harding (1978).

is realized, requires both historical and sociological investigation. The examination of sex differences research in chapters Six through Eight will provide a more concrete and extensive development of these ideas.

CONCLUSION

On the positivist analysis of scientific method it is hard to understand how theories purporting to describe a nonobservable underlying reality, or containing descriptive terms whose meaning is independent of that of so-called observational terms, can be supported. On the anti-empiricist wholist account it is just as difficult to understand how the theories that are developed have a bearing on intersubjective reality. Each of these approaches is also unable to account for certain facts about the actual practice of science. The absolute and unambiguous nature of evidential relations presented in the positivist view cannot accommodate the facts of scientific change. The incommensurability of theories in the wholist view cannot do justice to the lively and productive debate that can occur among scientists committed to different theories. Each of these modes of analysis emphasizes one aspect of scientific method at the expense of another, and each produces an individualist logic of scientific method that fails adequately to reflect the social nature of scientific discourse. Furthermore, the emphasis on theories distorts scientific growth and practice. Scientists rarely engage in the construction or evaluation of comprehensive theories. Their constructive, theoretical activity tends to consist much more in the development of individual or interrelated hypotheses (as laws, generalizations, or explanations) from the complex integration of observation and experiment with background assumptions. Success in expanding the scope of an explanatory idea via such complex integration plays as important a role in its acceptance as the survival of falsifying tests. Accounts of validation in the sciences must take account both of the role of background assumptions in evidential reasoning and of the roles of (sometimes) conflicting goals of inquiry with respect to which hypotheses and theories are assessed. The logic that reflects the structure of this activity will have to abandon some of the simplicity of the positivist account, but what it loses in elegance it will surely regain in application.

The analysis conducted in this chapter means that values can enter into theory-constructive reasoning in two major ways—through an individual's values or through community values. The fact that a bit of science can be analyzed as crucially dependent on contextual values or on value-laden background assumptions does not necessarily mean that someone is attempting to impose his/her wishes on the natural world without regard to what it might really be like. More customarily such analysis should be taken as showing the way in which such contextual features have facilitated the use of given data or observations as evidence for some hypothesis by an individual or by a community. Because community values and assumptions determine whether a given bit of reasoning will pass or survive criticism and thus be acceptable, individual values as such will only rarely be at issue in these analyses. When an individual researcher's values enable her or him to make inferences at variance with those of the scientific community, this is less evidence of strongly eccentric individualism than of allegiance to some other social (political or religious) community.[34]

The contextualist view produces a framework within which it is possible to respect the complexity of science, to do justice to the historical facts and to the current practice of science, and to avoid paradox. In addition, it is possible to articulate a standard of comparison independent of and external to any particular theory or research project. In making intertheoretic comparison possible it offers the basis (an expanded basis) upon which to develop criteria of evaluation. Finally, the social account of objectivity and scientific knowledge to which the contextualist account of evidence leads seems more true to the fact that scientific inquiry is not always as free from subjective preference as we would wish it to be. And even though the resulting picture of objectivity differs from what we are used to, our intuition that scientific inquiry at its best is objective is kept intact by appealing to the spirit of criticism that is its traditional hallmark.[35]

[34] This should not be taken to mean that social inequality and marginalization are necessary for objectivity but rather that differences in perspective are. A scientific community existing in a (utopian at this point) society characterized by thoroughgoing inclusivity and equality might indeed encourage the persistence of divergent points of view to ensure against blindness to its own assumptions.

[35] Note added in proof. Three books read since completing the manuscript also draw attention in varying degrees to the social character of cognitive processes in science: Peter Galison, *How Experiments End* (Chicago, IL: University of Chicago Press, 1987); David Hull, *Science as a Process* (Chicago, IL: University of Chicago Press, 1988); and Sharon Traweek, *Beamtimes and Lifetimes: The World of High Energy Physicists* (Cambridge, MA: Harvard University Press, 1988).

CHAPTER FIVE

Values and Science

THE argument so far has established that contextual values, interests, and value-laden assumptions *can* constrain scientific practice in such as way as to affect the results of inquiry and do so without violating constitutive rules of science. That is, the very character of reasoning in science makes it vulnerable to the influence of context. This is not yet to show that contextual values are always or necessarily implicated in scientific reasoning, or even that they must be implicated in cases of conflicting interpretations of the same experimental or observational data. Background assumptions, it is clear from the previous chapters, may be held for and defended on analytical and metaphysical grounds as well as inadvertently or on normative considerations. Once contextual considerations of any sort are admitted as relevant to scientific argumentation, however, values and interests can no longer be excluded a priori as irrelevant or as signs of bad science. The argument, therefore, does establish the legitimacy of examining research and research projects that are perfectly "good science" for the influence of value-laden considerations. This activity is, of course, immensely important in assessing claims that some scientific research projects can or should displace arguments in terms of values about a subject with purely "scientific" considerations. I shall examine two such areas of research in chapters Six and Seven. The argument as so far presented also legitimates the deliberate choice of assumptions because of the values they embody or support. What can be justified is somewhat more complicated than this simple formulation suggests, and I shall explain this idea more fully in Chapter Nine. In the present chapter I wish to discuss the variety of possible research and value interactions, or constitutive-contextual interactions, to place in context what I will say about the behavioral neuroendocrinological program.

VARIETIES OF SCIENCE VALUE INTERACTION

Scholars have already recognized a limited range of ways in which contextual values affect the practice of both pure and applied science. The first is the channeling effect on inquiry of broad values of its social and cultural context. In this country, for instance, while a certain amount of research, especially biological field research, can be pursued at the inclination of the researcher, much work requires major financial support from sources other than the individual, that is, from corporate or governmental sources. The research, pure or applied, that gets funded, and hence, pursued, is that which is seen to further governmental, societal, and corporate goals, whatever those may be.

According to the Mertonian school of history and sociology of science, even before the establishment of this direct and crass connection between social goals and scientific research, social needs and cultural values (for example, the interests of the seventeenth-century bourgeoisie) had an impact on the kinds of research undertaken.[1] From this perspective the questions thought important to investigate are determined as much by the social/cultural context in which science is done as by problems and puzzles internal to scientific inquiry. Merton, however, also thought that the conduct of research, the actual production of knowledge, was governed by internal norms of universalism, disinterestedness, communality, and "organized skepticism"—moral norms that guaranteed the integrity of the products of scientific practice and its insulation from more intimate influence by contextual factors. Contemporary sociologists of science have been exploring the limits of these norms and, as noted earlier, attending to the roles of social interests and values and of the social organization of scientific disciplines in the production of scientific knowledge.[2] Some of this work is in the Mertonian tradition to the extent that it sees problem areas, rather than specific content, determined by these social factors.

A second type of influence involves the explicit policy decisions about the application of technological developments of scientific knowledge. The debates over the adoption of nuclear energy and, now, over certain aspects of genetic engineering involve both factual and normative disagreements. The perceived conflict and conformity of these technologies with a number of different values has generated explicit conflicts and dissonance between those values and thus between social groups assigning different weights to those values. To a major extent the future of these technologies and of the scientific research associated with them will be determined by resolution of the normative disagreements, that is, by the ascendancy of certain values (for example, public health, popular control of energy sources) over their competitors (for example, centralized governmental or corporate control of energy sources).

[1] Merton (1938).
[2] Mulkay (1977).

A third major type of interaction involves the potential conflict between moral values and specific ways of carrying out research, particularly research with human subjects or research that could endanger
the public. As the risks of harming subjects (as in various types of drug
research) or violating their rights, such as that to privacy, have become
better appreciated, professional associations have developed guidelines
for their members. Morally based restrictions on experimentation are
not new, as the old prohibition on dissection of human cadavers reminds us, are not always imposed when they should be, as the fate of
syphilitic black men in Tuskegee reminds us, and are not always obvious, as the histories of both the Milgram obedience experiments and
the NIH guidelines on recombinant DNA research make clear.

Varied as they may be, each of these kinds of interaction between
science and values can be analyzed according to an "externality"
model. According to this model, while those points of contact between
science and the values of the social and cultural context in which it is
done may determine the directions of research or of its applications,
within the boundaries so determined scientific inquiry itself proceeds
according to its own rules. The points of contact with the social and
cultural context determine to what areas the rules will be applied. The
effect may be a broad one determining what questions will be investigated, for example, astronomy or mechanics, or which practical applications of knowledge will be pursued and which neglected, for example, nuclear technology or conservation technologies. It may be more
narrow, determining what paths to the knowledge we want will be
followed, which tests and experiments are permissible and which not.

The rules of inquiry, on the other hand, are a function of the constitutive values of science, themselves a function of the goal of science,
which in this model is simply assumed to be the development of an
accurate understanding of the natural world.[3] While the choice of areas or aspects of the world to be illuminated by application of the rules
is a function of social and cultural contextual values, the conclusions,
answers, and explanations reached by means of their use and guidance
are not. Even those contextual values that do affect science remain external to the real thing, to the doing of science. When they do not, we
have a case of bad science. This represents, as I have said, the classical
understanding of the relation of knowledge and values, of the value
freedom of science.

---

[3] The existence of multiple and possibly conflicting goals for scientific inquiry must,
of course, be disregarded in order to suppose that a mechanical application of such rules
would result in a uniquely correct understanding of the natural world.

The contextual account of reasoning and argumentation in science I have offered raises the possibility that some cases are not correctly analyzed according to this "externality" model. It allows us, therefore, not only to extend the list of expected interactions but to see the examples usually cited in a different light.

The extended list of ways in which values apparently contextual with respect to a given research program can shape the knowledge emerging from that program includes at least five distinct types:

1. *Practices.* Contextual values can affect practices that bear on the epistemic integrity of science.
2. *Questions.* Contextual values can determine which questions are asked and which ignored about a given phenomenon.
3. *Data.* Contextual values can affect the description of data, that is, value-laden terms may be employed in the description of experimental or observational data and values may influence the selection of data or of kinds of phenomena to be investigated.
4. *Specific assumptions.* Contextual values can be expressed in or motivate the background assumptions facilitating inferences in specific areas of inquiry.
5. *Global assumptions.* Contextual values can be expressed in or motivate the acceptance of global, frameworklike assumptions that determine the character of research in an entire field.

These are not exclusive categories, for example, 5 and 4 can include 2 and 3. The types of interaction listed *can* but need not occur independently. The detailed discussions of research purporting to establish a biological basis for behavioral and cognitive sex differences contained in the following chapters present examples of the influence of contextual values on data, specific assumptions, and global assumptions. I wish in the remainder of this chapter to describe some examples of the influence of contextual values on practices and data, as well as to illustrate their influence on global assumptions with an example taken from a less controversial area than the biology of behavior.

MILD CASES

Practices (Case 1)

A moment in the history of the study of human interferon provides the first example. Industrial microbiology has spawned the phenomenon of small firms founded by biochemists, stock in which is owned in part by their founders and in part by large pharmaceutical corporations.

These firms have been developed in order to commercially manufacture and market biological substances produced by the new technologies of recombinant DNA. These corporate arrangements both provide funds for present and future research and ensure that the scientist-entrepreneurs involved in the companies receive a greater share of potential profits than they would as academic scientists only.

In January 1980 interferon was being tested for effectiveness against cancer and as an antiviral agent generally. In that month the microbiological firm Biogen announced in a press conference featuring its director and one of its active researchers that it was the first laboratory to achieve the bacterial production of human interferon.[4] This announcement was followed by a jump in Biogen's stock, a major increase in demand for the substance on the part of cancer victims and their families, and a flurry of corporate-sponsored research as other microbiological and large pharmaceutical firms vied to climb onto the "interferon bandwagon." Unmentioned at the time was a similar experiment in Japan that had been published several months earlier, without the fanfare. Also unmentioned was the fact that Biogen had not succeeded in preventing the death of the bacteria synthesizing the interferon, so that the development of techniques for large-scale production was not yet assured by the experiment. Six months later American studies were published and presented at oncological conferences suggesting that interferon was only marginally more effective and for some cancers even less effective than therapies already in use. Four years later interferon was described as a "miracle cure in search of a disease,"[5] and we now hear sporadically of potential uses for it, none of which seem to bear out the original hope.

This episode involves transgressions against (at least two) folk traditions in science. While these traditions do not have the same status as methodological rules, they concern practices connected with the constitutive ideal of truth as well as with considerations of justice. The first holds that scientists don't or ought not to profit commercially from their scientific activity. The considerations of justice underlying this maxim are that just as no individual scientist deserves sole credit for her or his discoveries since each stands on the "shoulders of gi-

---

[4] The basic elements of the Biogen interferon story are available in the news section of *Nature* 283 (24 January 1980), 284 (13 March 1980; 17 April 1980), and 285 (1 May 1980); in the "News and Comment" section of *Science* 207 (1 February 1980; 21 March 1980), and 208 (16 May 1980); and in *Science News* 117 (26 January 1980; 15 March 1980; 7 June 1980). An account is also available in Gurin and Pfund (1980). See also Yoxen (1986).

[5] Hillel Panitch, quoted in Benowitz (1984), p. 231.

ants," so none should profit exclusively from discoveries made possible by the work of others. The epistemological justification is that scientists ought not to have a stake in the outcome of their research because, scientists being human, such a stake might bias their interpretations of results in directions that favor their interests at the expense of the facts. The traditional ban on profit taking is violated by the ownership by scientists of commercial firms formed precisely to profit from the new advances in the biological sciences. It can be argued, of course, that since the firms will only make money if their products work, the epistemological, constitutive concern is inapplicable in this instance, making the issue one of justice solely.

The second tradition is not so easily brushed off. This is a rule about the communication of results—that research should first be presented in professional journals or in papers read at conferences. The justification is again twofold. A standard way of publicizing research results provides a way of justly adjudicating priority of discovery. From the epistemological point of view it is better to submit claims to the scrutiny of those capable of evaluating them before presenting them to the general public. Most members of the public do not for the most part have the time or the familiarity with contemporary science to carry out such scrutiny and are also generally unaware of the context that gives results their significance (or lack of it). When results are communicated by means of a press conference, there is no opportunity to study them for their soundness before they are absorbed into and begin affecting the public mind. The dramatic style of presentation required for newsworthiness undermines attempts at critical understanding or evaluation.[6]

The potential of interferon was, it seems, highly overestimated. Had the announcement of its bacterial production been made by normal or traditional procedures (had it not been a commercial undertaking in the first place), it would have reached the public, if at all, along with disclaimers about its therapeutic value. Biogen's stock would not have experienced its dramatic rise in value, and cancer sufferers and their families would have been spared the disappointment of false hope. The communication of results is an activity engaged in by scientists as scientists. The choice of a mode of communication warranted in the ethic of profit making in preference to a mode warranted in the ethic of truth seeking is an instance of the displacement of constitutive by contex-

[6] This is effectively illustrated by comparing the coverage of the press conference in both daily newspapers and scientific journals (see note 4) with the scientific paper describing the achievement. See Nagota et al. (1980).

tual—in this case, commercial—values. Unlike the expected types of case mentioned above, in this instance values of the context are not so much directing research from outside as entering into and affecting the professional practice of scientists.[7]

Questions (Case 2)

An example of the second type of interaction is provided by the history of the development of systemic means of birth control. In a study of the role of values in testing toxic substances, endocrinologist Carol Korenbrot argues that in the course of the development of oral contraceptives the selection of risks to be measured was a function of the extrascientific values of those performing or supervising the testing.[8] She takes as her text Gregory Pincus' *The Control of Fertility*, which is an account of the history and biology of oral contraception by one who was deeply involved as a major researcher and developer of the product "Enovid."[9] While it is true that Pincus was supported by a drug company and so may have been influenced by commercial considerations, the one social/cultural theme to which he continually harks is that of the dangers of unchecked population growth and the necessity for its control.[10] Korenbrot suggests that his explicit commitment to the need for an effective method of limiting population growth strongly influenced how he tested Enovid for effects other than its inhibition of ovulation.[11] In spite of the availability of data showing a relationship between estrogens and reproductive tract cancers and between estrogens and blood coagulability, the chapter in Pincus' work entitled "Some Biological Properties of Ovulation Inhibitors in Human Subjects" emphasizes their prophylactic and therapeutic properties and minimizes their hazards.[12] The tests reported on and tables presented are concerned, to a great extent, with conditions that improve or might improve or be prevented with use of oral contraceptives, conditions such as dysmennorhea, endometrial dysplasia, endometritis, and even breast cancer. The data included on conditions that may deteriorate—cervical erosion and thromboembolism—are presented with extensive qualifications and explanations tending to exonerate Enovid as a causal factor.

[7] For additional examples and reflection on the impact of commercial interests in science see Dickson (1984), especially pp. 56–106.

[8] Korenbrot (1979), pp. 11–42.

[9] Pincus (1965).

[10] Ibid., p. viii.

[11] Korenbrot (1979), pp. 17–19.

[12] Pincus (1965), chap. 12, especially pp. 252–259, 263, 281.

Korenbrot claims that Pincus' extrascientific commitments biased him in favor of oral contraceptives. This bias in turn led him to actively seek positive rather than negative effects—additional inducements to use oral contraceptives rather than possible reasons to be wary of them. This approach makes sense when one remembers that those concerned with population growth are primarily concerned with population growth in Third World countries where there are often strong cultural and economic inhibitions against limiting births or against "artificial" birth control.[13] Surely one's case for use is strengthened if users find relief from painful or life-threatening conditions, especially if relief from pregnancy or reducing the number of one's children are not immediately perceived as benefits. If one regards the issue as one of potential opposition to what one perceives to be in the long run beneficial, one will want to make the strongest case possible. Pincus' concerns in this regard and his treatment of the biological effects of internally administered contraceptives make it likely that this attitude is in part responsible for the inadequate testing of oral contraceptives before they were commercially distributed. This instance is, by the way, one of the cases that made apparent the need for more rigorous control of food and drug testing by an independent agency.[14]

Reflection

Each of these cases requires a bit more discussion. The issues raised by the commercialization of industrial microbiology tend to be perceived as primarily moral ones, involving fairness and freedom of inquiry. I have suggested that the practices that raise moral questions also raise epistemological ones. The problem identified above is only one of many ways in which scientific communication is affected by its new commercial context. Trade secrecy, for instance, generates problems similar to those generated by the requirements of public image and identity. The need to establish priority, rights, and, through the patent laws, ownership, is already stifling interchange among biological researchers just as alleged requirements of national defense have imposed secrecy on weapons-related aspects of research in physics, chemistry, and computer science.[15] Such privatization of knowledge cannot help but influence the development of knowledge if only by insulating

[13] Djerassi (1981); Hardin (1968).

[14] As Ruth Doell points out in conversation, it also raises the question of what constitutes adequate testing of a substance that will have borderline effects at certain concentrations of use. The decisive implication of oral contraceptives in thromboembolism required a study involving sixty thousand women.

[15] This is discussed in Longino (1986).

mainstream investigation from discoveries in classified and "privately held" inquiry. I argued in the previous chapter that a central feature of scientific objectivity consists in the availability of the research process and its results to criticism. While the press conference format may protect claims temporarily from disputation or refutation, the witholding of results for patenting purposes prevents that knowledge from being used to enrich, refute, or otherwise alter hypotheses in mainstream research. The dual circumvention of traditional norms and constraints governing the communication of scientific information that is imposed by commercial requirements will surely produce a body of scientific knowledge that is different from what might have been produced under a different set of circumstances.

This concern may be dismissed by observing that the supervenience of constitutive values by values of the commercial context effects only temporary interruptions in the development of scientific knowledge, interruptions whose effects will be corrected over time. Over time, however, not only will public confidence in the institutions of science be eroded but the ability of the scientific community to make the distinctions between the true and the false, the sound and the unsound, the plausible and the implausible, will be undercut. One solution might be the adoption of professional protocols enjoining scientists from making a commercial profit from the results of their work. The overriding of epistemologically sound conventions by nonconstitutive values is simply a function of role conflict: individual scientists taking on roles governed by nonscientific values, for example, the commercial values governing the behavior of entrepreneurs. The particular difficulty in the interferon case is that both roles, the scientific and the entrepreneurial, are focussed upon the same activity—the production of a substance with possible medical, and hence commercial, value. The lure of discovery and the lure of profit dangle together.

Disentangling them in this instance, however, will not address the full dimensions of the problem because commercial values are not the only values putting these kinds of pressures on the profession. We live in a society increasingly dependent on science-based technologies, a society reliant on scientific research for new modes of production and of communication, new materials for consumption, new sources of energy, and regulative guidelines for the use of all of these. As the demands for new resources and ways to develop them become more critical, there will be greater and greater pressure on science for immediate answers regardless of the lack of consensus among scientists.[16] This

---

[16] This point was made in conversation by Paul Schulman.

impatience will tend to undercut more and more the time-consuming procedures, such as publication in professional journals, necessary to achieve genuine consensus and relative certainty regarding the possibilities and consequences of particular technologies.

The determining factor in the oral contraceptive case discussed by Korenbrot is not the fusion of activities structured by quite different goals that generate incompatible rules but ignorance. Endocrinology was still, in the early 1960s, not well enough developed to provide much guidance regarding the potential somatic effects—harmful or beneficial—of estrogen compounds.[17] It is easy to see how an almost messianic (if also paternalistic and ethnocentric) belief in the necessity of population control would incline one towards testing for their beneficial rather than their harmful effects. Where we do not know enough about a material or phenomenon either to predict its activity or to choose appropriate methods for predicting its activity, there arises the opportunity for the determination of scientific procedures by social and moral concerns that have little to do with the factual adequacy of those procedures. The demand for information about a phenomenon, which originates in the particular context in which research is done, means that choices must be made about what sorts of effects to test for and what sorts of methods will be used in those tests. When ignorance about the phenomenon frees those choices from the constraints imposed by constitutive norms, they are left vulnerable to other contextual pressures such as beliefs in the social utility of population growth and skepticism regarding its value or interest in competing concerns such as health. Constitutive norms and values are not so much displaced, as they were in the interferon case, as replaced, when lack of sufficient initial data makes them inapplicable, by nonconstitutive, contextual considerations.

GLOBAL ASSUMPTIONS (CASE 5)

The third type of science and values interaction that I wish to discuss in this chapter is the interplay between contextual values and those global assumptions that determine the character of research in an entire field. It is harder to establish that any given case instantiates this type because the development and adoption of global frameworks is a very complex phenomenon with many formative influences. Nevertheless it is, I think, possible to tell the outlines of a story and in the telling

[17] There was data for mice, but not for humans, on the connection between estrogens and reproductive tract cancers.

address some of the concerns about the relation of physical and chemical sciences to contextual values.

What is troubling about claims that even these sciences might be value-laden is their instrumental success. Were they subject to the vagaries of shifts in contextual social and political values (think of the early Soviet condemnation of relativity theory) we should not have the pragmatically fruitful theoretical structures we have. This observation is reminiscent of a protoargument that Hilary Putnam gives in *Meaning and the Moral Sciences*, albeit for the referential character and truth of theories, that is, for scientific realism, not for the independence of inquiry from contextual values. "But if these objects [gravitational fields, the metric structure of space-time] don't really exist at all, then it is a *miracle* that a theory which speaks of gravitational action at a distance successfully predicts phenomena; it is a *miracle* that a theory which speaks of curved space-time successfully predicts phenomena."[18] The nuclear plant produces electricity, our rockets get to the moon and send back pictures of Saturn and of Jupiter, the hybrid corn survives the drought, the bacterial plasmid produces interferon. When we rely on the theoretical claims of science to guide our technological interventions in the natural world, they work. What else would explain their working, if not that they refer to and accurately describe real things? This somewhat transcendental argument considered in conjunction with Francis Bacon's remark nearly four centuries ago that "the roads to human power and to human knowledge lie close together and are nearly the same"[19] provides a clue to the interplay of constitutive and contextual values in these successful sciences.

That a theory "works," that it can be used to predict correctly the empirical consequences either of naturally occurring events or of human intervention and manipulation of events in nature is often taken to be a reason for accepting it. But accepting a theory for practical or instrumental purposes and asserting it to be true are quite different acts. "Working" is not an epistemological notion. The scientific realists' arguments that would give it epistemological significance were seen in Chapter Two to fail to establish that the predictive success of a theory requires us to conclude that such a theory refers to and veridically represents real objects. As Bas van Fraassen has put it in his formulation of constructive empiricism, the success of science can be explained by supposing only that science aims for empirical adequacy.[20]

[18] Putnam (1978), p. 19.
[19] Bacon (1960), p. 122.
[20] For van Fraassen's arguments that truth is not required to explain the instrumental success of theories, see Bas van Fraassen (1980), especially chapters 2 and 3.

Acceptance of a theory on this view involves belief not in its truth but in its empirical adequacy. We can use a theory to guide our interactions with the natural world, even be committed to so using the theory, without being committed to belief in its literal truth. "Working" is a practical notion, then, one connected to the practical goals of gaining greater control of our lives and our environment. This goal represents a value belonging to the context in which science is done. It also provides a constitutive goal of (some) science that sanctions the mechanistic analysis of phenomena in such a way as to facilitate our interventions. Such analysis has since functioned as a desideratum guiding reasoning about the physical world. I will develop these ideas through a consideration of scholarly research on the development of early modern science and the mechanistic philosophy of nature that nurtured it.[21]

While we take it for granted, sixteenth- and seventeenth-century philosophers and scientists created and argued for a conception of matter whose real properties were common to all matter, were quantitatively characterized, and were capable, at least in principle, of precise measurement. The mechanistic philosophy had its origin in an analogy between natural phenomena and machines, but during this formative period it developed into a general theory of the motion of material objects. The theory of instruments, tools, and machines was only one of many applications. Historian E. J. Dijksterhuis describes this as the emancipation of mechanics as a science from its origin in the study of machines.[22] Mechanism itself evolved from a philosophy of nature that saw the world as a very large machine to one that saw the world as composed of essentially lifeless, inert matter describable in mathematical terms. All change, according to this view, was to be explained by reference to external forces or impact, and the relevant properties of matter were shape, size, and motion.

It is important to remember that the mechanical conception of nature did not arise from a newly unprejudiced examination of the data. Many historians of science have commented on the congruence of new fundamental needs of European societies in the fifteenth and sixteenth centuries and the mechanistic model of nature that emerged from this period, swamping organicist and hermeticist alternatives. Even those historians of science who resist "externalist" explanations of the scientific revolution describe the competition between empirically indistinguishable mechanistic and antimechanistic explanations of the same

[21] In addition to the historians whose work is mentioned in the text, I have benefited from reading Burtt (1927).

[22] Dijksterhuis (1961), p. 498.

phenomena. Richard Westfall, for instance, relates the different uses of the same experiment by both Boyle and van Helmont. The experiment involved placing a small tree in a pot containing a carefully measured amount of earth, watering the tree regularly, and after measurable growth by the tree, removing it from the pot and weighing the earth. What the experimenter discovered is that there is very little, if any, diminution in the quantity of earth. (Presumably the times of measuring are in the same relation to the prior times of watering.) Van Helmont believed that nothing (whether organic or inorganic) comes to be in nature save "by a getting of the water with childe."[23] For him all matter is water that is constrained into its living form by a "vital" principle. So the fact that the earth's weight is constant is for van Helmont evidence that the increased weight of the tree represents the added water that was converted to wood by the vital principle.[24] Robert Boyle, on the other hand, saw the experiment as confirmation of a quite different hypothesis. For Boyle all bodies are formed of a uniform matter consisting of particles that differ only in shape and motion. Transformation in bodies occurs by the addition and subtraction of matter and not by the action of vital principles. So he took the experiment as showing that water, earth, and wood are all ultimately made of a uniform stuff in such a way that they are all changeable into one another.[25]

Mechanism of course was not always applied to such ambiguous situations and when applied to problems involving not transformation but translocation produced useful results. Mechanism as a philosophy of nature, moreover, was compatible with a variety of theories of mechanics, for example, the otherwise quite different Newtonian and Cartesian theories. As a philosophy of nature mechanism facilitated certain interpretations of observed phenomena (for instance, the tree experiment), and it made certain aspects of phenomena (the mathematically representable so-called primary qualities) more central than others. Once one has decided that these are the properties that matter, then one can go about ascertaining and measuring them and making inferences about their functional dependencies on one another.

Not surprisingly, given the origin of mechanistic thinking, the phenomena most susceptible to such treatment turned out also to be those of concern to craftworkers involved in the projects of the developing economy. Dijksterhuis lists the classes of craftworker whose practices

[23] Westfall (1977), p. 28.
[24] Ibid., pp. 28–29.
[25] Ibid., p. 77.

and needs in the fifteenth and sixteenth centuries provided fertile ground for the development of mechanics. They included artist-engineers and architects who designed and built canals, locks, military fortifications, and weapons, and who developed new tools with which to carry out these endeavors, as well as instrument makers catering to the needs of navigation, clock making, cartography, military technology, and others.

> A good deal of the knowledge and skill displayed by these men was still purely empirical, but the constant handling of matter, which is always refractory, could not fail to stimulate the desire for a causal explanation and to induce efforts to devise a more rational working-method. It thus becomes understandable that the first branch of science in which the revival was to take place was mechanics (at first still in the sense of the science concerned with tools and implements). In this case empirical knowledge did not have to be sought deliberately, but arose naturally from the pursuit of technical trades; the waiting was only for theoretical reflection, which however, was helped by the fact that there is no single department of physics which calls more urgently for mathematical treatment and lends itself more naturally to it than mechanics.[26]

Though he does not reject social explanations in principle, Dijksterhuis rejected a number of specific explanations of the rise of modern science that link it directly to socioeconomic developments of the period. And certainly thinkers like Galileo and Newton were not directly catering to the needs of the emerging capitalist class. But as Carolyn Merchant has demonstrated, the degradation of the environment—for instance, the destruction of the great European forests for marine and other construction—required that new forms of production be developed and new resources made available.[27] These requirements could in turn only be satisfied if a new conceptualization of the relationship between humans and nature were developed to legitimate these new forms of interaction with (or action upon) the natural world. What the social and economic developments associated with the rise of the emerging bourgeoisie did was to provide an environment in which could thrive a science that rationalized and extended the powers of craftspersons and artisans, whose products were necessary to that class. The idea of the world as a machine need not have been derived from or inspired by or otherwise caused by economic factors in order

[26] Dijksterhuis (1961), p. 243.
[27] Merchant (1980).

that we should see these as playing a major role in the eventual triumph of the mechanistic way of thought. The idea of the world as a machine or a mechanically organized collection of machines decomposable into quantitatively describable and manipulable parts makes real the ideal of control articulated by Bacon. Knowledge and power may not be two aspects of the same phenomenon, as he claimed, but mathematical mechanical knowledge and manipulational power are one another's intellectual and manual correlates.

And so it seems perfectly reasonable to suppose that the reason (or a major reason) for the eventual triumph of mechanism is that, unlike the hermetic tradition with which it contended, the overall philosophy of nature that guided research was compatible with the needs of the socioeconomic climate in which it developed. This would explain why mechanical rather than hermetic theories reached a stage of development and elaboration that enabled their adherents to persuasively claim demonstration of their views. In addition to being able to solve real problems, as a philosophy of nature it legitimated certain modes of exploitation of resources—for instance, mining—it put control of phenomena, at least in principle, in human hands rather than in control of independent vital spirits, and it made understanding accessible to all rather than only to those who had special sympathetic abilities.[28]

Mechanism did this by characterizing matter in a particular way: from being the formless and so incomplete substratum of Aristotelianism it came to be all there really is in nature, and its properties—quantitatively determinate shape, weight, and motion—were the only real properties. The inertness of matter, which is a part of this picture, requires that explanations of changes in its state not only appeal solely to external forces or impact but that they be unidirectional, that is, that causal factors be independent of and temporally prior to their effects so that effects would not themselves influence the causal factors. It is this unidirectionality together with the mathematical expression of functional dependencies that makes possible prediction and sometimes control of certain features of the physical world.

This very general picture, of course, is not mechanics itself. As noted above, the science of mechanics was a field of contention between expositors of quite different theories. The general picture, however, did

---

[28] A number of recent scholars have also argued that it served important political uses. The radical distinction it introduces between the scientist and nature mirrors or is mirrored in the construction of human others: women and a rebellious working class. See Merchant (1980); Keller (1985), chaps. 2 and 3; Thomas (1980); Jacob and Jacob (1980). Legitimation of control is also at issue in the debates highlighted by these scholars. Political control is understood as analogous to technical control.

provide an overall characterization of the natural world, and contending theories can be understood as contesting for the best way to articulate the overall characterization for particular phenomena observed. "Working," that is, achieving pragmatic success, directly vindicates not the philosophy but a particular theory of mechanics. The philosophy of nature, however, is vindicated indirectly as the source or generic model of the successful theory.

The Object of Inquiry

These reflections on the development of early modern science are intended to provide an illustration of one type of contextual value influence on scientific inquiry, that in which values are expressed in or motivate the adoption of frameworklike assumptions that determine the character of research in an entire field. What I've tried to show is that a very general conception of the sort of phenomenon they were investigating permeated the questions early modern scientists asked of nature, and that those questions were themselves linked to the needs and interests of the socio-economic-cultural context in which they conducted their inquiry. This is not an original idea, but the contextualist account of scientific inquiry can provide an analysis of science and values interaction that denies neither the genuineness and integrity of the science nor its shaping by contextual interests. I've suggested the directions such an analysis might take, primarily (1) highlighting the role of mechanistic assumptions about appropriate elements of description and explanation in mediating reasoning between observations and hypotheses, and (2) an explanation of the persistence and eventual triumph of mechanistic philosophy in terms of its provision of a world picture that satisfied emerging needs and interests of its European social and economic context. That such a story *can* be told of early modern science frees us from supposing that the pragmatic successes of physics and chemistry are proof that the theories involved are *true* in the sense of being accurate representations of an underlying or fundamental reality, or that these models of what science is are achieved through value-free inquiry. I would like now to draw out some general reflections suggested by this story.

Any science (or any methodical inquiry) must characterize its subject matter at the outset in ways that make certain kinds of explanation appropriate and others inappropriate. This characterization occurs in the very framing of questions. Teleological questions, for instance, unlike mechanistic questions, are not appropriately addressed to the behavior of matter conceived as inert. The first difference is the one emphasized in early debates about teleology, namely the difference between causal and purposive accounts of change of state. In addition, the answers to teleological questions, unlike those to mechanistic questions, do not satisfy practical goals, and so teleological explanations have no place in sciences whose goal is the practical one of control of natural processes. A complete articulation of the goals of any scientific inquiry includes a description of the *kind* of explanation or understanding (for example, mechanical) that such inquiry aims to provide. This description, or preliminary characterization of the inquiry's subject matter, can be called the specification, or constitution, of the object of inquiry.[29]

The object of inquiry is never just nature or some discrete part of the natural world but nature under some description, for example, nature as a teleological system or nature as a mechanical system or nature as a complexly interactive system. Certain descriptions make certain kinds of questions meaningful and appropriate that would not be so in the context of another overall characterization. Because the characterization of the object of inquiry depends not on what nature tells us but on what we wish to know about it, that description will link the inquiry to the needs and interests it satisfies. Mechanistic philosophy, which characterized the natural world in a particular way, made certain kinds of questions appropriate and others inappropriate. It also, as we have seen, functioned as the source of assumptions mediating between data and explanatory hypotheses. Both proponents of and audience for a particular inquiry bring such assumptions to bear on the subject of investigation. As long as data are brought to bear on the choice of those hypotheses, they will be evidentially supported albeit via the mediation of background assumptions.

In addition to being the source of such assumptions the conception of the object of inquiry is a stabilizing factor that limits the range of hypotheses that are even candidates for consideration. In Chapter Two I distinguished between two missions of the scientific enterprise: knowledge extension and true representation. In the course of extending a given explanatory framework to more and more phenomena, the conception of the object of inquiry prescribes the character of hypotheses and determines the character of reasoning. As a greater number and variety of data are brought under a field's explanatory umbrella,

[29] This phrase is, of course, Michel Foucault's. Our accounts of the construction of the object differ, however, reflecting our divergent disciplinary orientations. His complex theory of the emergence of objects of inquiry is outlined in Foucault (1982). Donna Haraway has also used this concept in her studies of twentieth-century primatology. See my discussion of Haraway's work in Chapter Nine.

the assumptive character and contestatory history of its formative ideas fades from view. What matters is success in meeting practical objectives and that success moots the metaphysical and conceptual questions previously at issue. Only when philosophical analysis reminds us of the underdetermination of theories by their evidence (if even then) is the possibility of an alternative conceptualization of the objects of knowledge leading to equally supportable alternative hypotheses and theories even entertained. And for scientists these abstract philosophical possibilities are much less compelling than substantive contextual or constitutive reasons to seek alternatives.

The idea of the object of knowledge can help to show how contextual values are transformed into constitutive values. The picture I'm suggesting is the following: in any historical period one can find a variety of research traditions, ways of conceptualizing either the natural world generally or particular corners of it more specifically. These conceptualizations, that is, characterizations of the fundamental properties and relations of the objects studied, are what I am calling the constitution of the object of study. This constitution is a function of the kind of knowledge sought about these objects and hence a matter of *decision, choice, and values as much as of discovery*. It is important to acknowledge that these choices are not often, if ever, perceived as such and thus could as well be described as the unconscious projection of human needs onto nature. And it is community adherence to the values and assumptions dictated by one (contextually fixed) set of goals that provides some measure of protection against the influence of individuals' idiosyncratic values.[30] Paradoxically, such community adherence also protects the daily practice of science from contextual incursions, especially from the direct encoding of socio-economic needs into scientific hypotheses. Thus contextual values are transformed into constitutive values.

The kind of knowledge sought and represented in a specification of the object of inquiry functions as a goal determining constitutive values. It stabilizes inquiry by providing assumptions that highlight certain kinds of observations and experiments and in light of which those data are taken to be evidence for given hypotheses. It also provides constraints on permissible hypotheses, as celestial mechanics is guided by

[30] These play a crucial role in the criticism of theories and hypotheses discussed in Chapter Four. As Evelyn F. Keller suggests, the scientific community's identification with a particular set of values is a selective factor which ensures that, for the most part, only those who also hold those values will attempt to join it. The identification of scientists with values is never total or complete, nor are the values entirely consistent. This makes it possible for factions to form and mavericks to join.

the goal of explaining the mechanisms of celestial motion. But the decision to seek a particular kind of knowledge, for example, the decision to seek proximate causes rather than functions and purposes or vice versa, reflects contextual rather than constitutive or epistemological values. The sciences seek not simply truths but particular sorts of truths.

It is quite possible for incompatible research traditions to coexist. Kuhn, perhaps because of his exclusive focus on the physical sciences, thought that the presence of several paradigms indicated the immaturity of a field. The continued coexistence of research traditions guided by incompatible ideas of the object of inquiry could be as well explained by the complexity of the phenomenon studied. The more complex, the less likely that all its features will be adequately accounted for in any one set of models generated by a given set of interests or needs. This is an idea to which I shall return in the concluding chapters.

I've discussed the way the characterization of the object of inquiry is a pivotal meeting point of contextual and constitutive values with respect to some field of inquiry. Let me complicate things a bit. First, fields can be demarcated in different ways, and their correlated objects of inquiry may differ depending on how the lines are drawn. Are the objects the same for the general field of psychobiology and any of its subfields, for example, the study of aging in sensory nervous systems or the study of biological bases of behavioral sex differences? One needs to examine the structure of argumentation in these fields in order to answer this question. Secondly, much of the work that gives us some understanding of complex processes and events is interdisciplinary. How do interdisciplinary inquiries settle on a common object of inquiry? Finally, not every undertaking identified as scientific is carried out under the aegis of an object of inquiry. Toxicity testing, for instance, seeks to predict the health effects of exposure to various substances. Here we are not seeking to understand a phenomenon but simply to know its effects in a restricted set of circumstances. This requires the application of several disciplines, at least physiology (of the organisms exposed) and chemistry (of the substance in question). The application of these disciplines to such a problem does not seem to require the conceptualization of an object of inquiry. Toxicity testing looks on the surface like a simple correlation problem, solvable by techniques of simple induction. As the discussion of Enovid testing suggested, there was no guiding set of assumptions that could guide research. The absence of an object of inquiry left decisions about what effects to test for open to contextual influences. These examples, therefore, point from another direction to the role that the assumptions involved in the characterization of a domain or object of inquiry play in reducing the vulnerability of an area of inquiry to individuals' subjective preferences. Individual values are held in check not by a methodology but by social values.

CHAPTER SIX

Research on Sex Differences

THE biological study of sex differences in behavior, temperament, and cognition is particularly amenable to treatment in the analytic terms developed in the earlier chapters of this book. The attempts to show a biological basis for such alleged differences have both provoked angry and hostile reactions from feminist scholars and activists and inspired popularizers of science to wax ever more lyrical about sexual difference and complementarity. I shall consider the cultural dimensions of this work more closely in later chapters, focussing here and in Chapter Seven on the structure of the scientific arguments. To this end I shall review recent work in physical anthropology, physiological psychology, and neuroendocrinology. These areas of research house work on human evolution, the dependence of human gendered behavior on gonadal hormones, and the sexual differentiation of the brain.

All the studies have as part of their purpose the elucidation of human nature and behavior. The light they intend to throw is of quite different kinds. The evolutionary studies are concerned with the description of human descent: what happened—the temporal sequence of changes constituting the evolution of humans from an ancestral species; and how it happened—the mechanisms of evolution. Behavioral neuro-endocrinology and physiological psychology are concerned not to tell a story but to articulate general laws of the hormonal control of (or influence upon) anatomical development, physiology, behavior, and cognition. In the former case, researchers, using principles of the general synthetic theory of evolution, seek a historical reconstruction that can help clarify what is human and what is natural about human nature. In the latter case no history is sought but rather universals about the natural, in the form of causal generalizations, are developed on the basis of contemporary observations made primarily in experimental settings.

Both types of inquiry take place within established programs or directions that address particular kinds of questions and abide by particular conventions concerning how to go about answering these questions. By carefully examining the data permitted as evidence and the hypotheses entertained or supported on the basis of that data, it will be possible to see the role of background assumptions in creating the evidential relations. I shall focus on the examples provided by these studies of three of the science-values interactions listed in Chapter Five. The evolutionary studies can be read as an example of type 3—contextual values affecting the description of *data*, that is, value-laden terms employed in the description of experimental or observational data and values influencing the selection of data or of kinds of phenomena to be investigated—as well as of type 4—contextual values expressed in or motivating the *background assumptions* facilitating inferences in specific areas of inquiry. As the descriptive problems of anthropology, whether cultural or physical, have been well-discussed elsewhere, I shall explore the human evolution material primarily as an example of type 4. The physiological psychology and behavioral neuroendocrinology can be read as examples of type 3 and of type 5—contextual values expressed in or motivating acceptance of global, frameworklike assumptions that determine the character of research in an entire field. I shall concentrate in this chapter on the ways in which contextual values affect the description and labelling of phenomena in these fields and in the following chapter on the ways in which contextual values affect the global background assumptions in light of which evidential relevance is assessed.

In chapters Two through Four I argued that evidential relevance of data is assessed in light of background assumptions. This would suggest that in order to understand research reports and programs they be analyzed in such a way as to distinguish data from hypotheses. This makes it possible to ask how the data acquire the status of evidence for the hypotheses they are said to support, that is, to ask how they come to be described and to ask about the assumptions that link the data so described to hypotheses. Only then can we fruitfully ask about the contextual values that may have shaped a particular inquiry. These two chapters present the scientific material in enough detail to allow the reader to see how the philosophical approach works for these cases.

Human Evolution

The main questions addressed in the search for human origins are standardly grouped into two categories: anatomical evolution and social evolution. In addition, there are some changes central to human development that are captured by neither of these categories. These are individual behaviors like locomotion that, although likely facilitators, do not of themselves involve social interactions. In addition to behavior, students of evolution are interested in capacities and dispositions manifested by behavior, such as intelligence and sociability. And finally, there is a set of questions concerning the relations between anatomical and social (or behavioral) evolution.[1]

Data

Our theories about the mechanisms of evolution tell us what data to use as the evidence for any particular theory of human descent. About the evolution of our anatomy the theory is clear and simple, if ungenerous: fossils, primarily bits of ancient bone, teeth, some partial and disassembled skeletons, and a few footprints, constitute the base upon which to build our reconstructions of the way here. There are relatively few fossil remains of the earliest hominids—so few that the finding of a tooth can throw accepted truths into dispute again. However, developments in the physical and chemical sciences of the twentieth century have given us additional direction in how to read those fossils we do have. Relying upon those theories, we are able to assign dates and thus place the bones in evolutionary sequence. About data relevant to the evolution of our behavior there is more question. Individual, or noninteractive, physical behaviors such as mode of locomotion and diet seem to pose the fewest problems. The development of bipedalism—when? how long?—is read from fossil footprints and skeletal remains. Dietary habits are read from such phenomena as the size, shape, wear, and thickness of enamel on fossil teeth. A primary difficulty here is that these ancient teeth are often (usually) found singly; and, while some finds can be dated quite accurately, it is not always possible, without further identifying bones, to say with certainty whether they came from the jaw of a human, an ape, or a transitional hominid. Some claims about tool use are based upon the presence of what appear to be functional objects with hominid remains. The more elusive feature of developing intellectual capacity is based on study of the fossil craniums: both of their size and of markings indicative of brain structure left in their interiors.

About the data relevant to the evolution of social, interactive behavior and their relation to the development of our anatomies there is greater contention. The material appealed to includes not only the fossils used in the reconstructions of individual capacities and behaviors and the estimated size of and quantity of remains in hominid sites but also observations of modern ape, monkey, and human societies. As they differ from one another considerably—from traditional gatherers such as the African !Kung San and the many Australian aboriginal peo-

[1] A good review of principles and methodology in the study of human evolution is available in Jolly (1978).

ples to traditional hunters such as the Eskimo and Indian peoples of Alaska and northern Canada, and from the relatively sociable and playful chimpanzees to the relatively unsociable and aggressive baboons—the relevance of the observed behavior of any one of these societies to the reconstruction of the behavior of early hominids is constantly in question. Critics noted early on the tendency of researchers to rely on male informants, to ask questions reflecting male preoccupations, and to pick as models societies that supported their conclusions—to use perceived aggressiveness in male baboons, for example, as a model for aggressiveness in male humans.[2] Developments in immunology and biochemistry suggesting a very close relationship between humans and chimpanzees have made it possible to narrow the field of candidates for ancestry and relation among the primates. Even if it were possible, however, to develop an account of interspecies relationship that determined one among the possibilities as closest to hominids morphologically and physiologically, the description of the social behavior of any species or society is fraught with uncertainty, anthropomorphism, and various forms of centrism based in race, sex, or ethnicity. The behavior of contemporary apes, who themselves represent an evolved rather than an original species, is, in any case, a questionable model of the behavior of our hominid ancestors.[3]

Hypotheses

In recent years stories of human descent have congregated around two central images: "man-the-hunter" and "woman-the-gatherer." Both approaches attempt an integrated story of anatomical and behavioral development that would answer the questions set by the theory of evolution: how those developments that we deem central to an emerging human species were those favored by the processes of selection in the particular environments in which their remains are found. The approaches differ, as might be expected, in their assessment of the relative contributions of males and of females to the evolution of the species. The androcentric "man-the-hunter" perspective assigns a major role to the changing behavior of males. It was promoted by thinkers otherwise as diverse as Edward O. Wilson and Sherwood Washburn.[4] The gynecentric "woman-the-gatherer" perspective assigns a major role to

[2] Leibowitz (1979); Weisstein (1971).

[3] This point is stressed by Martin and Voorhies (1975), pp. 109–110, and by van Gelder (1978), pp. 431–449.

[4] The classic source for the "man-the-hunter" view is Washburn and Lancaster (1968). See also Laughlin (1968). Wilson's version can be found in Wilson (1975), pp. 271–301.

the changing behavior of females. It was first proposed by Sally Slocum,[5] and received extensive development by Nancy Tanner and Adrienne Zihlman, working together and independently.[6] Each perspective assumes the centrality of one sex's changing behavior (or "adaptive strategies") to the evolution of the entire species. Neither assumption is apparent from the fossil record or dictated by principles of evolutionary theory. Each is an example of a contextually driven background assumption facilitating inferences from data to hypotheses.

The development of tool use by early hominids is regarded as a pivotal behavioral change in both perspectives. As an aid to survival it is said to have favored the development of the bipedalism and upright posture necessary for effective tool use, and hence of the anatomical changes that made the new postures possible. Tool use and the conditions of its invention are also linked in both accounts to the development of characteristic human forms of intelligence and sociability.

In the androcentric account the development of tool use is understood to be a consequence of the development of hunting by males. The development of tool use is also seen as a major contributing factor to changed dentition, that is, the reduction of the size of the (male) canines. In fact, Sherwood Washburn argues for stone tool use dating to an earlier time than the finding of manufactured tools would suggest on the basis of the apparent timing of this reduction in the male canines.[7] Defensive threats and shows of aggression, not to mention actual aggression, could be accomplished via the brandishing and throwing of objects rather than via the baring and use of the canines. Once smaller canines were no longer a liability, selective pressures for reduced canines (for example, diets requiring more effective molar functioning) were free to operate. This account, thus, ties the behavioral changes that contribute to selective pressures favoring the development of hominid morphological characteristics to male behavior. And not just any male behavior but behavior that, still in the twentieth-century mind, epitomizes the masculine. In an echo of contemporary androcentrism male hunting is said to provide the conditions requiring the development of distinctively human forms of intelligence and of cooperation.

By contrast, the gynecentric story explains the development of tool use as a function of female behavior, seeing it as a response to the

[5] Slocum (1975).
[6] Tanner and Zihlman (1976); Zihlman (1978); Tanner (1981); Zihlman (1981, 1982).
[7] Washburn (1978), especially p. 201.

greater nutritional stress experienced by females as the abundance of the forests was replaced by the more challenging grasslands and as the conditions of reproduction changed. Females experience greater stress than males because they feed not just themselves but their young through pregnancy, lactation, and beyond. Gathering foods from a distance is necessary in the less abundant savannah, and this new mode of food acquisition itself placed new demands on hominid behavior. Changing female behavior makes possible and is required by longer infant dependency. This in turn is a function of increasing brain size, which demands that a greater portion of development take place outside of the womb. A greater inventiveness was thus both required (by the life conditions) and expected (by our reconstruction) of females.

Whereas most man-the-hunter theorists focus on stone tools, woman-the-gatherer theorists see tool use developing much earlier than the emergence of stone implements and with organic materials such as sticks and reeds. Objects of these materials were opportunistically appropriated or deliberately fashioned to serve in digging, carrying, and preparing foods. Females alone, gathering, also invented the use of tools in defense against predators. Because no remains would be expected, tool use in this account can be assigned to an earlier date than in the account that identifies the first tools as the stone manuports found in suggestive collections near riverbeds and streams. In this story females are seen as the innovators and thus as greater contributors to the development of such allegedly human characteristics as increasing intelligence and flexibility. As for the change in male dentition? The gynecentric view sees female sexual choice as an effective selection mechanism: males with less prominent canines, less prone to aggressive displays and behavior, and more sociable, were more desirable partners for females than their more dentally endowed fellows.

Reasoning and Assumptions

How can the sorts of phenomena admissable as data support either of these two accounts of tool use? As we are concerned with behavior, fossil bones and teeth are no more helpful than the tools themselves. The other types of data include the items identified as tools, the behavior of contemporary hunters and gatherers, and the behavior of other contemporary primates. Focussing on reasoning that moves from the finding of appropriately shaped stones (manuports and chipped stones) in the vicinity of fossil skeletal remains of *Australopithecus* and *Homo Erectus* or massed by streambeds to conclusions about the uses and users of those early tools, we can see several problems. There is, first of all, the inference from the objects themselves to their artifactual or (minimally) implemental character. The features of the stones that lead anthropologists and archeologists to classify them as tools are their roughly similar size, suitability for manual grasping, and (in the case of chipped stones) rough isomorphism (that is, there is a limited number of chip patterns). The odds of finding such uniformity are low enough that those features indicative of intentional selection or manufacture in connection with their presence at sites of a creature who could have made and used them is evidence that they are indeed crude tools. The background assumption here seems to be that, in the absence of countervailing factors, what seems to be is a good indication of what is. Or as L. G. Freeman puts it: "When [patterned occurrences of the elements the prehistorian studies] are derived from undisturbed contexts they indicate that patterned human behavior was responsible for their existence."[8]

Trying to say something about the uses and users of these tools is another matter. They could have been used to kill small animals, to scrape pelts, section corpses, to dig up roots, to break open seed pods, to hammer and soften tough roots and leaves in preparation for consumption. In attempting to give a specific use (which then serves as the basis for more elaborate accounts of the behavior of their users), anthropologists often have recourse to analogies with contemporary populations of hunters and gatherers. The difficulty is that, unlike the distinctive features of human anatomy, the behavior and social organization of these contemporary peoples is so various that, depending on the society one chooses, very different pictures of *Australopithecus* and of *Homo Erectus* are developed. Man-the-hunter theorists will describe the role of the chipped stones in the killing and preparation of other animals, using as their model the behavior of contemporary hunting peoples. Woman-the-gatherer theorists will describe their role in the preparation of edible vegetation obtained while gathering, relying, for their part, on the model of gathering behavior among hunter/gatherers. Similarly, the fact that some contemporary primates use sticks to dig in ant and termite nests does no more than establish the possibility that creatures as much like them as like us could have done the same.

None of the admissable data, thus, provides any sort of decisive or even unequivocal evidence for or against either of the two accounts. How the data are read depends on whether one is working within the framework of man-the-hunter or woman-the-gatherer. In an earlier discussion of these matters biologist Ruth Doell and I compared this

[8] Freeman (1968), p. 265.

state of affairs with other problematic evidential situations in human evolution studies.[9] For instance, a set of footprints preserved in volcanic ash at Laetoli and discovered by Mary Leakey in 1976 is cited as evidence that bipedal hominids had developed at least 3.59 million years ago. Here, too, assumptions are required to connect the data to the hypothesis. In this case the assumptions are generalizations embedded in coherent and accepted understandings (theories) of sets of phenomena. For instance, simple and readily made observations enable us to gauge the pressure exerted by the feet of fully upright walkers and quadrupeds or knucklewalkers, and to establish the foot design necessary for these forms of locomotion. This facilitates the inference that the prints were left by hominids rather than by incompletely bipedal or nonbipedal creatures. Contemporary physics and chemistry have seen the development of a number of different but mutually consistent tests for dating fossils and other remains. This mutual coherence supports reliance on the potassium-argon tests that assign to the volcanic tuff an age of 3.59 to 3.77 million years.

A different challenge is presented by the problem of the "missing link," that is the problem of tracing the complete evolutionary transition from primeval apes such as *Dryopithecus* to *Australopithecus*, now generally accepted as directly ancestral to humans. Until recently *Ramapithecus*, whose fossil remains are dated at 8 to 11 million years ago, was a prime candidate. The fossils, however, consisted only of some teeth and jaw fragments and a few postcranial fragments. While the jaw (and dentition) reconstructed on this basis seemed to diverge in the direction of hominid characteristics, nothing can be said about the rest of *Ramapithecus* anatomy. The jaw and teeth remains are consistent with any degree of uprightness and any degree of brachiating or nonbrachiating structural adaptions. More finds, more bones, which would permit a more complete reconstruction of *Ramapithecus*, could either confirm or disconfirm the hypothesis that *Ramapithecus* is indeed the transitional species. The problem here is not one of settling the evidential relevance of the data available but one of the incompleteness of the data. In light of general evolutionary principles the fragments *are* evidence, but they are only partial evidence.[10]

Assessing the evidential relevance of stone tools in respect of hypotheses regarding behavior, however, is unlike both of these cases. There are no theory-embedded generalizations in light of which we may as-

[9] Longino and Doell (1983). See also Mary D. Leakey (1979); Leakey and Hay (1979).
[10] Longino and Doell (1983). See also Simons (1968a, 1968b); Leakey (1968); and Pilbeam (1977). For a recent review of the controversy and new evidence related to *Ramapithecus* see Pilbeam (1984).

sign them significance, nor is it a question of waiting or looking for more data. It is rather a matter of choosing or using a framework of interpretation—male- or female-centered—and assigning evidential relevance to the data on the basis of the assumptions of the framework. On their own the data are dumb, requiring such assumptions in order to function as evidence. The frameworks belong to ways of seeing and being in the world that assign different degrees of reality and value to male and female activities. If female gathering behavior is taken to be the crucial behavioral adaptation, the stones are evidence that women began to develop stone tools in addition to the organic tools already in use for gathering and preparing edible vegetation. If male hunting behavior is taken to be the crucial adaptation, then the stones are evidence of male invention of tools for use in the hunting and preparation of animals. Although at this stage the woman-the-gatherer framework offers the more comprehensive and coherent theory, this may be due to its having been developed after and partly in response to man-the-hunter theories. A determined partisan of the latter group could, no doubt, improve upon that account.[11] Certainly there is no dearth of anthropologists and biologists defending ever new versions of the hunting story and its centrality to the human one.

In time, a less gender-centric account of human evolution may eventually supersede both of these current contending stories. Such an account would focus on elements common to both sexes, perhaps communication. At this point, however, a great value of the female-centered framework is that, in addition to telling a compelling story, it showed how dependent upon culturally embedded sexist assumptions the man-the-hunter story is. The issue is, however, that there is direct evidence for neither of the interpretive frameworks within which the data, in this case chipped stones, acquire status as evidential support for hypotheses regarding the dietary and social behavior of *Australopithecus* and *Homo Erectus*. Not only do we not now have such evidence but we cannot have it. The distance between evidence and hypothesis is not closed by more fossil data, by better anatomical and physiological knowledge, by principles from the theory of evolution, nor by common-sensical assumptions. It remains an invitation to further theorizing. The availability of (at least) two different frameworks both keeps the gap open as far as nonpartisan observers are concerned and reminds us of the need for background assumptions to secure the relevance of data to specific hypotheses.

[11] For an account of human origins that incorporates some of the research on gathering, abandons hunting, yet retains an androcentric view, see Lovejoy (1981).

BEHAVIORAL NEUROENDOCRINOLOGY

Hormones regulate a variety of physiological functions. The role of the gonadal hormones, the estrogens and androgens, in the development and expression of sexually differentiated traits and functioning constitutes only a small portion of the entirety of hormonal effects. Nevertheless, it is an intensely studied portion. The questions about the relation of sex hormones to sexual differentiation that are or have been studied can be grouped into three large categories: their effects on anatomy and physiology, their effects on temperament and behavior, their effects on cognition. These categories correspond to the three areas in which sexual differences are believed to be manifest. Hormones have both organizing and activating effects. An organizing effect is one that occurs during the development of an organism and that irreversibly primes or programs tissues to respond in certain set ways to later physiological events. The development of sexually differentiated reproductive organs is one of the organizing effects of fetal gonadal hormones. An activating effect is one produced by circulating hormones in the mature organism, as adrenalin secretions increase the heartbeat or the attainment of a certain estrogen level triggers the release of luteinizing hormone in women. It is important to keep in mind during the following discussion that male and female organisms produce and use both androgens *and* estrogens. Distinctive organizing and activating effects are a function of the *level* of concentration of any given hormone and not its mere presence in the organism.[12]

It is tempting simply to argue against the soundness of any studies that purport to show hormonal determination of sex-linked behaviors. Many writers, in fact, do try to show that most of these studies are simply instances of bad or incorrectly done science. I think that the situation is more complex. Certainly some of the research in the area of sex differences just is bad (sloppy, silly, poorly conceived) science. But many cases of good science, or of scientific inquiry that conforms to the constitutive values of a particular tradition, can be shown to be bad science if considered out of the larger research contexts that give them shape and meaning. My point, then, in the ensuing discussion is not so much to dismiss the studies I discuss but to exhibit their logical

[12] The analysis of this and of the following sections was prepared using material in Bermant and Davidson (1974); Eleftheriou and Sprott, eds. (1975); Maccoby and Jacklin (1974); Money and Ehrhardt (1972); Moyer, ed. (1976); Baker (1980); and the review articles on the biological bases of sex differences in a special issue of *Science*: Wilson, George, and Griffin (1981); Bardin and Catterall (1981); MacLusky and Naftolin (1981); Ehrhardt and Meyer-Bahlburg (1981); Rubin, Reinisch, and Haskell (1981).

structure and to show how assumptions and values belonging to the social and cultural context in which the research is done have a bearing on that structure. The discussion of this chapter will focus primarily on the role of such contextual features on the description of data. The following chapter will focus on the role of contextual features in assigning evidential relevance to data and thus to shaping reasoning.

Data

There is a large amount of observational and experimental data available to serve as evidence for hypotheses regarding the relation of sex hormones to sexually differentiated characteristics. It is not all consistent nor is it all of the same quality.

The information relevant to questions regarding morphological differentiation includes, first, the observation of male and female body types and the correlation of these with higher and lower than average levels of androgens and estrogens circulating in the body and, second, the correlation of developmental and other abnormalities in sex-linked anatomical and physiological characteristics with deficiencies or excesses in hormonal levels, for example, the effects of estrogen therapy on secondary sex characteristics, the association of several varieties of hermaphroditism with elevated or depressed levels of the different sex hormones or with the incapacity of normal target tissues to utilize a particular hormone. In addition to the information available regarding humans there are numerous animal studies assessing the physiological effects of deliberate manipulation of hormone levels both perinatally and postnatally.

Data relevant to behavior also include animal experiments and observations of humans. Animal experiments are performed to determine the effects of hormone levels on reproductive behaviors, such as mounting, lordosis, and female receptivity, and on nonreproductive behaviors. One of the most intensely studied of these latter is the relation of early testosterone exposure to frequency of fighting behavior in a variety of strictly controlled laboratory situations. In addition to the animal studies there are a number of attempts to correlate hormonal secretions with human behavioral differences. There are first of all the commonly accepted stereotypes of sex-linked behaviors and their presumed correlation with the different fetal hormonal levels that are implicated in anatomical and physiological sexual differentiation. These cannot be regarded as genuine data because of their unrigorous and presumptive character. They do, however, provide the starting point and underlying context for more serious and rigorous explorations. There have been numerous social and behavioral studies of differences between males and females. While more rigorous than cultural stereotyping, such studies are not beyond controversy. Another source of more reliable information would be the observation in a controlled setting of the behavior of individuals with hormonal irregularities. A number of such groups have been studied, among them young women with CAH (congenital adrenocortical hyperplasia), a condition leading to the excess production of androgens during fetal development, also refered to as AGS (adrenogenital syndrome); young women and men exposed *in utero* to progestins (administered to pregnant women to prevent miscarriages); and male pseudohermaphrodites (genetic males whose appearance from birth to puberty is female, becoming virilized at puberty). These clinical groups provide data for claims about the organizing or predisposing role of fetal hormones on later behavior. Because they involve hormonal levels and effects at variance with chromosomal sex, they are analogous to groups of perinatally neutered or castrated animals who are artifically administered hormones in doses at variance with chromosomal sex.

Other studies are concerned with the relation between circulating hormones and simultaneous behaviors. One favorite type of study attempts to correlate levels of hostility and aggression and levels of circulating testosterone. Such testing on "normal" persons has failed to reveal any consistent association between aggressive tendencies and testosterone levels, while studies of incarcerated males convicted of violent crimes seem to show some correlation.[13] Another type of study measures circulating hormone levels or neuroendocrine system responses to circulating hormones in lesbians and gay men.[14]

In the area of cognitive differences the most notable work is on alleged differences in the mathematical ability of males and females. Researchers claim to observe that average male performance on standardized math tests is consistently superior to that of females. Studies to discover a hormonal basis for this superiority include animal and human studies. Animal studies—for example, testing the effects of androgen on spatial behavior in rats—have not been very fruitful. Recently, however, certain mathematical abilities of a group of hypogonadal men were tested in an attempt to link spatial and mathematical abilities to the pubertal androgen surge.[15]

[13] Rubin, Reinisch, Haskell (1981). It is important to keep in mind that elevated testosterone levels in incarcerated men may be a result, and not a cause, of their incarceration.

[14] Dörner (1976); Gladue, Green, and Hellman (1984).

[15] Hier and Crowley (1982).

Hypotheses

Behavioral endocrinology is, as I have noted, a very active field of research in which lots of hypotheses are articulated and investigated. Just to give a sense of the range of this work, I'll mention a few representative samples in the categories of inquiry I've distinguished before discussing any of these studies in detail. For reasons of space the list is restricted to hypotheses regarding sex differences in humans.

There is widespread consensus that the mechanisms of development of the male and female reproductive systems are fairly well understood. Thus, it is generally accepted that during the third and fourth month of fetal life the bipotential fetus will develop the internal and then the external organs of the male reproductive system if exposed to an androgen (a function of an earlier event that is itself dependent on the presence of the Y chromosome) and will develop the internal and external organs of the female reproductive system if not so exposed. While the details of sexual differentiation are understood, it must be noted that the role of testosterone has been much more studied than that of estrogen. Recent studies indicate the hitherto unappreciated importance of estrogen for both male and female development.

The mechanisms of central nervous system development, while increasingly studied, are not yet as well understood. Many researchers are now studying the differential roles of gonadal hormones in brain organization. Robert Goy and Bruce McEwen have hypothesized, for instance, that androgen receptors play a primary role in sexual differentiation of the human brain.[16] Another group of researchers have hypothesized that peripheral gonadal hormones alter the sensitivity to neurotransmitters such as serotonin.[17]

The hypotheses regarding the influence of sex hormones on behavior attribute their effectiveness either to their perinatal "organizing" effects or to their direct activating (or permissive) effects. Researchers distinguish three types of behavioral effect: sexual orientation, gender identity, and gender role behavior.

In the arena of sexual orientation attempts have been made to attribute homosexuality to both prenatal and circulating endocrine imbalances: deficiencies in the sex-appropriate hormone or excess amounts of the sex-innappropriate hormone.[18] Most recently Gladue, Green, and Hellman have suggested that the "intermediate level of neuroendocrine responsiveness to estrogen in some male homosexuals [consti-

---

[16] Goy and McEwen (1980), p. 79.
[17] Fischette, Bigon, and McEwen (1983).
[18] Goy and Goldfoot (1975).

tutes] a biological marker of their sexual orientation" and that "there may be physiological developmental components in the sexual orientation of some homosexual men."[19]

The area of nonsexual behavior has seen a proliferation of hypotheses. "Gender identity" refers to an individual's primary self-identification as being of one sex or the other, while "gender role behavior" refers to "aspects of behavior in which normal males and females differ in a given culture."[20] Julianne Imperato-McGinley has argued for a hypothesis of hormonal determination of gender identity.[21] Anke Ehrhardt, one of the most active of these researchers, working first with John Money and later with Heino Meyer-Bahlburg, disagrees, arguing that gender identity is determined by environmental factors, especially parental sex assignment. Ehrhardt's main focus is gender role behavior ("physical energy expenditure," "play rehearsal of parenting and adult behavior," "social aggression," "career choice"), which, she argues, is influenced by exposure perinatally to sex hormones.[22]

Sex differences in aggression and their hormonal determinants are studied in many species. The following statement by F. H. Bronson and C. Desjardins can be taken as a cautious summing up of the accepted wisdom in this area: "We may expect both the organizing and adult modulating roles of testosterone to be important in any species in which there exists a reasonable sexual difference in aggressiveness in favor of the male."[23] As for humans, even such thorough and nonpatriarchal scholars as Eleanor Maccoby and Carol Jacklin endorse the claims that males on the whole exhibit higher levels of aggressive behavior and that aggressive behavior is a function of perinatal and circulating testosterone levels.[24] They are much more tentative about linking aggression with such phenomena as leadership and competitiveness.[25] Certain anthropologists throw caution to the wind, however, and argue that the social dominance of males is a function of their hormonally determined behavior.[26] They have also interpreted this theory as implying that males are naturally superior (whatever that means) to females. Such theorists are imputing to aggression the determination of position in hierarchical social structures and then attrib-

[19] Gladue, Green, and Hellman (1984), p. 1499.
[20] Meyer-Bahlburg (1982), p. 681.
[21] Imperato-McGinley et al. (1979).
[22] Ehrhardt and Meyer-Bahlburg (1981), p. 1312.
[23] Bronson and Desjardins (1976), p. 101.
[24] Maccoby and Jacklin (1974), pp. 243–247.
[25] Ibid., pp. 263–265, 274, 386–371.
[26] Goldberg (1973).

uting aggressive behavior to the level of testosterone circulating in the organism, either perinatally or in maturity. Parallel theorizing about women imputes maternal behavior and temperament (for example, nurturance, patience, a certain kind of attentiveness to infant needs) to hormonal status.[27]

Finally, a number of hypotheses about the connection of prenatal hormones and cognition have been entertained. These include the supposition by Norman Geschwind that testosterone exposure increases brain hemispheric asymmetry, leading to greater specialization for function. This specialization is linked to superior performance on tests of spatial ability and in mathematics generally.[28]

Reasoning and Assumptions

The promulgation of such hypotheses as are mentioned in the previous section in today's sociopolitical climate cannot but be controversial. While I shall examine the cultural, social, and political dimensions of the controversies in a later chapter, the very existence of controversy— the disputing of findings and the development of alternative hypotheses to explain data—makes the task of analyzing these studies much more feasible than it would be in the absence of controversy. Inferences and assumptions that in a different context would go (and formerly went) unchallenged are subject to more detailed scrutiny by other scientists, which in turn assists the external analyst and critic in her reconstruction. I am indebted, therefore, to those feminists in and out of the sciences who have raised questions about the soundness of sex differences research. I shall limit my analysis in this chapter to the studies of gender role behavior, cognition, and brain differentiation.

As in evolutionary studies the relation between data and hypotheses becomes much more complex in the attempt to link hormonal levels with behavior. I will analyze the inferential steps in Ehrhardt's hypothesizing about young females with CAH as it is expressed in her 1981 article with Heino Meyer-Bahlburg because, unlike some of the authors exploring this topic, Ehrhardt is directly engaged in some of the research that forms the basis of her thinking.[29] In addition, because she is examining the relation between *prenatal* hormone exposure and later behavior, there is no question of the hormone levels being an effect of the behavior rather than vice versa. From the point of view of hereditarian theories of gender, moreover, Ehrhardt's work, if sound,

[27] Rossi (1977).
[28] Geschwind and Galaburda (1985).
[29] Ehrhardt and Meyer-Bahlburg (1981).

would indicate a mechanism that mediates between the genotype and its behavioral expression. Finally, hers is the work that *Science* chose to represent research on gender role behavior in its special issue on sex difference research. Whether merited or unmerited, this fact confers a certain professional imprimatur. All these factors together confer upon her work pivotal significance.

The data brought into the reasoning include human observation and animal experimentation as indicated above. The human observations are of the girls affected by CAH and (sometimes) their female siblings as controls. The data consist of correlations between the prenatal exposure of the CAH girls to greater than normal quantities of androgens and the girls' behavior (or alleged behavior) as children and as adolescents. These young women and other groups of persons who, like them, have experienced anomalous fetal levels of gonadal hormones, are in effect "experiments of nature." While ethical considerations prevent researchers from conducting on humans the sorts of experiments conducted on animals, that is, castration and artifical administration of gonadal hormone, the occurrence of syndromes such as CAH or hypogonadism and the effects on fetuses of hormone administration to pregnant women provides them with substitutes. Members of such groups, when so identified, are the object, therefore, of intense scrutiny.

As mentioned above, CAH involves the excess production of androgens by the adrenal gland. It also involves a failure by the adrenals to produce cortisone. Infant girls with CAH are born with large clitorises sometimes mistaken for penises and usually surgically altered in later life. All individuals with CAH require lifelong cortisone treatment to compensate for their nonfunctioning adrenals. The majority of the CAH girls studied are described as exhibiting "tomboyism," characterized as a behavioral syndrome involving preference for active outdoor play (over less active indoor play), greater preference for male over female playmates, greater interest in a public career than in domestic housewifery, less interest in small infants, and less play rehearsal of motherhood roles than that exhibited by "normal" young females. The significance of the apparent correlation of abnormally high fetal androgen levels with these behaviors is the apparent relative insensitivity of these so-called gender role behaviors to environmental factors such as parental and other forms of conditioning. Other commentators have noted that one of the difficulties with these behavioral observations is that they are obtained from parents and teachers who know of the girls' abnormal physiological condition and from the girls themselves.[30] Thus it is difficult to know how much the reports are influenced by the observers' expectations. I will assume for purposes of this analysis that the reports are more or less accurate, that is, that the behavior of these young women does on average differ to some degree from that of their female siblings or peers.

Having claimed that the CAH girls' behavior is singular in this respect, Ehrhardt explains it as a function of their prenatal exposure to androgens. Upon arguing this hypothesis for the CAH girls, she then generalizes over all humans, claiming that gender role behavior, that is, behavior thought appropriate to one gender (or sex) but not to the other, is importantly influenced by prenatal exposure to sex hormones. So boys' preference for active outdoor play and relative disinterest in small infants and in parenting is explained by their fetal exposure to androgens. And girls' preferences are explained by their fetal hormone exposures. What facilitates the inference from apparent correlation to causation? Ehrhardt explicitly refers to work purporting to show that in other mammalian species behaviors analogous to the ones in question *are* hormonally determined. In addition, she refers to hypotheses regarding the role of hormones in brain organization, thus suggesting a mechanism for the behavioral expression of fetal hormone exposures. While in both instances she is relying on the assumption of continuity of physiological and behavioral phenomena across mammalian species, its deployment in behavioral studies on the one hand and brain organization studies on the other raises different problems. I will therefore discuss them separately.

Experiments show that mounting behavior and some types of "aggressive" behavior in rodents are functionally related to androgen exposure during critical periods in development.[31] Female rodents exposed during critical periods to greater than normal quantities of androgens will attempt to mount other animals significantly more often than untreated females will, and perinatally castrated males will attempt to mount other animals significantly less often than normal males. In addition, a variety of experiments with rodents show a correlation between perinatal androgen exposure and certain types of aggressive behavior.[32] Thus, sexually dimorphic patterns of behavior in rodents are attributed to perinatal hormone exposure during the critical period. The importance of the perinatal exposure is that its effect is not activational but organizational, that is, it does not induce the

[30] Fausto-Sterling (1985) and Adkins (1980) discuss Ehrhardt's earlier publications on this subject.
[31] Bermant and Davidson (1974), pp. 195–202.
[32] Edwards (1976); Bronson and Desjardins (1976).

behavior in question at the moment but predisposes the organism to respond to stimuli in particular ways in later life. It should be mentioned that even different rodent species differ quite widely in the types of sexual dimorphism they display and in the role of hormones in mediating that display of dimorphism.

The appeal to rodent experiments—taking the "zoocentric" view, as one researcher has charmingly put it—assumes that the rodent and the human situation are similar enough that demonstration of a causal connection in the one species is enough to support the inference from correlation to causation in the other. This presupposes that the behaviors exhibited by the several species—human, other primates, rodents—are the same phenomenon, just as, say, reproduction in these species is the same phenomenon. The situation is much more complicated for these gender role behaviors, however.

First, it is not at all obvious that the behaviors of experimental animals are sufficiently analogous to those of the human children and adults studied. Fighting behavior in a laboratory cage is not clearly analogous either to rough and tumble play or to active outdoor play. Nor is frequency or intensity of rough and tumble play a dimension that matches propensities to athleticism as opposed to propensities to reading. The human child and adult behaviors, for instance, all exhibit a degree of intentionality not characteristic of the stereotyped rodent behaviors studied.[33]

Second, the experiments with rodents all involve single factor analysis. The conditions of the animals' lives can be highly regulated (more than those of human life, at least), making possible experiments that attempt to vary only one factor at a time and make no attempt to understand interactions between factors. The human situation, including that of the CAH girls, is always interactive. Humans are in a social context from the first moments of their lives. We have no way of isolating the variables operating in real life, in which any one feature is a function of a multiplicity of interacting factors. Thus, the larger contexts in which behaviors are identified are not sufficiently analogous.

The analogy between the human behaviors and the stereotyped nonhuman behavioral dimorphisms seems obvious if one expects sexual dimorphism and classifies behavior as masculine or feminine. Without this expectation or the assumption that behavior is so gendered, however, the behaviors of the children seem more various and classifiable under different schemas. Hand-eye coordination, for example, cuts across indoor and outdoor, feminine and masculine behavioral classi-

---

[33] Doell and Longino (1988).

fications. The assumption of dimorphism makes certain features of the behaviors—for example, level of expenditure of physical energy—more salient than others, and thus makes the behaviors appear suitable as evidence for the hormonal hypothesis. In addition, the sample results are never uniform. The assumption of gender dimorphism makes the clustering of individuals around certain behavioral poles more significant than the amount of individual variation that is as much a feature of the data as the clustering.

The second source of instability for the assumption facilitating the transformation of correlation to causation is the mechanism proposed to link hormone exposure to later behavior: hormonal organization of the brain. Ehrhardt and Meyer-Bahlburg refer to several studies of hormonal effects on central nervous system development. They acknowledge that in contrast to the situation for rodents "the evidence in primates and especially in human beings is inferential and . . . tentative" and that "the role of social learning is much greater in human behavior than in subhuman mammals."[34] Nevertheless, they go on to say that "there is sufficient evidence to suggest that biological factors influence psychosexual differentiation in human beings, too."[35] They mention in particular the similarity of subcortical regions of the brain in humans and other mammals and the cross-species correspondence in timing of androgen production and of hypothalamic differentiation. These questions about the brain will be explored further in the next chapter. Here I will again focus on the effects of assumptions on description of data.

Brain Organization

There are currently two suggestions regarding the nature of hormonal organizing effects. One is that critical period exposure to hormones affects the threshold of response within neurons to environmental and hormonal stimuli in later life. The other is that hormones affect the development of the neural circuits responsible for certain behaviors. Ehrhardt's and Meyer-Bahlburg's mention of the organizational hypothesis is intended to suggest that the correlations they cite between fetal hormonal exposures and later behavior are terminal points of a causal chain that is mediated by brain and central nervous system organization. Brains are sexually differentiated anatomically and thereby predisposed to produce sexually differentiated behavioral responses. Researchers in this field, which involves primarily rodents and some bird species, have introduced the terms "masculinization," "feminiza-

[34] Ehrhardt and Meyer-Bahlburg (1981), p. 1312.
[35] Ibid.

tion," "demasculinization," and "defeminization" to describe the various differentiation processes. The major idea is that gonadal hormones induce brain differentiation much as they induce reproductive tract differentiation. Ehrhardt and Meyer-Bahlburg's summary reference to work on the role of gonadal hormones on brain organization fails to note that the use of the key terms cited above is itself inconsistent. The following are some examples of the resulting difficulties.

In their introduction to the volume *Sexual Differentiation of the Brain* Goy and McEwen state that "masculinization" is reserved for "hormonal effects involving the enhancement of male-typical behaviors in genetic females," and "feminization" is reserved for "hormonal effects involving the enhancement of female-typical behaviors."[36] The reader can be forgiven for feeling confused when, within a few pages, the authors are talking about the masculine state of the brain of androgen-insensitive genetic males,[37] or when much later in the volume they refer to incomplete masculinization of the brain in 5-α-reductase deficient individuals (genetic males).[38] The definitions offered of the key terms suggest that males can be feminized or demasculinized and that females can be masculinized or defeminized. These definitions leave us no way to name the process whereby intact genetic males or females develop the behavioral traits or brain morphology thought to be typical of their sexes, yet the researchers talk as though masculinization is what happens to normal males and feminization is what happens to normal females. (Or more precisely, masculinization is what happens to the as yet undifferentiated fetus that has a Y chromosome and no functional abnormalities and feminization to the undifferentiated fetus with two X chromosomes.)

This inconsistency between definition and use is resolved in a definition McEwen offers in a different publication: "Masculinization is defined as the enhancement during development of masculine traits."[39] This definition, however, leaves open the character of the enhancement and, of course, assumes that we can identify masculine traits. This lack of clarity in definition is mirrored by the use of these terms, which are used sometimes to refer to hypothesized but unknown determinants of behavior, sometimes to behavior, and at other times to specific events in neural development. That is, the use wavers between referring to some mechanism of differentiation or to differentiation itself. In each

[36] Goy and McEwen (1980), p. 5.
[37] Ibid., p. 8.
[38] Ibid., p. 132.
[39] McEwen (1981), especially p. 1309.

of these cases the colloquial meanings of "masculine" and "feminine" are both doing all the work.

The creation of terms whose meaning is primarily behavioral for processes of neural development only hypothesized to exist leads researchers to highlight some aspects of the biochemical processes they can trace at the expense of others. For instance, that the gonadal hormone involved in brain development in males starts out as testosterone is made more important than the fact that it is aromatized to estradiol before being taken up by neurons. Richard Whalen makes a similar point regarding the nomenclature of gonadal hormones. Their grouping into androgens and estrogens, he suggests, reflects hypotheses about their mechanism of action when that is often unknown.[40] Brain organization research seems governed by a conviction of the deep differences between the sexes involving sharp biochemical distinctions and cleanly separable lines of masculine and feminine development. This conviction has resulted in a classification system for gonadal hormones generated by their purported effects rather than by chemical structure or mode of action. The assumption of behavioral dimorphism parallel to anatomical dimorphism, then, results in a bivalent classification system for gonadal hormones that mirrors their postulated effects on sexual differentiation, regardless of the studies showing that their effects vary depending on other physiological factors. The nomenclature both masks the complexity of hormone action and leads people to think of gonadal hormones as themselves male or female.

Mathematical Ability

Many of the programs attempting to articulate a biological basis for alleged differences in mathematical abilities between the sexes suffer from problems similar to those just outlined. The grounds for claiming that there are differences in ability are of two kinds: studies of performances on various spatial ability tests and studies of performances on the standardized tests given to secondary school students who plan to go on to college or university. The sorts of biological bases appealed to in explanation of these differences include different degrees of brain hemisphere laterality, differential hormone exposure, as well as a combination of these. Commentators have directed searching criticism at both the biological mechanisms proposed to explain the differences and the claim that the differences discerned are significant enough to warrant an explanation of any sort.

The work linking spatial ability to greater degrees of brain asym-

[40] Whalen (1984).

metry and both of these to sex is the weakest of these research programs. For instance, Paula Caplan and her fellow researchers point out that many of the spatial ability testers failed to perform the elementary statistical analyses, such as regression analyses, that would support the claim of significantly different performances.[41] This elimination of an explanandum calls into doubt the explanation offered. Sex differences in brain laterality researchers, however, take as basic data the research purporting to demonstrate sex differences in spatial ability. The paper by Hier and Crowley claiming that hypogonadal men (men who did not experience the typical androgen surge at puberty) perform more poorly on spatial ability tests than normal males also loses its significance for sex differences when those sex differences disappear.[42]

By contrast, the data produced by researchers Camilla Benbow and Julian Stanley on Scholastic Aptitude Test performances seem more robust. Benbow and Stanley are affiliated with the Johns Hopkins University Study of Mathematically Precocious Youth. They have studied the performances of almost 50,000 children under the age of thirteen on the mathematics SAT normally administered to sixteen- and seventeen-year-olds. A first report, published in *Science* in 1980, reported on a group of 9,927,[43] and a second report in 1983 reported on 39,820 children.[44] The children studied have all been identified (by teachers and by their performance on standardized tests) as having a high degree of mathematical ability. Among this group Benbow and Stanley have consistently found a thirty- to forty-point difference in the mean scores of girls and boys, with the boys scoring higher. Even more striking, according to Benbow and Stanley, is the ratio of boys to girls achieving very high scores (above 600 about 4:1 and above 700 about 12:1).

Benbow and Stanley clearly prefer biological to social explanations for the differences that they have unearthed. While they do not endorse any particular biological hypothesis, in the *Science* papers reporting the sex differences they are at pains to argue that their data are inconsistent with several hypotheses about social/environmental determinants of sex-associated differences in mathematical performance. In a paper by Camilla Benbow and Robert Benbow, dedicated to Stanley, the preference for biological explanations is much more explicit.[45] In this paper they report on following up some of Norman Geschwind's

[41] Caplan et al. (1985).
[42] Hier and Crowley (1982).
[43] Benbow and Stanley (1980).
[44] Benbow and Stanley (1983).
[45] Benbow and Benbow (1984).

suggestions regarding testosterone, right brain hemisphere development, and several phenomena attributed by Geschwind to excess fetal testosterone exposure: left-handedness, myopia, and immune disorders (allergies).[46] Finding levels of left-handedness, nearsightedness, and allergies higher among their talented youth than in the general population, they conclude by endorsing Geschwind's hypothesis that fetal testosterone exposure is responsible for the difference in M-SAT performance that they record:

> Geschwind and Behan (1982) proposed that exposure to increased levels of testosterone in the developing fetus retards neuronal development of the left hemisphere. This implies that the developing individual would have a (relatively) stronger right hemisphere. Because the left hemisphere, which is better at language processing, does not dominate over the right hemisphere, which is specialized for non-verbal problem-solving tasks (e.g., spatial problems), such an individual would have a greater chance at developing his/her spatial or mathematical reasoning abilities through environmental interactions. By contrast, an individual with a dominant left hemisphere would rely more on his left hemisphere and would attempt to solve problems using a verbal approach. Such initial biases are then accentuated by the environment, which shapes the development of cognitive abilities. In our hypothesis, sex differences occur because males are more likely than females to be exposed to increased levels of testosterone. Males are indeed more likely than females to be left-handed or to suffer from immune disorders, which would be consistent with this hypothesis. Moreover, the two consequences of fetal exposure to an increased level of testosterone, as predicted by Geschwind and Behan, were in fact found for mathematically precocious youths. This would be necessary in order to validate our model.[47]

Necessary, perhaps, but not sufficient. Like the work in biological bases of gender difference this work on mathematical ability/performance floats on a sea of assumptions. While the researchers have controlled for variation in courses taken by males and females, they assume that this is the only significant social factor to be considered. This and similar assumptions about the backgrounds of the children tested will be discussed further in Chapter Eight. In addition, however, in order to use the test performances as they do it is necessary to assume

[46] Geschwind and Behan (1984); also Geschwind and Galaburda (1985).
[47] Benbow and Benbow (1984), pp. 485–486.

that they are indicators of inherent ability rather than of acquired knowledge. Accepting the data as a reflection of real differences in ability, in turn, requires assuming that there is one form in which mathematical ability is expressed and that that form is expressed in performance on standardized tests such as the M-SAT. In addition, one must assume that the content of a problem has no bearing on the formal properties of a problem nor on an individual's grasp of those properties. Many critics have argued that the content of the quantitative word problems in these tests reflects the typical experience and preoccupations of men and boys rather than those of women and girls.[48] To the extent that this is so, the above assumption must be established before the performance data can read as ability data.

Comparison with Anatomical Research

This situation can be compared with that of the hormonal determination of *anatomical* sexual differentiation. For contrast we can take the studies of the hormonal influence on differentiation of the external genitalia in humans. The current view is that testosterone secreted by the fetal testis is required for normal male sex organ development and that female differentiation is independent of fetal gonadal hormone secretion.

As is the case in the behavioral studies, among the relevant human observations the most significant are those of persons affected by various hormonal abnormalities. Even here the assumption of dimorphism affects the description of the phenomena. Cases diverging from prototypical male or prototypical female development are treated as cases of partial or incomplete male or female development. Such individuals are treated as inadequate males or females rather than as instances of types with their own integrity or as points on a continuum of which prototypical males and females are the extremes. In this respect the anatomical studies parallel the behavioral studies. Genetic males who lack intracellular androgen receptors and are thus unable to utilize testosterone exhibit a female pattern of development of external (though not internal) genitalia. Genetic females exposed in utero to excess androgen, the CAH youngsters or women whose mothers were treated with progestin during pregnancy, exhibit what is described as partial masculine development, including enlargement of the clitoris and incomplete fusion of the labia. Because of this descriptive bias it is safer to continue the comparison by concentrating on what is

[48] See Graf and Riddell (1972).

known about the role of testosterone in the development of prototyp-
ically male genitalia.

The human studies do support the idea that exposure of the primor-
dial tissues to testosterone or one of its metabolites, for example, 5-α
dihydrotestosterone, at the appropriate time is both necessary and sufficient for masculine development of the sex organs.[49] This inference is
further corroborated by experimental data in a variety of mammalian
species whose reproductive anatomy and physiology are analogous to
those of humans. In contrast with the animal experiments used to support claims about behavior, the systems here really are analogous: penises, testicles, seminal vesicles are all quite similar across mammalian
species.[50] Furthermore, the anatomical effects of hormone exposure
or its failure in the animals studied are invariable rather than probabilistic.

Researchers have also been able to establish in large part the biochemical pathways of action of testosterone. The similarities in the
physiological systems involved and in the relation of the presence or
absence of testosterone to sex organ development allow the model of
action established in nonhuman mammalian species to be applied to
humans as well. The uncertainties here have to do not with the functional interactions of different anatomical areas but with completion
of the biochemical pathway analysis. For example, because the exact
mechanism of hormonal action at the cellular level is only partially
understood, it is not yet certain how testosterone or its metabolites act
in the cell nucleus. In this respect this issue in endocrinology is analogous to the questions regarding *Ramapithecus* in evolutionary studies.
The lack of certainty will be allayed by more information and more
analysis. The biochemical data we do have, however, make the hypothesis regarding male sex organ development that we have been discussing as unassailable as biochemical theory itself. This, of course, is
not to say that biochemical theory is unassailable but that the assumptions involved belong to a well-established body of theory currently in
use. In this respect the strength of the support offered the hypothesis
by the human observations mentioned is comparable to that provided

[49] The other half of this story usually is: "and no particular hormonal secretion from
the fetal gonad is required for female development." In many texts testis development is
simply identified with sexual development. Undoubtedly when more is known about
female sexual development, our understanding of male sexual development will correspondingly shift. For an illuminating discussion see Fausto-Sterling (1988).

[50] The analogy is structural and functional. Relative sizes of these structures vary
across species.

for the hypothesis of bipedalism in *Australopithecus* by the physical evidence of the footprints.

THE ROLE OF VALUES

The evolutionary studies and behavioral studies that have been the focus of attention resemble inquiry on related questions in relying on assumptions to join data with hypotheses. What the comparisons show is that the difference consists in what I've been calling the stability of those assumptions. In dating bipedalism or establishing the pathways of sexual differentiation of the external genitalia, researchers rely on assumptions that are closely intertwined with accepted theory in other or related disciplines. This is an example of the public function of scientific knowledge as a resource for argumentation. Even here, of course, value-laden assumptions, for example, dimorphism, are mingled with empirically supported generalizations. The research on human evolution and on contemporary behavioral sex differences relies on less stable assumptions, some of which are explicitly androcentric and which play different roles in the research programs. As argued earlier, the reliance on assumptions directly encoding contextual values is not by itself grounds for rejecting the work as science. It is often the case in new fields that reasoning and inference rely on assumptions that become established only after the field has sufficiently developed. Prior to the articulation of such inferential networks, however, the influence of values and contextual interests and commitments is more clearly discernible. I wish in this section to consider the implications of the preceding analysis for understanding the role of such contextual factors in the development of theory in these areas.

The aims of the two kinds of research examined above are quite different. The aim of the evolutionary studies is to reconstruct a history, to recover particulars and interrelate them in such a way that the course of development of a particular species, *Homo sapiens*, can be described. On this basis generalizations concerning the interrelations of various aspects of human existence become possible, but their development is not the immediate aim of these studies. In contrast, the aim of the neuroendocrinological and behavioral research is to discover the hormonal substrates of certain behaviors, that is, to develop causal or quasi-causal generalizations relating hormonal states and behaviors. To the extent that we take evolutionary studies to reveal certain behaviors or dispositions to behave as expressions of human nature and neuroendocrinological studies to reveal hormonal determinants of those behaviors, the otherwise quite disparate aims of these studies interconnect.

Just this kind of interconnection is emerging today. Evolutionary studies undertaken within the man-the-hunter framework have been taken to show that the sexual division of labor observable in some contemporary human societies has deep roots in the evolution of the species. The stories of males going off together to hunt large animals and females staying home and nurturing their young seems to some to prefigure contemporary, if rapidly disappearing, Western middle-class social life: men engage in public affairs, management of production and governance, and women in domestic affairs, childrearing, housekeeping, and husband maintenance.[51] If these broadly described behaviors or behavioral tendencies can be correlated with the more particularized behaviors and dispositions to behave studied by neuroendocrinology, a picture of biologically determined human universals emerges. Evolutionary studies provide the universals: genders and sex roles that remain fundamentally constant throughout the history of the species; neuroendocrinology provides the biological determination: the dependence of these particular behaviors or behavioral dispositions on (prenatal) hormone distribution, itself genetically controlled.

It is instructive to note not only the ways in which these inquiries intersect but their differences, particularly in their expression of patriarchal values. In the following discussion I shall follow convention in distinguishing two forms of expression of masculine values. "Androcentrism" is generally used to refer to perception of social life from a male point of view with a consequent failure to accurately perceive or describe the activity of women. "Sexism" is generally used to refer to statements, attitudes, practices, behavior, or theories presupposing, asserting, or implying the inferiority of women, the legitimacy of their subordination, or the legitimacy of sex-based prescriptions of social roles and behaviors. Neither of these terms quite captures a third expression of patriarchal values, the assumption of thoroughgoing dimorphism or sexual essentialism. In part it is the idea that "they" are made for and hence complementary to "us." As such it is a form not only of sexism but of heterosexism. The latter is generally identified as homophobia. Certainly opposition to, or denial of, homosexuality is part of heterosexism, but I see the tendency toward heterosexism as a more far-reaching imposition of complementary duality, which denies a whole range of possible human variety.

[51] Compare Wilson (1978), p. 95.

In the evolutionary studies the assumption of dimorphism plays as much of a role as it does in the endocrinological studies: males and females are assigned distinctive roles that parallel contemporary Western stereotypes. In addition, in the evolutionary studies assigning central significance to man-the-hunter androcentric values are expressed directly in the framework within which the data are interpreted: chipped stones are unequivocal evidence of male hunting only in a framework that sees postulated male behavior as central not only to the evolution of the species but to the survival of any group of its members. The following premise of one argument for treating the stones as hunting weapons is illustrative of this tunnel vision: "If *A. robustus* was a vegetarian, it is difficult to imagine what he [*sic*] was doing with tools. On the other hand, tools became useful to a bipedal hunter because they do facilitate killing."[52] This passage exhibits the tendency of theorists to think only in terms of male activity and their reluctance to ascribe to early human males any behavior other than hunting. In its association with aristocratic ways of life hunting, along with self-assertion and courage, carries an aura of nobility that scavenging or digging, both of which are also facilitated by tools, simply lack. Not only does the man-the-hunter framework fail to perceive the contribution of females to early human life but it insists on characterizing male behavior in ways dictated by our culture's contemporary evaluation of males and male activities.

The woman-the-gatherer framework, on the other hand, does the same for female behavior: it makes female contributions to early human life the focus of inquiry, it reinforces our contemporary views about the nurturant quality of women's activity, and it describes uses for tools consistent with women's postulated behavior. It puts women at the center of the evolutionary story, but the women bear a remarkable kinship to contemporary stereotypes. While this framework is as gynecentric as its rival is androcentric, its great value from a logical point of view is its revelation of the epistemologically arbitrary character of the man-the-hunter framework. As long as both frameworks offer coherent and comprehensive accounts of the relevant data, neither can displace the other.

There are several points worth noting about this example. Human behavior is complex and varied enough that relations between particular hypothesized behaviors and anatomical evolution may never rest on as secure a basis as the relationship between footsteps and bipedalism. There will always be room to dispute any proffered theory. This

[52] Laughlin (1968), p. 319.

may account in part for the relative success of the woman-the-gatherer model. Another reason may be that proponents of this model have not strayed from fundamental sociobiological principles concerning the relation between behavioral and anatomical evolution. It is offered as an alternative to the androcentrism prevalent in human evolution studies and exemplified in the image of man-the-hunter, but it continues to rely on such concepts as kin selection and sexual selection.

In the neuroendocrinological behavioral studies at the moment there is no comparably explicit androcentric framework for the interpretation of data. At the level of description of data, however, both description and selection are influenced by heterosexism, or sexual essentialism, that is, by the idea that there are sex-appropriate and sex-inappropriate behaviors. The assignment of lively activity to one sex and the relegation of the other to quiet, domestically oriented play is cultural mythology, although admittedly mythology acted out in many lives. The language used to describe the CAH girls' behavior—for example, "tomboyism"—reflects uncritical acceptance of this mythology from the start.[53] This description implies the inappropriateness of the behavior. The myth it expresses may also influence the selection of data, that is, may lead investigators to highlight the presence or absence of certain behavioral factors and overlook or downplay others, to design studies that look for culturally assigned masculine qualities in hormonally unusual females and the converse for males.[54] Finally, if sexual differentation were a less central concern, other aspects of the observed behaviors might become more salient leading to a reclassification of the data. This point will be further explored in Chapter Seven.

These data selection and organization questions are primarily problems of description and presentation. They serve as examples of theory-laden observation as discussed in Chapter Three. Choosing a less value-laden term than "tomboy" may allow for the description of a genuine difference, if there is one, in the behavior of the CAH girls from that of their siblings. Thus, it is at least theoretically possible that the description of the data could be "cleaned up" so as not simply to reflect back these particular contextual values and assumptions. In fact, researchers in this field do seem to be trying to develop cleaner data, partly in response to feminist criticisms.[55] If they are successful, we would have a catalogue of human behavior and dispositions and of

[53] Fried (1979).
[54] Fausto-Sterling (1985).
[55] See, for instance, Ehrhardt (1985) and Linn and Peterson (1985).

behavioral differences that might or might not correspond to the socially important differences of sex. Similarly, the dual classification system that results from systematizing the data in light of assumed sexual essentialism could be abandoned. A new classification system that treated sexual variety as providing examples of integral types or of a sexual continuum rather than of truncated males or females could replace the present one if we were finally to abandon sexual essentialism. The finding of physiological correlates for some of these differences would constitute a less suspect data set than the one so far provided.

The choice of a physiological rather than an environmental framework of interpretation of such data is not directly related to androcentric or sexist values. Some feminists have suggested that the search for (presumably immutable) physiological determinants of gender reflects sexist concerns (for example, for the permanence of sexual inequality). Other feminists, however, have happily accepted the idea of physiological determinants of sexually differentiated traits. Their perspective celebrates so-called female qualities, such as nurturance, and condemns males as biologically incapable of escaping a heritage of aggression and violence. Their viewpoint might be characterized as a feminist, rather than patriarchal, heterosexism. If the physiological framework does reflect androcentric or sexist values, it does not do so in as straightforward a way as man-the-hunter theorizing reflects androcentric values.[56]

What about the assumptions involved in the interpretation of such reconstituted data as evidence for physiological causal hypotheses? I suggested above that this theoretical orientation is not on the face of it expressive of androcentric or sexist values. But I have also argued that the assumption of cross-species uniformity, that is, of the analogy between humans and other animals, is highly questionable in its application to behavior. One might well ask, What would explain its persistence, if not the role it can play in the sexist project? I think that there is another explanation. Developing such an explanation involves seeing research on the biological bases of presumed gender differences in a broader scientific context, acknowledging, for example, its relations to the aspirations of more established research programs. This is one of the tasks of the next chapter.

[56] Harding (1986) offers an interpretation of sex difference research that sees it as directly expressing androcentrism. She sees such research as the outcome of the fragility of masculine identity. This strikes me as an empirical hypothesis about the causes of interest in such research. It might be true, but it needs some evidential support. And the high number of women in this field would then be quite puzzling. In any case I'm not sure what this hypothesis adds to our understanding of the logical structure of the field.

CHAPTER SEVEN

Explanatory Models in the Biology of Behavior

IN THIS chapter I will examine the assumptions that underlie studies in a variety of sex- or gender-related areas and show their role in the inferences either made or suggested by authors of the studies. The ubiquity of the assumptions I will discuss might seem to preclude their ideological or value-related character. I will argue in this and the following chapter that, to the contrary, their application in the study of human behavior reflects a deep ideological commitment.

In Chapter Five I suggested that the ideological or political value of the assumptions framing a scientific research program may not be apparent to practitioners within the program and that practitioners are not all motivated to pursue a research program because of the political or social implications that it may have. But that such a program thrives and has an audience is often very much a function of its ideological power. Researchers who do not examine the presuppositions of their work may, therefore, quite unintentionally be furthering some ideological program as well as a scientific one.

The sociopolitical implications of research on sex and gender difference have an even broader sweep than the sexist assumptions discussed in the previous chapter. I will examine these implications in the next chapter. To understand this ideological dimension of the research, however, requires looking closely at its logical structure, which I propose to do in this chapter. This examination will also illustrate a point made in Chapter Four in connection with the social character of scientific inquiry. Studies do not stand or fall simply on their own internal merits but also in light of their relationship to other studies (which may together constitute a research program). If they have no connection to other work or such a connection is not recognized, they will sink in the sea of academic periodical literature. By the same token, when their connection to ongoing work is recognized, they acquire meaning beyond the experiments and observations reported. The authors of many of the biobehavioral studies to be discussed here do not all explicitly or strongly endorse causal inferences. The meaning of any individual study, however, in the context of the hormonal research program, goes beyond whatever particular correlational findings are reported. The credibility that such work confers on a hormonal causal framework is a primary reason for its receiving attention and support.

My strategy in the present chapter will be to explore explicit statements by researchers in the hormone-behavior field as well as instances of what I call the linear-hormonal model in their work. Perhaps the most effective way to reveal the assumptive character of this model is to compare it with other possible biological approaches to the material. Feminist critics of the behavioral neuroendocrinological program, notably Ruth Bleier and Anne Fausto-Sterling, have argued that neurobiological research emphasizing the plasticity of the brain shows the hormonal program to be out of date or mistaken.[1] I propose to develop the contrast by exploring a particular theory in recent neurobiology, the selectionist model of higher brain function developed by Gerald Edelman, exploring its implications for the explanation of behavior. I will compare the reasons that can be given in support of these two approaches in the biology of behavior, arguing that internal and contextual considerations are inextricably linked to each other.

EXPLANATORY MODELS

Background assumptions are rarely made explicit in research reports but must be reconstructed from an analysis of the evidential reasoning in individual reports read in the context of a research program. In analyzing the neuroendocrinological and neurophysiological research discussed in this chapter, I have found it useful to single out an important class of background assumptions, which I call "explanatory models."

By an explanatory model or model of explanation I do not mean the very abstract models such as "deductive-nomological" or "simulacrum" models discussed by philosophers of science, which are attempts to describe the logical structure of any explanation. What I mean instead by this term is a normative and somewhat general description of the sorts of items that can figure in explanations of a given sort of phenomenon and of the relationships those items can be said to bear to the phenomena being explained. Such descriptions can be abstracted from particular studies by replacing specific descriptive terms with more general terms, for example, "enzyme" for the names of particular enzymes. They are normative with respect to classification in the following sense: a description M_1 is normative for a given research

---

[1] Bleier (1983); Fausto-Sterling (1985).

program RP_t if any individual study or research project must aspire to provide or contribute to the provision of an explanation of form M_t in order to be classified as belonging to RP_t. For example, in behaviorist psychology explanations must appeal to environmental stimuli as independent variables and treat externally (extensionally) described behavior as the variable dependent on these environmental stimuli. Explanations that describe behavior by means of agents' intentions or that treat states of consciousness as independent variables do not conform to this model and are ruled out by the behaviorist program.

Explanatory models, then, embody hypotheses or assumptions about the sorts of entities and relationships relevant to the explanation of a given sort of phenomenon. Such hypotheses may or may not be part of an explicit theory of the phenomena. If a given research program is successful, the hypotheses embodied in the explanatory models abstractable from it will generally become part of a theory of the relevant phenomena. In large part, however, explanatory models exist through their exemplars in scientific research design and reports rather than as explicit statements. In the conduct of research they serve as background assumptions against which data are ordered, in light of which data are given status as evidence for particular hypotheses and as a context within which individual studies gain significance.

THE LINEAR-HORMONAL MODEL

The studies attempting to establish a prenatal hormonal basis for behavioral sex differences exemplify what Ruth Doell and I have called a linear-analytic model of explanation.[2] What we mean by this is a model of or prescription for explanation that aspires to treat a dependent variable O_t as the deterministic result of one (or more) original independent variable(s), $I_t \ldots I_n$. The connection between O_t and $I_t \ldots I_n$ may be mediated by intervening events—metabolic transformations, aromatization, enzymatic reactions, et cetera. The process is linear if O_t is the straightforward outcome of a unidirectional and irreversible sequence of (biochemical) events. Linear-analytic explanations result from attempts to trace an outcome serially to some (set of) isolable and independent initiating events. The tracing can produce a sequence of single events, one following upon the other, but more typically it produces a branching structure.

The diagrams in Figure 1 illustrate the linearity of the model in various of its permutations. There is a fixed direction of change/causality,

[2] Doell and Longino (1988).

a fixed pattern of transformation and of interactions. Obviously it has proved extremely fruitful in biology. Various processes such as glycolysis and cell respiration can be represented as instances of one of these patterns. In hormones and human behavior studies it is employed in a variety of contexts—in the gender role behavior studies mentioned, in studies of the etiology of homosexuality, in studies of cognitive performance. I will call the linear model as it is expressed in these studies the linear-hormonal model. In research conducted under the aegis of the linear-hormonal model behavior is treated as the outcome of fixed and irreversible sequential processes initiated by pre- or perinatal gonadal hormone exposure, for example, exposure of the fetal organism at a critical period to testosterone, to one of its metabolites, such as 5α dihydrotesterone, or to an estrogen or estrogen metabolite such as estradiol. In interactive versions some later stage in the physiological sequence may work in combination with social or environmental factors to produce the behavioral effect.

Application of the model to human behavior, temperament, and cognition involves several stages. One stage is the invocation of animal experiments, which purport to demonstrate the dependence of certain forms of behavior—sexual behaviors like mounting behavior or lordosis, or social behaviors like rough and tumble play or fighting behavior—on fetal or perinatal exposure to a given hormone (mounting and fighting behavior are thus linked to testosterone exposure).

A second stage is the invocation of work showing the dependence of certain aspects of neuroanatomical and neurophysiological development on gonadal hormones. In the rat perinatal exposure to gonadal hormones is implicated in the development of a variety of subcortical morphological differences.[3] Even more significantly, in most mammals, including humans, the pituitary gland's secretion of luteinizing hormone (LH) is controlled by the hypothalamus. Whether the secretion pattern is cyclic or acyclic depends on the prenatal organization of the hypothalamus by gonadal hormones. Such phenomena are presented as supporting the more general hypothesis that mammalian brains are organized in sexually differentiated ways by perinatal gonadal hormones. This organization is thought to take the form either of neural circuit development or of setting neuronal threshold levels for response to stimuli. The brain, then, as described in Chapter Six, is thought to be programmed by fetal hormones so that the organism—animal or human—is disposed to respond to environmental changes,

---

[3] See Goy and McEwen (1980); McEwen (1981); and Pfaff (1980).

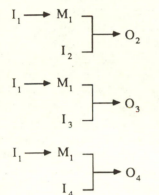

$$I_1 \longrightarrow M_1 \longrightarrow M_2 \cdots \longrightarrow M_N \longrightarrow O \qquad \text{SIMPLEST LINEAR}$$

$$\left.\begin{array}{c} I_1 \\ + \\ I_2 \end{array}\right\} \longrightarrow \left.\begin{array}{c} M_1 \\ + \\ I_3 \end{array}\right\} \longrightarrow O \qquad \text{LINEAR - INTERACTIVE}$$

$$\left.\begin{array}{c} I_1 \longrightarrow M_1 \\ I_2 \end{array}\right\} \longrightarrow O_2 \qquad \begin{array}{c}\text{LINEAR - INTERACTIVE} \\ \text{(RANGE OF DIFFERENT OUTCOMES)}\end{array}$$

$$\left.\begin{array}{c} I_1 \longrightarrow M_1 \\ I_3 \end{array}\right\} \longrightarrow O_3$$

$$\left.\begin{array}{c} I_1 \longrightarrow M_1 \\ I_4 \end{array}\right\} \longrightarrow O_4$$

LINEAR WITH FEEDBACK

$$I_1^1 \longrightarrow M_1^1 \longrightarrow \ldots M_n^1 \longrightarrow O_1^1 \nearrow^{O_2^1 \ldots} I_2^2 \longrightarrow M_1^2 \longrightarrow \ldots M_n^2 \longrightarrow O_1^2 \nearrow^{O_2^2 \ldots} I_1^1{}_{\text{etc}}$$

FIGURE 1

such as the introduction into a rat's cage of another rat, in certain set ways.

In general, according to the view being developed by this research, animals have male brains, programmed for characteristically male behavior, or female brains, programmed for characteristically female behavior. Not all behavior is sexually differentiated but that which is is dependent on this pre- or perinatal neural organization by gonadal hormones. In the linear-hormonal model, then, sexually differentiated behavior in mature animals is linked to prenatal gonadal hormone levels via the mechanism of brain organization. These animal studies establish the form of the general model to be used in the human case. Figure 2 demonstrates the general schema. In some cases the environment serves only as a stimulus to prompt the expression of the behavior in question, while in others researchers allow that past environmental conditions may affect the expression of the behavior in some way.

The work of Anke Ehrhardt discussed in Chapter Six provides good examples of the application of this linear-hormonal model to human behavior.[4] Although I shall again concentrate on Ehrhardt's work, other researchers, for example, June Reinisch of the Kinsey Institute, apply the model in similar ways.[5] Once the model is elaborated in a general way, it remains to show that it applies to humans. This involves finding appropriate correlations between prenatal hormonal exposures and later behavior. The clinical populations constituted by individuals experiencing the effects of abnormal fetal exposures can be seen as experiments of nature, making available data that we would not otherwise have. Most of Ehrhardt's published reports, whether under her name alone or with collaborators, whether dealing with subjects' play behavior, career aspirations, or social interactions, and whether dealing with androgenized females or "feminized" males, can be read as attempts to fit the data they provide into the model and then to generalize from the results in the clinical groups to human behavior at large. It is interesting to note that Ehrhardt is at pains to distinguish phenomena that can be understood as significantly influenced by prenatal steroid hormones, such as "gender role behavior," from phenomena that in her view cannot be, such as "gender identity." There are, of course, others to champion theses of hormonal determination in these cases.

In Ehrhardt's view gender role behavior, including play behavior (indoor or outdoor), degree of "parenting rehearsal," and career preferences can be understood as the product of a series of events, the initial one being exposure to a given hormone. This event can be the result of normal developmental processes (as when, in a male fetus, testosterone is released in the course of sexual differentiation of the fetal gonads),

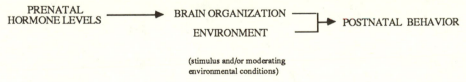

FIGURE 2

[4] Ehrhardt and Meyer-Bahlburg (1981). See also Ehrhardt and Meyer-Bahlburg (1979); Ehrhardt, Ince, and Meyer-Bahlburg (1981); Ehrhardt, Meyer-Bahlburg et al. (1985).

[5] Reinisch and Sanders (1984).

or of developmental abnormalities (as when female fetuses are exposed to high levels of androgen because of malfunctioning adrenals), or of hormones circulating in the uterine environment (as when progesterone is administered to the woman carrying the fetus). Other researchers attribute sex differences in aggressivity and parenting to prenatal hormone levels as well.[6] Ehrhardt has also postulated another intervening step that is closer to the behavior to be explained, is only sometimes invoked, and can be invoked without the organizational hypothesis. Its link to brain organization is not explained. This step is energy level or energy expenditure. The behaviors associated with high fetal levels of androgens tend to involve greater expenditure of energy than those associated with low levels. Ehrhardt, therefore, suggests that fetal androgens dispose individuals to high energy levels and that these result in the gendered (or masculine) behaviors.

One complication in applying the linear-hormonal model to humans is the degree of individual variability in behavior even within hormonal groups. Another is the very complex social environments in which humans develop as compared to most animal species, and certainly as compared to those reared for experimental purposes. Ehrhardt attributes some of the within-category variability observed both within her samples and in the general population to social and environmental factors. She has proposed an interactive model that moderates the influence of alleged prenatal brain organization of later behavior.[7] In her interactive model the organized brain will be disposed to display some subset of a set of behaviors. Which among the subset is expressed by any given individual depends upon environmental factors. Even though the environment is given some role, the hypothesis of the sexually organized brain is retained in this model. It should also be noted that no real suggestion about what such environmental factors might be or how they might operate is provided. The expository attention is reserved to aspects of the hormonal model. Ehrhardt's interactive model is an example, therefore, of the linear-interactive models of Figure 1, a variation of and not a competing alternative to the hormonal model.

The picture that emerges from the work of Ehrhardt and colleagues is displayed in the following diagrams of Figure 3 and Figure 4. Figure

[6] Ibid. For maternal behavior see Rossi (1975, 1978).

[7] Ehrhardt (1979, 1985). These discussions of an interactional model make clear how much depends on establishing that the gender-innappropriate behavior of the CAH and other hormonally abnormal youngsters is hormonally dependent. Without this claim there is no nontheoretical reason to argue for the involvement of biology generally in the expression of behavioral sex differences in humans.

3 presents the full model, while Figure 4 presents its energy expenditure variant. Clearly, the behavioral neuroendocrinological program is engaged in expanding an explanatory framework by extending the scope of fetal hormone effects to include not just anatomical and physiological sex differentiation but behavioral sex differentiation as well. Behavioral sex differences in this model are, like the cyclicity or acyclicity of LH secretion, under the control of sexually differentiated brains, themselves the result of prenatal gonadal hormones.

Explanations of other aspects of human behavior related to sex or to sex differences show a similar pattern. Homosexuality and alleged cognitive differences are both approached through a framework that sees postnatal (child and adult) behavior as an outcome, to some degree, of prenatal hormonal influences. I will focus on those studies in both areas that implicate brain organization as well as prenatal hormone levels.[8]

Homosexuality in men and women is extremely complex, and only a few researchers attempt to link all homosexuality to the prenatal hormonal environment. Others, like John Money, distinguish between "facultative" and "obligative" homosexuality (behavior chosen in certain circumstances—for example, single sex environments—versus behavior expressed exclusively in any circumstances) and even in the case of the latter are willing to consider the role of familial environment and other social factors in its development. Ehrhardt, to her credit, has in one context wondered about the wisdom of treating homosexuality as a single category of behavior to be approached within the hormonal framework: "To put people into one category simply on the basis of their sexual life-style and to ignore the many individual differences between such people may very well be a naive assumption of a unifying principle that may prove to be of little relevance."[9]

In spite of such caveats researchers in the behavioral endocrinology program continue to try to link some or all homosexuality to prenatal hormones. Ehrhardt herself, in a paper written with Meyer-Bahlburg, argues for the dependence of homosexuality in women whose mothers took hormones to prevent miscarriages on their exposure to the maternal hormone.[10] Some programs, notably that associated with G. Dörner, treat homosexuality as a form of cross-sexuality.[11] Homosexuals

[8] There are, of course, other more sociological approaches to these topics. I am not talking about all the research about these phenomena but about a particular and widespread scientific treatment of them.

[9] Ehrhardt (1979), p. 153.

[10] Ehrhardt, Meyer-Bahlburg et al. (1985).

[11] Dörner (1976).

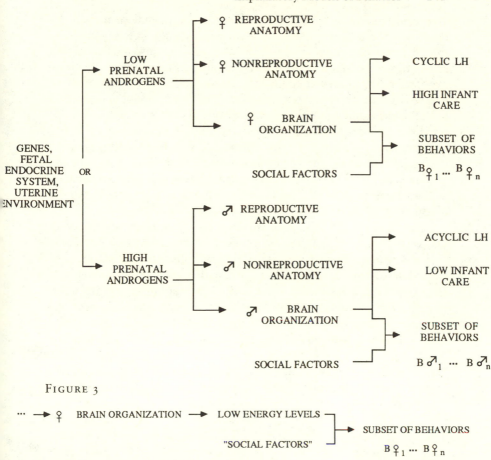

FIGURE 3

FIGURE 4

are treated as having the sexual/erotic orientation appropriate to the other sex. They are thus perceived as analogous to the androgenized women whose childhood behavior is appropriate to that of the other sex and so as appropriately modelled by animal subjects. Dörner originally posited separate male and female mating centers in mammalian brains. As in genital differentiation the level of androgen to which brains are exposed would determine which center would predominate:

high androgen level leading to development of a male center in the medial hypothalamic region of the brain, low androgen level leading to development of a female center in the ventromedial nuclear region of the brain, and intermediate levels leading to development to some extent of both. According to this picture, individuals with the genitalia of one sex and mating center of the other are (or tend to be) homosexual and individuals of either sex with both centers somewhat developed will be bisexual. In spite of its attraction to clinicians working in the area of homosexuality this approach has encountered numerous problems within the hormonal framework. Not the least of these is the fact that the majority of those individuals known to have been exposed to abnormal levels of sex innappropriate hormone are heterosexually oriented.

As a clue to finding the prenatal antecedents of homosexuality, researchers have been seeking physiological reactions in adult homosexuals that can be tied to fetal hormone exposure. In 1984 a team of United States researchers created a stir with a report published in *Science* indicating a distinctive neuroendocrine response to estrogen administration in homosexual men.[12] Under normal circumstances LH (luteinizing hormone) is released continuously (acyclically) in males and cyclically in women. The female cyclicity is keyed to the female menstrual cycle: serum levels of LH in women (but not in men) show an immediate drop and then a surge following the release of estrogen in the system. As mentioned above, this sex difference is thought to be brought about by early hormonal organization of the hypothalamus. In sampling twelve heterosexual women, seventeen heterosexual men, and fourteen homosexual men Brian Gladue and his coworkers found that the male homosexuals showed a LH secretion pattern that deviated towards that of the heterosexual females from that of the heterosexual males. The researchers are careful, at some points, not to overstate the implications of their study, saying in discussion of their results, "This invites the idea that there may be physiological developmental components in the sexual orientation of some homosexual men."[13] Nevertheless, at the beginning of their report they explicitly place their work in the context of pursuit of biological explanations of sexual orientation. Their work thus can be seen as filling in part of the sequence of steps in a linear unidirectional explanation of sexual orientation that could be applied to some homosexual men. For those individuals to whom it would apply sexual orientation would be understood to be an outcome of prenatal hormonal organizing effects on

[12] Gladue, Green, and Hellman (1984).
[13] Ibid., p. 1498.

the brain and nervous system. While this study, which is one of the most recent on possible biological determinants of homosexuality, focusses on men, there are a number of other studies attempting to demonstrate comparable conclusions about homosexuality in women.[14]

Similarly, the attempts to link cognitive differences, especially "spatial ability" and, via that, mathematical ability, to differential hormone exposure conform to this explanatory model. Writing in the *New England Journal of Medicine*, Hier and Crowley advanced one version: the superior performance of males on spatial ability tests is dependent on the testosterone they experience during puberty.[15] Norman Geschwind's theorizing provides another version: left-handedness, susceptibility to allergies, learning disabilities, and superior mathematical performance are all dependent on prenatal androgen exposure.[16] Neither of these programs has been taken very far: little is said about *how* androgen pre- or postnatally is supposed to exercise its causal influence, although Geschwind guessed that fetal testosterone might influence the degree of hemispheric functional asymmetry.

Proponents of the hormonal model often claim that there is no plausible alternative explanation for the data they present. While they are correct to the extent that there is not currently an alternative biological explanation, they are not correct in supposing that there *could* not be. The hormonal theorists treat the brain very much as a black box. They search for hormone receptors in various parts of the brain but have no explicit theory about how the brain actually works. Implicitly the brain is viewed as a fixed unit that translates sensory inputs into behavioral instructions but not as an organ with indigenous operations that may profoundly transform not only those sensory inputs but itself as well. Recent work in neurophysiology offers a quite different view of the brain than is presupposed by the hormonal model. I shall discuss one particular line of theorizing, use it to develop an alternative account of brain-behavior relationships, and then compare the hormonal and the enhanced neurophysiological accounts. The logical insufficiency of constitutively derived arguments will help to show the relevance of contextual values and interests to this debate.

THE SELECTIONIST THEORY OF HIGHER BRAIN FUNCTION

Perhaps the first thing to be said about this model is that it is not in use to explain any particular category of behavior. Rather it has been de-

[14] Compare Foss (1951); Perkins (1981); Saghir and Robins (1973).
[15] Hier and Crowley (1982).
[16] Geschwind and Galaburda (1985).

veloped in response to the problem of consciousness: What would a theory of brain physiology have to look like and incorporate in order to be an adequate biology of human minds? What is of central interest here is the material basis of a set of cognitive capacities: memory, learning, association, self-correction of memory, the mediation between action and experience, awareness and self-awareness.

Many neuroscientists are currently working on understanding higher brain function and distinctive human (or primate) capacities.[17] I shall focus here on the work of Vernon Mountcastle on brain structure and of Gerald Edelman on brain function, which coincide to provide an initial sketch of an answer to the above question. Two essays of theirs on the structure and function of the neocortex have been brought together in a volume *The Mindful Brain*, and Edelman has a later essay in a volume of the MIT Neurobiological Research Program series and has recently published a book, *Neural Darwinism*, that presents the theory.[18] Edelman calls his theory a group selectionist theory by analogy with the selectionist theory of immune system function. This theory is not the group selectionist view in evolutionary studies, although there are superficial resemblances. I will briefly summarize the central features of their analysis and then speculate on the implications of their work for the forms of explanation of human action and behavior. Comparison with the linear-hormonal model will make it possible to identify further distinctive features of each set of explanatory forms.

In the group model of higher brain function the minimal unit of function is a neuronal group, that is, a group of 50 to 10,000 nerve cells. Mountcastle's anatomical work identifies these groups with cortical columns, vertically arranged groups of cells throughout the layers of the cortex. Mountcastle estimates that in the human neocortex there might be 600 million "minicolumns" consisting of 110 cells each. Edelman postulates two types of interneuron connection: the cells constituting groups or columns are densely interconnected ("intrinsic connectivity"), and the groups are multiply connected with each other ("extrinsic connectivity").

Because of the multiplicity of extrinsic connectivities many groups will receive (recognize) a signal emitted by any given group, and each group can simultaneously receive signals from different groups or sources. Groups have a distinctive response to each kind of signal rec-

[17] Changeux (1985) provides a good review of recent human neurobiology. See also Schmitt, Worden, Adelman, and Dennis, eds. (1981).
[18] Edelman and Mountcastle (1978); Edelman (1981, 1987).

ognized and so different subsets of a group's total external connections will transmit a processed signal to other recognizing groups. Because groups differ in their intrinsic connectivities (are "nonisomorphic") and are embedded in similar but nonidentical patterns of external connectivities, the fact that many receive an identical signal from some transmitting group is called "degeneracy" rather than redundancy by Edelman. Unlike isomorphic units, they are capable of doing different things with a signal once it is received or "recognized," and they can respond to different signals as well. Group degeneracy is the solution to the problem of specifying a system that is capable both of a wide range of signal recognition and specificity of signal recognition.

The selectional aspect of the theory lies in Edelman's account of the development of intergroup connectivities. As the brain forms, he proposes, the groups are densely but weakly interconnected. Functional patterns of external ("extrinsic") connectivities will be selected from these preexistent connections. Such functional patterns are called repertoires. Figure 5 is a highly schematic representation of the stages of connectivity of one cell group with others. Edelman postulates two forms of repertoire: primary and secondary, reflecting time of development rather than degree of importance or centrality. In Figure 5A the initial genetically determined development of the brain results in a system of cell groups characterized by extensive degeneracy and consisting of many more cell groups than are ultimately used in making connections. The primary repertoire is formed by a selective process based on function, in which certain connections stabilize and others vanish. Thus, at this stage of development (Figure 5[B]) many synaptic connections and many neurons are eliminated. Secondary repertoire, depicted in Figure 5C, is formed from primary repertoire by a second selective process occurring in the course of experience. This process consists in the amplification (represented by thicker lines in the diagram) or inhibition of responses to a given signal pattern by a cell group. This alteration in probability of response occurs as the result of synaptic alteration that changes intrinsic and/or extrinsic connectivity.

Secondary repertoire is in constant formation and reformation in response to experience. The extensive degeneracy that persists in secondary repertoire means that different combinations of cell groups will respond to the same signal type at different times in the same individual and that different cell groups and combinations of cell groups will carry out the same recognition function in different individual brains. This feature of the selective theory seems consistent with observed diversity in characteristic mental function among individuals. In addition, Edelman postulates that after the formation of secondary reper-

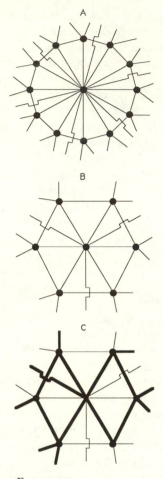

FIGURE 5

toire there is still lots of primary repertoire left for additional development of secondary repertoire. This means, among other things, much flexibility and opportunity for additional learning. According to this view, memory and other brain functions are distributed rather than localized or assigned to particular brain regions.

Consciousness or awareness is a function of what Edelman calls "phasic reentry." Each neuronal group is a processing unit that receives and transmits signals. In describing the functioning of these groups, Edelman postulates two levels of signal recognition: one type, labelled "R," recognizes an incoming signal from noncortical areas such as the thalamic nuclei; the second type, labelled "R of R," recognizes a signal from a recognizer group in the cortex. The main idea is that if signalling is discontinuous, an original signal can be processed by a recognizer group and reentered along with subsequent incoming signals. This enables linkage among successive phasic inputs, which in turn facilitates continuity of awareness and the integration of multiple sensory modalities (Figure 6). Thus, my awareness of the cup before me as a continually existing object is made possible by the matching of earlier with subsequent signals from the primary receiving areas of the cortex stimulated by optic signals as well as by the reentry of signals generated by the activation of association networks (that is, signals generated within the brain rather than outside it). This is represented as step 4 between cycles 1 and 2 in Figure 6. Phasic reentry also makes possible the coordination of multiple modalities of signal, thus integrating, for instance, auditory and visual neural representations of the same object. This somewhat oversimplifies the actual processes but makes clear how, on this view, (1) no higher order processes are required to establish the connection between successive incoming signals, and (2) consciousness is less a property of the physical brain than a process of the brain.

Unlike the theories associated with the linear-hormonal model, this theory of brain function is not presented as an explanation of specific behaviors and it is not developed in order to explain specific behaviors or types of behavior. Rather, it is a theory addressed to the question, What sort of structure and functioning must characterize a brain capable of long- and short-term memory, learning and correction of memory, observational as distinct from conditioned learning, self-awareness, creativity, and mediation of action and experience? These

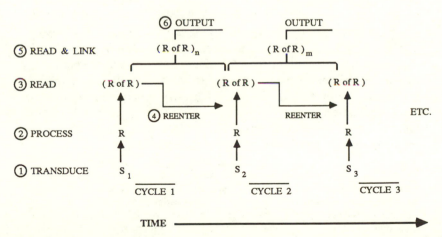

FIGURE 6
SOURCE: Edelman and Mountcastle 1978.

different theoretical aims make direct comparisons between the explanations generated by the linear model and the group selective theory difficult. It is possible, however, to think (very speculatively) about the *form* that explanations of behavior consistent with the selective theory might take.

The theory, first of all, would be relevant to nonreflex behavior, that is, to intentional or voluntary behavior, which involves the representation of self, action, world, and the consequences of action to oneself. Instances of such behavior would be explained by appeal to a complex set of neuronal interactions in the cortex. These neuronal interactions would be identified with states of consciousness, and partly because they include a historical component, each set postulated as underlying a given instance of behavior would be unique. The theory postulates the continual alteration of neural networks in response to experience and action and a role for "self-inputs," (via the phasic reentry mechanisms), which include not just past associations (memory) of externally generated signals but representations of self as well in the generation of action. Moreover, the secondary repertoires formed in the context of experience and action are those engaged in the processing of non-novel signals. Experience (including social experience) and self-image, therefore, play a primary role in the *biological* explanation of the behavior/action of species with a highly developed cortex. These features of the selective theory distinguish it quite sharply from any theory like the linear-hormonal theory.[19] While such a theory attributes a certain set of behaviors to a prewired brain, according to the selective theory, there is no constant association between a type of behavior and a type of brain state because the brain is continually changing. Figure 7 is a schematic representation of the complex interconnectivity that enables self-modification of the brain and that underlies intentional behavior.

The role of prenatal brain organization by gonadal hormones in the explanation of particular behaviors in humans is minimized because of the role of the neocortex, as opposed to the hypothalamus, in mediating human action and experience. Such early gonadal hormone exposure might affect certain very general properties of cortical functioning, such as speed of processing, but it is not likely to be involved in the formation of specific intergroup connectivities, understood as the

---

[19] Theories similar to the linear-hormonal model are proposed in human sociobiology, which treats all social behavior as determined at some level of description genetically. See, for example, Wilson (1978). The precise mechanisms of brain programming proposed by the sociobiological theorists might be different than that outlined in the linear-hormonal model, but the idea that some kind of brain programming occurs would be common to both.

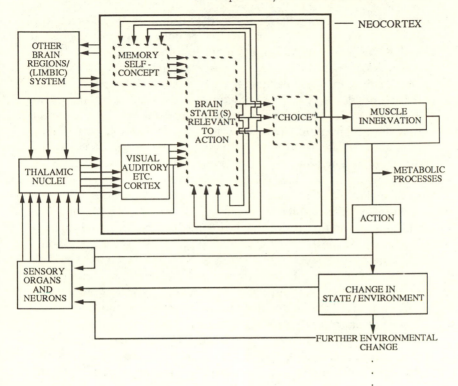

FIGURE 7

NOTES: --- Indicates distributed functions in neocortex.
___ Indicates discrete areas or localizable states.

selection through reinforcement or amplification of certain neural network pathways. The effects of prenatal hormone exposure on other
areas of the brain such as the hypothalamus would presumably be experienced in the cortex as incoming signals on a par with other incoming signals, to be processed in ways established in the secondary repertoire. In the cortex, therefore, these effects are not causes but inputs,
or information to be acted on. Because of the mutability of secondary
repertoire, their processing by the neocortex and hence their "meaning" for the organism, can change over time. These remarks hold for
the behaviors encompassed in the linear model as well as for the activities cited by Edelman—the composition of symphonies or the construction and solution of elaborate mathematical problems.

The linear-hormonal model seems to account for the otherwise extraordinary association between gonadal hormone exposure and later behavioral patterns not just in the human subjects of the studies cited but in the general population. It's simply not the case that all men and women conform to behavioral patterns correlated with their genetic reproductive capacity, but there is enough of a rough dimorphism to support the idea that there is something to explain. According to the selective theory of brain development, the correlation could receive the following explanation. Gonadal hormones determine the appearance of the newborn, which prompts different responses from parents and other adults depending on the newborn's perceived sex. These responses, from its first moments of life through years of growth, are ingredients in the complex interactions that constitute complete brain development. This explanation can appeal both to aspects of social conditioning and to attempts by the infant/child to conform to socially communicated ideals of what certain types of person are or should be.[20] What we, in our culture, identify as femininity is simply that collection of temperament, disposition, and behaviors characteristic of someone who has been responded to in ways deemed, in our culture, appropriate for someone with female genitalia and who has herself/himself continued to act in ways that prompt such responses.

As for the CAH children who provide the strongest evidential base for the hormonal model, one can say that their behavior is a specific response to their situation as they perceive it. They are not, after all, unconscious entities responding blindly to their physiology or external environment but persons who (1) have a medical history productive of greater self-consciousness and self-knowledge than is usual for young people, (2) are quite aware of their uniqueness, and (3) are very likely uncertain of their "femininity" and possibly of their femaleness as well. This combination of circumstances may account for their choosing as children behavior less restrictive in its implications for adult life than traditional girllike behavior is. Finally, such direct effects of testosterone as do exist could be on muscle development, with a consequent need for exercise. The hormones in this case would not be seen as organizing behavioral syndromes but as effecting a physiological state to which the individual responds as best she can.

The selectionist model of brain function thus permits the development of a biological explanation of behavior, including sex-differentiated behavior, quite different from that generated in the neuroendocrinological tradition. Social and intentional factors in behavior are not peripheral but central to this new biological approach which we might

---

[20] For a presentation of this kind of theory see Bem (1985).

call social cognitive or intentional. Before addressing the evidential status of these two approaches, I wish to develop some further contrasts between them as regards the theoretical importance of human gendered behavior, the nature of human agency, and modes of causal interaction.

ADDITIONAL CONTRASTS BETWEEN THE TWO MODELS

In the first place, human gendered behavior loses its significance to biology in the selective model. In the exemplifications of the linear model considered above alleged gender difference is a clue, as well as a major explanandum, that leads researchers to explanatory theories involving sexual differentiation of the brain. In the concluding paper of a recent volume of review essays in reproductive neurobiology David Goldfoot and Deborah Neff defend behavioral endocrinology as follows:

> Many hormone-behavior experiments are better construed as *behavioral bioessays* of endocrine function rather than as studies in which the primary purpose is to explore behavioral sex differences. Often the strategy has been to find a dimorphic response that can be shown to be modifiable by endocrine manipulations, so that additional target organs influenced by the endocrine system (e.g. the brain) can be studied.[21]

If the point of the behavioral endocrinology research is to understand hormone effects (and not behavior), then it is easy to see how sex-differentiated behavior would be seen as a possible important clue to the full power of hormones, since we already know that female and male fetuses are ordinarily exposed to different levels of gonadal hormone. Furthermore, the Goldfoot and Neff quotation makes clear that the object of inquiry in this research is not sex differences but hormone effects. The contribution to understanding behavioral sex difference is incidental to the main point of the biological research, although that contribution is what draws the attention of outsiders. Sex differences are crucial to the research because they support the claim that the causal efficacy of hormones extends to behavior, not because any theory in this field must explain behavioral sex differences.

In the theory of higher brain function, on the other hand, the object of inquiry is the biological substratum of complex cognitive function-

---

[21] Goldfoot and Neff (1985), p. 772.

ing. Thus, the kinds of behavioral difference that would be of interest would be differences in amount of cognitive processing involved in different kinds of behaviors, or differences in degree of intentionality or other variations in subjective states involved in action. Since this would differ from individual to individual and even over time for a specific individual, only a very general and abstract form of conceptualization would be possible; that is, only under a different level of description would behavior be brought under general causal laws, if at all. In any case, sex differences in the behaviors cited earlier, which, it can be argued, involve a good measure of intentionality, could disappear as significant biological categories. One might expect instead distinctions and categories more closely tied to distinctions relevant to the processes postulated by the selective theory or any comparable neurophysiological theory. This is not, of course, to deny that a researcher determined to maintain the importance of behavioral sexual dichotomy could not attempt to develop these views in the context of the selective theory. The point is that, whereas such difference is central to the linear-hormonal program as it is currently structured, it is inessential in the group selective program.[22]

A second interesting contrast concerns agency and the understanding of action. In the linear-hormonal model behavior is seen as a product of forces out of the control of the individual, that is, prenatal gonadal hormone exposure and environmental influence. In the group selective theory agency is restored to individuals. Action is the activation of muscles by the motor cortex. Activation occurs via the pathways of the neuromuscular system in consequence of decisions reached or intentions formed via the neural processing involving the cortex, neocortex, and associated areas. Mental action presumably is the activation of neural circuits in consequence of decisions reached/intentions formed via cortical neural processing. Clearly there is as yet only the promise of a theory. Nevertheless, the reentrant signalling that makes possible self-consciousness makes possible agency, or, to hyphenate wildly, self-conscious, self-directed acting-in-the-world. Moreover, as Edelman and Mountcastle both emphasize, this is agency of a biological nature—no ghost in the machine, homunculus/a, or even central higher level control center is required to explain conscious action. If the general approach of the selective theory is successful, then presumably the developed account of agency will offer a picture con-

---

[22] This dislocation of sex difference would facilitate a more subtle understanding of the complexity of sexual diversity. This point will be developed in Chapter Eight.

gruent with our experience of the limitations as well as the efficacy of consciousness, intention, and deliberation.

A related difference lies in the origins and immediate contexts of these two research programs. Even though the behavioral endocrinology work is not entirely dedicated to finding solutions to particular practical problems, it does originate in the clinic. This is especially true of the work on humans. One of the main points of the work is to gain sufficient understanding to permit chemical intervention in or management of various psychosexual traits. This issue will be pursued at greater length in the following chapter. The selective theory, however, was developed not in a clinical context but in a more purely academic context. Edelman thought that the selective model he had used to solve the problem of antibody specificity could be applied to what he took to be somewhat similar problems in understanding diversity and specificity in neural function. While the theory could form the basis of intervention efforts to change individuals, it points in a quite different direction and would enable quite different sorts of intervention (that is, social rather than chemical) than does the linear-hormonal model.

The final major difference I will highlight is the strongly interactive character of the selective theory in contrast to the at best weakly interactive character of the linear model. According to Ehrhardt's version of interactionism, usually unnamed "social factors" combine with a fixed biology in the production of one or several among a range of behaviors. I call this a weak interaction because the biological and social factors are unchanged by their contact. They are independent coactors, as jointly causative factors, in behavior.[23] In the selective theory "social factors" as experienced by the individual are implicated in the development of the biological structures themselves. The self-ordering of the cortex occurs as synaptic connections in the secondary repertoire are committed (stabilized) in consequence of the individual's sensorimotor experience. I call this a strong form of interaction because neither the biological structures nor the environmental factors can be considered as independent unmodified elements cooperating to produce a joint effect but instead influence each other, thereby altering the effect either could be said to have on behavior. This picture avoids two kinds of reductionist traps: gene/internal programming, which is clearly inadequate to completely account for the complexity and plasticity attributed to the brain, and environment/external programming,

[23] This form of interactionism and the limitations it places on the prospects of assigning causal efficacy to either factor considered independently is discussed in relation to research on I.Q. in Lewontin (1974).

the instructionist view that understands the *formation* of connectivity, rather than its *selection*, to be consequent upon experience, and that would also have the result of reducing flexibility to the organism.

These two approaches to thinking about the role of the brain in behavior thus have quite different implications and reverberations. From an evidential point of view, however, they resemble each other in that internal, evidential considerations alone are not sufficient to support one rather than the other. I will develop this point in the next section which examines the data relevant to particular hypotheses associated with both models as well as the assumptions that establish that relevance.

Evidence

Evidence for the Hormonal Theory

Two types of empirical data are relevant to claims about the causal role of prenatal levels of gonadal hormone in child and adult behavior. One type is neuroanatomical and neurophysiological, and was discussed above. The presence of hormone receptors in the hypothalamus is evidence that gonadal hormones have some function in the nervous system. The presumed role of gonadal hormones in organizing the hypothalamus for cyclic or acyclic luteinizing hormone secretion supports the idea that some brain functions are an outcome of prenatal hormonal organization. Most of the data, however, are correlations between behavior and prenatal hormone exposures. In the behavioral endocrinology work reviewed above, researchers are applying the general linear-hormonal model in the construction of specific hypotheses: particular adolescent or adult behavior patterns are traceable to prenatal levels of some particular hormone, which is presumed to have had a central organizational role in their development (or the absence of which is linked to some developmental deficit). It is instructive to notice the nature of the correlational data and their relationship to the explanatory hypotheses advanced by researchers.

In the gender role cases and cognition cases the data regarding behavior are statistical averages from small populations: thirty-two androgenized women here, sixteen hypogonadal men there, et cetera. These averages are then compared to some average drawn from a control population of "normal" individuals. Homosexuality, in the literature I've looked at, is not statistically measured (though surely, even if of questionable relevance, there must be quantifiable phenomena here: for example, percentages of males and females among those persons a subject reports as finding sexually attractive). An average departing from that of the control population is then connected with another average that so departs—namely exposure or nonexposure to a given hormone, usually an androgen, but as in some cases of "feminized males" sometimes an estrogen. It is usually not possible to state precisely the amount of hormone to which individuals were exposed, which constitutes another unremarked difference from experimental manipulation of laboratory animals. Thus the basic data are described in collections of statements of the following form: in a sample of n women/girls exposed to higher than normal levels of androgen in utero k percent displayed an interest in athletics as compared with l percent in a control population of m women/girls; or: in a sample of n hypogonadal men the average score obtained on XYZ tests of spatial ability was K as compared with an average score of L for a group of m normal males. Various statistical tests are employed to determine whether the differences between K and L or n and m are significant.

Absent any background theory or assumptions, there is not much one could project from this data. At best one could by generalization develop hypotheses such as "In the general population, *ceteris paribus*, young women exposed to higher than ordinary levels of androgens will on average exhibit a greater degree of interest in athletics than young women who have not been exposed" or "In the general female population a correlation between interest in athletics and prenatal exposure to levels of androgens higher than j may be expected." More boldly, one might abstract from the sex of the subjects and hypothesize that in the general population, *ceteris paribus*, a correlation between (significant) androgen exposure in utero and high interest in athletics may be expected. In each of these cases one would be inferring that the distributions of a set of properties in a sample was representative of their distributions in larger populations. The test for any of these hypotheses would involve more sampling.

To what kinds of *causal* hypotheses are the data relevant? One might hypothesize that in a given sample or in a general population a given level of hormone exposure at a particular stage plays a causal role in the relative frequency of expression of a given characteristic, for example, .5 in exposed versus .35 in unexposed. The kind of evidence that might support such a hypothesis would be some statistically significant correlation between the occurrence of the alleged cause and that of the alleged effect. In the case of a correlation of this sort the characteristic in question could easily be epiphenomenal, that is, a by-product of some intermediate effect of the hormone exposure in conjunction with other factors. Absent these additional factors, the difference in frequency of expression of the characteristic could conceivably drop to 0. Data that are averages of sample results and that are measurements of states or characteristics for which there may be considerable overlap among contrasted groups do not on their own support causal inferences about individuals or populations. Some additional assumptions or information are needed to make the data relevant to claims that in an individual hormone exposure is causally responsible for the expression of a particular characteristic. This is the role of the linear model. For a researcher working with that general picture of the pattern of causation of certain kinds of behavior, the data do become relevant to claims about the causal role of hormones. The role of animal modelling and of the associated theories of brain organization is to provide some support for the linear model. What needs to be established, however, is that the behaviors studied in humans—athletic play versus reading, choice of sexual partner, cognitive performance—really are analogous to those studied in animals—aggressiveness versus passivity, rough and tumble play, mounting versus lordosis, and maze performance. Among the researchers whose work I've discussed so far in this chapter, with the noted exceptions, there seems little doubt about the appropriate classification of their objects of study and (in spite of obligatory warnings against hasty generalizations across species) surprisingly little doubt about the applicability of rodent brain organization to human brains.

Turning to support for the model itself, the various human studies conducted under the umbrella of the model obviously cannot be considered to offer direct evidence for it. They do constitute indirect evidence in the sense that the model provides an explanatory framework within which the studies can be interpreted. Several other arguments that appeal to constitutively prescribed features can also be offered in support of the model. For instance, if indeed the animal studies are appropriately understood in terms of the model, then its application to the human case exhibits the virtues of theoretical unification and simplicity in at least two regards: (1) mammalian species are treated together under one explanatory paradigm, and (2) certain social behaviors can be treated as on a continuum with other effects (like reproductive anatomy and physiology) of prenatal gonadal hormone exposure.[24] A crucial part of the methodology in human endocrinology and in physiological psychology (indeed in human physiology generally) involves the reliance on animal models. The kind of inference being examined here is simply standard procedure in this field.

[24] An argument to this effect is presented by Pfaff (1980), pp. 245–246.

Whatever weight such considerations might have with practitioners in the field, there are criticisms, also driven by internal or epistemic values, that can be made of this research. The animal model, as noted in the preceding chapter, presupposes a sufficient analogy between the human and animal phenomena. In the case of much anatomy and physiology the analogy holds—mammalian reproductive systems are sufficiently homologous across species that one species supports inferences about many. In the case of behavior, however, there are several significant disanalogies. The human child and adult behaviors all exhibit a degree of intentionality not characteristic of the more stereotyped animal behaviors. Specific forms of play, as well as human sexual orientation, involve a degree of self-consciousness not required in the animal situation.[25] One organ that does differ across species is the brain—the human brain is both proportionately larger and more complex than the brain of any other mammal, including other primates and cetaceans. Intentional behaviors involve more and other areas of the brain than are involved in the hormonally influenced behaviors of the nonhuman animals. Finally, the experimental contexts of the animal and human studies are different.

For example, the experiments with rodents all involve single factor analysis. The conditions of the animals' lives can be highly regulated, making possible experiments that attempt to vary only one factor at a time and make no attempt to understand interactions between factors. The human situation, including that of the hormonally exceptional children, is always interactive. Humans are in a social context from the first moments of their lives. We have no way of isolating the variables operating in real life, in which any feature is a function of a multiplicity of interacting factors. Thus, it can be argued that neither the behavior nor the anatomy nor the larger contexts in which behaviors are identified are sufficiently analogous for the application of the animal model. In addition there are several weaknesses in the model as it is applied to nonhuman species. First, different mammalian species respond differently both behaviorally and morphologically to perinatal hormone manipulation. Such behavioral sex differences as exist are always observed within species and cannot be presumed general across species.[26] Second, researchers have shown, in particular, that certain organizational effects (on the system governing gonadotropin secretion) in rodents do not occur in rhesus monkeys, which considerably dampens the prospects for extending the hypothesis to humans.[27]

[25] This is argued in Doell and Longino (1988).
[26] Goy and McEwen (1980), pp. 5–11.
[27] Karsch, Dierschke, and Knobil (1972).

Just as the arguments for the model are not decisive, however, neither are these arguments against it decisive. The claim about the intentionality of behavior, for instance, is both contestable and based at least as much on philosophical as on strictly empirical considerations.

Evidence for the Selectionist Theory

Here, too, the relevant data are of two kinds. There is a body of neuroanatomical and neurophysiological data supporting the selectionist model of brain function. There is also a body of behavioral data relevant to the proposed theory of the role of the brain in behavior.

The neurobiological evidence includes observation or experimentation that indicates the brain actually is organized in groups of neurons and that these groups interact in the ways described. The Nobel prize winning work by David Hubel and Thorsten Weisel on the structure of the visual cortex of the cat is cited as providing significant experimental support for the idea of neuronal groups and more specifically for the idea that neuronal groups are organized along a vertical axis as columns.[28] For many aspects of the functional theory, such as the degeneracy of neuronal repertoires containing isofunctional but nonisomorphic groups and the alteration of synapses during formation of the secondary repertoires, it is not yet experimentally possible to get supporting data. The primary problem here is that to determine, for instance, the isofunctionality of groups it would be necessary to measure and correlate the simultaneous activity of hundreds to thousands of neurons. There is a fair amount of evidence, such as the elimination of massive numbers of nerve cells during the postnatal period of brain development, for the operation of selection in the development of cortical groups. Edelman claims as additional support the consistency of his theory with current work in cognitive psychology, for example, aspects of the work of David Marr on the modularity of vision.[29] One might add the work on parallel distributed processing to this category.[30] Edelman himself has turned to research on cellular adhesion molecules, which he expects to elucidate processes of development of neural networks.[31]

Just as the work proposing physiological causes of sex-differentiated behavior relies on a variety of correlational data, so defenders of the alternative approach outlined as an application of the selectionist theory can appeal to a bevy of studies demonstrating correlations between

[28] Hubel and Wiesel (1977).
[29] Marr (1982).
[30] Rumelhart, McClelland, and the PDP Research Group (1986).
[31] Edelman (1983, 1985). See also Edelman (1987).

sex-differentiated behavior and systematic social and environmental differences.

Some of the most famous of these are anthropologist Margaret Mead's cross-cultural studies from which she concluded that the typical behavior of males and females differed from culture to culture.[32] While Mead's work has recently come under fire,[33] the work of other cultural anthropologists bears out her general claim of cultural variation in the expression of sex-differentiated behaviors.[34] Some cultures seem to show no differences, in others the differences are the reverse of those common in Euro-American societies, while others show patterns similar to the European and American pattern.

Social and developmental psychology can be mined for intracultural data that are consistent with the cross-cultural studies. In particular, parents and other adults respond differently to children depending on these children's sex. This difference in treatment begins at birth and seems quite independent of parents' intentions.[35] A study by Jacquelynne Eccles and Janis Jacobs shows strong correlations between parents' attitudes about the value and difficulty of mathematics for their children and the children's performance in standard mathematics tests like the SAT.[36] And a variety of studies correlate homosexuality with certain social experiences and self-perceptions.[37]

As for the explanation given above of the results from the particular populations studied in behavioral endocrinological studies, the Dutch researcher Froukje Slijper carried out a very pointed study.[38] She administered a test of gender-related values to CAH children and to a group of young patients with diabetes mellitus and found that the two groups scored no differently. She argued that the significant common factor was the experience of chronic illness with consequent hospitalization and frequent medical visits. She interprets the behavior of both groups as a deliberate challenge to the intrusion of medical authority into their lives as well as the expression of insecurity about their own well-being. It is, in her view, a response to their awareness and interpretation of their experience. And finally, looking at the results of studies of sex role and sex-related behavior in the CAH and other popula-

[32] Mead (1935).

[33] Freeman (1983).

[34] Whiting and Pope-Edwards (1973); Minuchin (1965); Ember (1973). See also the essays in Rosaldo and Lamphere, eds. (1974).

[35] Seavey, Katz, and Zalk (1975).

[36] Eccles and Jacobs (1986).

[37] Van Wyck and Geist (1984).

[38] Slijper (1984).

tions, one might argue that the intentional or social cognitive model is more consistent with the high degree of variation. As I suggested in Chapter Six, the assumptions of the linear model may lead us to over-emphasize the clustering of the data. A different approach to explaining behavior makes other aspects of the same data stand out and would facilitate alternative classifications and descriptions, for example, along such dimensions as degree of intentionality or of contrariness.

Just as is the case for the studies in behavioral endocrinology, only in the context of an explanatory model can these studies be used to support any particular account of how the behaviors in question come to be distributed as they are or how any individual comes to express certain behaviors rather than others. Correlations of environmental and cultural factors, or of subjects' concepts of sex role, with behavior do not on their own support hypotheses about the causal role of such factors. An explanatory model that treats human behavior as the outcome of neurophysiological states which themselves are a function of individuals' social experiences and constitute individuals' intentional states legitimates treating those correlations as support for causal claims.

Such a model, of course, assumes the self-initiating, intentional character of human behavior, which biologically depends on higher brain function rather than on lower brain function exclusively. Again only indirect evidence can be offered in support of this assumption. One argument cites the much greater relative size of the human brain, particularly the neocortex, as compared to the brains of the species used to develop the linear-hormonal model. This fact can be used to support the claim that human behavior is under the control of those higher brain functions involved in cognitive processing. Another is the consistency of this assumption with our experience of ourselves and of others. Not only can we do much more than even the primate species studied, our doing it requires simultaneous self-consciousness, world consciousness, and projection of ourselves into the world. This aspect of subjective experience might plausibly be dismissed as mystical or wishful thinking if there were no theoretical alternative to the linear-hormonal model,[39] but the selectionist theory demonstrates that this is not the case.

Finally, the social-cognitive approach is subject to a variety of criticisms driven by internal epistemic considerations. First of all, it assumes the intentional character of human behavior, including sex role

[39] This position of Skinner's (1971) is echoed in the pronouncements of hormonal researchers; compare Witelson (1985).

or gender role behavior. It is not at all clear what could count as empirical evidence that behavior in general is or is not intentional. A critic might dismiss the introduction of intentionality as the introduction of suspect or forbidden metaphysics. Second, partly as a consequence of the introduction of intentionality, the social cognitive approach sacrifices the theoretical simplicity of the linear-hormonal model. The animal model cannot be extended, for different kinds of explanations are appropriate for sex-related behaviors in the two populations. And sex role or gender role behavior is removed from the theoretical umbrella of the hormonal model that does explain other aspects of differentiation. Thirdly, as is also the case with the hormonal model, while there is evidence to support the selectionist claims made about neural organization and function, the precise mechanisms at the molecular and cellular level have yet to be worked out.

THIS discussion of the evidential status of the linear-hormonal model and the social-cognitive model shows that there is no more reason to assimilate so-called human gender role behavior to the hormonal model than there is to assimilate it to the self-conscious and intentional activities of scientific theorizing, musical composition, or classical dance performance. Both rest on explanatory models that involve metaphysical assumptions about causality and human action. Neither theoretical perspective can muster constitutively based arguments sufficient to exclude the other—thus both can continue to generate studies that are used to support microhypotheses about the etiology of particular forms of behavior that are consistent with one or the other broader model. In the following chapter I will demonstrate some of the contextual interests and values that motivate and are served by these opposing models.

CHAPTER EIGHT

Science in Society

ONE OF the implications of the previous chapter is that the dependence of particular studies on the linear-hormonal model does not invalidate them as scientific research. While their conclusions are certainly contestable, they are not thereby the products of bad methodology. No set of data is evidence for a hypothesis independently of some background assumption(s) in light of which the data acquire evidential relevance. Thus, reliance on an explanatory model or set of background assumptions does not demonstrate bad methodology. Moreover, the label "bad science" can only be applied in light of criteria that are operative within a particular field of research. The generation and presentation of sloppy data, but not (or not necessarily) the interpretation of data, deserves the label of bad science.

Scientific research, however, is not only evaluated as "pure" inquiry answerable to internal standards but as a basis for social action and policy, and increasingly as a ground for values and ideals. Here a much more complex approach to assessment is required. This chapter has two main goals. I wish first to review the real or purported implications of biological research for social action and sociocultural values. This discussion of the material from the last two chapters will strengthen the claim that it is the linear-hormonal model that underlies the behavioral neuroendocrinological studies discussed in Chapter Six and Chapter Seven and not some other set of assumptions. My second main task is to show how the contrasting approaches to scientific knowledge support different attitudes towards these implications.

THE VALUE OF FACTS

The relationship between science and values in Euro-American culture has been transformed since the Renaissance. What Newtonianism accomplished on behalf of physics, Darwinism has promised to do on behalf of biology. As we all learn in elementary intellectual history a considerable part of the resistance to the Copernican account of heavenly motion is value-centered: the role of humans in God's plan, the uniqueness of the human habitat, and the place of God in the universe. John Donne's Anniversary poems are eloquent expressions of the disturbance caused by the ideas of the new physics and of the diminishing power of value in relation to brute fact. Once the universe was conceptualized as a machine, it was no longer suffused with value and no longer a suitable location for God. After the publication of Newton's *Principia Mathematica* the transfer of power as far as the physical sciences were concerned was complete. From then on theological claims had to pass the test of consistency with Newtonian physics: rational proofs of God's existence gave way to empirical arguments like the argument from design.

The introduction of evolutionary theory paralleled the earlier conflict. Even if ideas of God had had to be accommodated to the rigors of mechanical science, in the early nineteenth century humans and human life were still centers of value distinct from the world around them. God, too, could be thought of as having created the mechanical universe in the geological and biological form in which it was then known. New theories of geological change began the challenge that culminated with the publication of Darwin's *Origin of Species*. Outrage at yet another displacement of humans, this time into a species of primate, thundered from pulpits and reverberated through the Fleet Street press. Almost as immediately, however, social theorists embraced Darwinism and used it to legitimate social inequality.

We are still living in a period of transformation. In the United States the Scopes trial only temporarily vindicated science against religion. The last ten to fifteen years have witnessed a small but vocal and well-financed coalition of religious antievolutionists putting the fear of God into textbook publishers and school boards and bringing evolutionary theory back into courtrooms. The debate about evolution is, however, political rather than scientific, and most pundits (rightly or wrongly) perceive antievolutionists as part of the radical right-wing fringe rather than part of the mainstream.

The political impact of fundamentalism contrasts sharply with the centrality of evolutionary theory in areas of the biological sciences seemingly far removed from the study of origins. It contrasts also with the reverence accorded biological theorizing in the secular atmosphere of mainstream U.S. culture. The infiltration of sociobiology into sociology and political science, for instance, continues a trend begun in the nineteenth century, even though in some cases the naive crudities of Spencerism and social Darwinism are avoided. Just as Newtonian mechanics provided models and metaphors for eighteenth-century social, political, and psychological thought, so biology is the source of models and metaphors for twentieth-century thought. Secular culture in the United States does not provide alternative absolute values to substitute for religious ones. Rather, the sciences, buttressed by their contemporary spectacular practical successes, have come to fill the void left by religion. Contemporary journalists cite controversial scientific research as fact, reinforcing cultural stereotypes and prejudices. They treat Nobel Prize winning scientists as experts on topics far beyond their special competence, thereby creating a new priesthood.[1]

As should be clear from the argument of the preceding chapters, this as easily gives rise to circularity as to the grounding of value in the bedrock of fact. Here I will explore some of the ways in which ideas articulated or assumed in a scientific context are taken up in the culture or prepared for absorption by the culture. Both specific hypotheses and the frameworks within which they are evaluated are taken to have implications for cultural values and interests. Some of these implications are clear to and made explicit by the researchers; others are not. In a final section I shall develop the implications of different accounts of scientific knowledge for the understanding of this phenomenon.

SCIENCE IN SOCIETY

Scientific claims and ideas have an influence on public (governmental) policies, on the social values informing policy, on informal policies, and on cultural ideals. By informal policies I mean institutional practices or policies of action that are generally accepted but not legally or administratively articulated or prescribed. Many medical, educational, and social welfare practices are governed by informal policies as well as by official policies to whose violation is attached some form of official sanction. Informal policies have their source in social values, as for instance welfare policies and their implementation are informed by social attitudes towards motherhood. By cultural ideals I mean norms of behavior or types of individual behavior accepted as desirable within a culture. Such norms or types are presented as the best sort of variety within a kind to be. While there may be no official sanctions attached to failing to satisfy or to aspire to satisfy such ideals, one runs the danger of encountering derision and discrimination by such refusal.

My aim in this section is to explore the kinds of impact certain types of scientific research on the biological bases of human behavior, cognition, and temperament have on a chosen set of social values and cultural ideals. My focus will be on the work that has been reviewed in prior chapters, though I will bring in comparable associated research

---

[1] See Nelkin (1987) for an analysis of the effects of science journalism.

programs from time to time. The normative questions I will review include social equality, the ideals of personhood and the associated ideals of sexuality, and the ideals of personal liberty and responsibility.

Social Equality

By social equality we mean something both deeper and less tangible than political equality. Political equality means something like formal equality of access to the formal decision-making institutions of a community, state, or nation. Thus, "one person, one vote" is a slogan of political equality, while institutionalized means of limiting access to the vote such as poll taxes, literacy tests, and more blatant methods of disenfranchisement are signs of political inequality.

Social equality has in part to do with image and status—two individuals are social equals if they associate with the same group of people, go to the same status parties and entertainments, have similar weight in their communities—and in part to do with entitlement to a society's resources. Our equal opportunity policies guarantee (or are intended to guarantee) to everyone an equal chance at achieving high status and the entitlement to resources that accompanies such status. They represent a compromise between a commitment to hierarchy (in its contemporary guise of meritocracy) and a commitment to social equality—from each according to ability and to each according to contribution. (Never mind that we have a peculiar method of measuring contribution.) The idea of equal opportunity requires that each person not be hindered by societally created obstacles at the outset of her or his quest for a satisfying life. This idea has given rise to a variety of new education programs designed to compensate for the obstacles imposed by past discrimination and exclusion. Such programs assume that innate differences in ability are uniformly spread throughout social classes and that compensatory education will eventually mean a distribution of significant social groups—the sexes and racial groups—in proportion to their distribution throughout the population.

Research supporting the biological basis of observed group differences has a contrary implication, one not lost on the champions of such research. The implications of the work of A. A. Ehrhardt and her various collaborators and fellow gender role researchers, discussed in Chapter Six and Chapter Seven, extend quite deeply and subtly into the educational realm. Their behavioral neuroendocrinology attributes, at a minimum, higher levels of "energy expenditure" to the male hormonal profile than to the female one. This reinforces expectations of boisterous and aggressive behavior from boys and encourages teachers to treat the greater aggressiveness of males (noted, for instance, in classrooms with limited computer access) as inevitable. Similarly, the acceptance of a biological basis for the apparent emphasis placed by girls and women on relationships, family, and nurturance translates into reduced expectations for female achievement in nontraditional endeavors. The traditional practice of tracking boys into athletics and "shop" and girls into home economics and secretarial courses can be seen as giving educational expression to beliefs about natural differences. Affirmative action for women and girls can be expected to produce little or no change if women are biologically disposed to avoid the type of gainful activity hitherto reserved for males, if women instinctively gravitate toward activities involving less self-assertion and more other-nurturance. The type of affirmative intervention at an early age that encourages young women to think about nontraditional adult roles for themselves is equally doomed by biology. As the subtitle of a recent book indicates, we will have come to "the limits of nonsexist childrearing."[2]

The work of Ehrhardt et al. translates vaguely into support for traditional roles—whether in implicitly permitting teachers to allow boys to get away with less self-discipline and greater physical expressiveness or to encourage girls to be quiet and more domestically oriented. Research on cognition and intelligence translates much more dramatically into educational policy. The suggestion that racial differences in average I.Q. scores are biologically based was used explicitly to support claims that efforts at compensatory education for Black children were futile.[3] Similarly, the recent work arguing for a biological basis for sex-differentiated performance levels on mathematics and spatial skills tests is presented as (1) an explanation for the absence of women from the sciences (they can't do it) and (2) reason to abandon "math anxiety" or other compensatory programs for girls. A comment by Hugh Fairweather on a review of studies of sex differences in brain asymmetry applies just as aptly to this related work:

> All in all one is most distressed . . . at the lack of *thinking* as opposed to *data gathering* that has taken place in this area in the last decade. Surely it is time we looked to do more than collect suggestive, ostensibly value-free, isolated pieces of natural history. It is not so much that questions such as "why" and "does it matter" remain unanswered—they have yet to be asked.[4]

---

[2] Stein (1984). For an attempt to make explicit the political implications of this book (and therefore of the biological work on which it relies) see Sobran (1984).

[3] Jensen (1969).

[4] Fairweather (1980), p. 325.

Just as with the work on gender role behavior this work on cognition shows no sign of reflection or analysis on the part of the researchers. Correlation after correlation is produced with no attempt to understand just what it is that is being measured or its relation to associated phenomena. Nevertheless, again like the gender role behavior work, the cognition research is absorbed into the literature, creating in some circles a fact and its explanation. This work is appealed to in other contexts as explaining the low representation of women in such fields as engineering, architecture, and the physical sciences.[5] And, if women are underrepresented in these fields because of an inherent liability, then various programs, such as affirmative action recruiting or educational programs to help young women overcome "math anxiety" and other resistances to mathematics and the sciences, are a waste of time, energy, and money. Equal opportunity requires that we remove socially created obstacles, not that we erase individual differences. The danger of uncritical reception of the cognition research is not that women may not be given an equal opportunity to apply for positions in these fields but that the social programs designed to enable them to compete on an equal footing will be cut.

Benbow and Benbow and Benbow and Stanley warn that one cannot infer from their work that any individual woman will not score in the very high ranges or perform at very high levels in work requiring mathematical ability. The point they seem to be making with this warning is that one should not discourage a person from pursuing mathematical study just because she is a girl. The implicit message, however, is that nothing need be changed to ensure that those girls who do have mathematical ability will be able to exercise it. Thus, they quite miss the point of the "politically motivated" objections to their work. As Alice Schafer and Mary Gray put the matter in a *Science* editorial, objectors are concerned about the potential impact of this work on funding agencies such as the NSF.[6] These agencies are not likely to allocate money to remedy a situation that is brought about by "natural" causes rather than by social injustice.

Ideals of Personhood

Ideals of personhood are models to which we aspire or whose realization is urged upon us. Aristotle's magnanimous man of virtue was one such ideal. Such ideals characterize individuals more or less imperfectly. To attribute the status of ideal to a description implies that the

[5] For discussion see Haas and Perruci, eds. (1984).
[6] Schafer and Gray (1981).

better a person exemplifies that description, the better sort of person she or he is. The content of an ideal may be identical with that of a stereotype. The difference between ideal and stereotype is a difference of function. A stereotype has a descriptive function, and an ideal has a prescriptive function. Our concepts of masculinity and femininity are examples of such dual function contents. We stereotype males and females when we describe (and act towards) them as though all men equally exemplified masculinity and all women femininity. It is clear that these gender concepts are also prescriptive ideals. We have terms of derogation for those who depart noticeably from them: for instance, "sissy" and "tomboy," "bitch" and "wimp."[7] And the famous Broverman study of the early 1970s showed that psychotherapists, those guardians of personal identity, tended to have dichotomous conceptions of the "healthy," that is, ideal, personality for males and females.[8]

Models of masculinity and femininity confront us in the vehicles of popular culture, in children's toys, and in our imaginations. Their existence as ideals means that individuals will try to mold themselves to the appropriate image to some degree. The molding often involves reshaping of the image: the cowgirl in frilly pink but still serviceable western gear. It also means that individuals who endorse the ideals will see themselves and others as conforming to them even when they do not. This is less a matter of simple self-deception than of directing one's attention to certain features and not others: to the pink rather than to the sturdy leather.

The regulative or prescriptive character of masculinity and femininity is also evidenced in the character of the judgments we make of those whom we must acknowledge as not realizing those ideals. They are either moral failures (the sissy and the tomboy, the wimp and the bitch) or victims of nature. The category of transsexual is designed to accommodate those whose physical bodies fail to accord in some way with their subjectively felt gender identification. By defining the transsexual as in need of surgical or hormonal therapy to correct nature's mistake, the gender dimorphic ideal is preserved.[9] Its role as an ideal is further revealed by the study of cultures with nondimorphic gender. Some American Indian cultures, for instance, have (or had) the category of

[7] Sandra Harding usefully distinguishes three levels of gender attribution: cultural/symbolic, social, and individual. See Harding (1986), p. 18. What I am calling ideals of personhood are articulated at the level of culture and function as ideals to the extent that we expect individuals to conform to them.

[8] Broverman et al. (1970).

[9] See Kessler and McKenna (1985).

"berdache"; which refers to individuals who took on or became a gender other than that assigned to them at birth. The berdache was a socially recognized, often honored, kind of person in these societies. While the different cultures vary in the modes of institutionalizing cross-gender roles, cross-gender individuals are not victims of a mistake requiring surgical correction but a member of a distinct classification that stands alongside what Western Europeans would identify as masculinity and femininity.[10]

Gender concepts play a similar role in the discussion of homosexuality. Europeans identify gender in alien cultures using individuals' sexual attachments as a criterion. Given a dimorphic gender classification, homosexuality, like transsexualism, is viewed as an endocrinological/developmental pathology. The goal of studying homosexuality, as evidenced in the titles and conclusions of many of the scientific articles on the subject, is its management and control, including its prevention. In an interview with science journalist Jo Durden-Smith, neuroscientist Roger Gorski reveals this underlying aim:

> There's something reductive and scary about a situation in which you *might* be able to ask a mother whether she wants testosterone treatment to avoid having a homosexual son. And of course we know nothing like enough yet about the actions of hormones to come to such broad general conclusions. Nevertheless, what Dörner is saying is very suggestive.[11]

The issue is not whether Gorski finds this prospect "scary" but that such intervention is seen as the expected end of research on the hormonal bases of homosexuality. Gorski is referring here to some of Gunther Dörner's ideas. In the discussion in the previous chapter I noted some of the problems in Dörner's theory of dimorphic male and female "mating centers." In order to overcome those problems Dörner has invoked the notion of maternal stress to explain the selective inactivation of fetal testosterone. Gorski is presumably thinking of treatments that would circumvent or override the effects of maternal stress (or whatever else is preventing the release or utilization of testosterone by the developing male fetus). His response makes clear the direction of understanding towards the goals of management and control.

Dörner's theory also reveals the mutually reinforcing effects of scientific and cultural imagery. Homosexuality is (still!) proscribed by the culture as both contranormal and wrong. Science, in the person of the

---

[10] Blackwood (1984). See also Martin and Voorhies (1975) and Williams (1986).
[11] Durden-Smith (1980), p. 96.

behavioral endocrinologist, remains liberally neutral on the moral questions but provides marvelous imagery to support the culture's judgments of contranormality. Homosexuality as well as other deviations from the dimorphic gender ideal are rather like cases of switched parts. In the ideal or normal case all the female parts from genes to neurons are united in one body and all the male parts in another body. The result is two types of individual: one with female reproductive capacity, feminine behavior, and a sexuality oriented towards men, the other with male reproductive capacity, masculine behavior, and a sexuality oriented towards women. Differences from that norm are a matter of mixing parts—mating and other brain centers, hormones, genitals—innappropriately and can be prevented or corrected by proper hormonal management or surgical therapy. It's like an auto parts store. Proper management of the inventory means that the right parts will reach their destinations. Carelessness means that a part for the diesel model will be installed in the gasoline-powered model and vice versa, with eventual disfunction.

The power of this view is most clearly evidenced in the feminist thought that assumes as explanandum the problematic of gender dimorphism. Many feminists have felt that the appropriate response to the biological determinism just described is to seek social and psychological explanation for dimorphism rather than to attempt to explode the very idea as a category applicable to individuals. The highly influential work of Nancy Chodorow is an example of feminist research that reinforces the assumption of dimorphism. Her version of object relations theory attributes the persistence of gendered individuals to the asymmetric relations of male and female children to their primary attachment figure (their mother).[12] Androgyny theory, too, continues the myth of dimorphism by positing two axes of personality.[13] Its radical break is to suggest that each of the ideals actually represents incomplete personhood and that wholeness resides in their integration. In both these debates masculinity and femininity are thought of as real elements of a dichotomy emerging from the observation of human experience rather than as cultural constraints imposed on that experi-

[12] Chodorow (1978). See also Dinnerstein (1977). For criticism of such accounts of gender from a different perspective see Spelman (1989), pp. 80–113.

[13] For discussion of the concept and ideal of androgyny see Stimpson (1974); Warren (1982); Beardsley (1982). Psychologist Sandra Bem, who once advocated androgyny as an alternative ideal, now urges the development of "gender aschematism," which avoids some of the problems of androgyny. The concept of gender schemata also avoids the problem of treating masculinity and femininity as inherent characteristics. See Bem (1985).

ence. Even though the goal of these analyses is to point the way towards overcoming gender dichotomization—or at least the differential value placed on women and men—by accepting a dichotomous classification system and hence neglecting the actual variety of human expression, they reinforce the dichotomy as much as they challenge it.[14]

This form of response works synergistically with the biological determinism it opposes to reinforce the status of general gender dimorphism as an ideal of personhood. As long as feminists counter theories of biological determination of gender difference and sexual orientation with competing environmental explanations of their origin, the discussion will revolve around the dimorphic center. As long is it does so, biologically oriented scientists and thinkers will continue to advance biological determinist theories. As long as they do so, dimorphism will remain unexamined as reality and as ideal. As long as dimorphism remains an ideal, individuals will attempt to conform to it. And, finally, as long as individuals attempt to conform to it, dimorphism will appear to be enough of a reality to require explanation. This schematic loop suggests the ideological power of gender-dimorphic concepts. The etiology of gender role behavior and sexual orientation is certainly more complex—indeed, the fact of nonconformity demands a more complex account. My point here is that as long as dimorphism remains at the center of discourse, other patterns of difference remain hidden both as possibility and as reality. In particular, the idea that there could be a multiplicity of modes of personality organization linked to sex and sexuality—a multiplicity of genders constructed at the intersections of biological sex, sexual orientation, reproductive status, class, race, and sexual ideology or morality, for instance—remains submerged.

Political Ideals

The final aspect of influence I wish to address is the impact of biological research on our ideals of liberty, autonomy, and responsibility. These concepts are central to our traditions of moral appraisal and political equality. I shall briefly indicate their interconnections before discussing the implications of some of the biological research.

Political liberty involves two sorts of freedoms. The negative freedom is the individual's freedom from (unwarranted) governmental control in the conduct of her or his life. The positive freedom is the right and ability to participate actively in the decisions that must be

---

[14] The same can be said of the new celebration of femininity in some texts of French feminism.

made at a level, broadly speaking, of community. (City, state, nation are the traditionally recognized units of political authority. Some feminist political theory suggests that we include family as well, or at least that the exclusion of family from the domain of the political results in an incoherence when women are explicitly included.[15])

The ideal of political liberty presupposes both personal autonomy and personal responsibility. By personal autonomy I mean independent decison making. This does not imply random or arbitrary choice but decision making resting primarily on one's own values, beliefs, and deliberation as opposed to action or decision that is primarily a product of forces outside the self. Nor does it imply decision making divorced from a social context. The values, et cetera, upon which autonomous decision making rests may have their origins in an individual's culture; what makes them one's own is that one endorses them as such. By personal responsibility in this context I mean effective decision making. This means that those decisions reached independently for the most part result in actions described in the decisions' propositional contents. This idea is the basis of our colloquial notion of responsibility, that is, that an individual's actions can be attributed to her or his intentions. Clearly the status of political liberty as an ideal rests on assumptions regarding the empirical possibility of self-determination by those on behalf of whom personal liberty is claimed. Autonomy and responsibility, while empirical assumptions relevant to personal liberty, also partake of the status of ideals. They acquire this status through being perceived as the achievements of the maturing human, realized to a greater or lesser degree in each of us. As ideals they receive different interpretations and different valuations in different cultures. What concerns us here in the context of biology is the relation of these assumptions underlying our political values to assumptions and claims in biological theorizing.

The research discussed in Chapter Seven presents us with distinctly contrasting sets of relevant assumptions. The behavioral endocrinology work which supports the view that certain behaviors result from prenatal hormonal organization of the brain proceeds on the basis of assumptions about animal modelling and what was termed linearity as well as on the basis of methodological atomism. I shall discuss each of these and contrast their implications with those of the quite different group selective theory of cortical function.

The implications of the assumptions of linearity and "zoocentric" theorizing are apparent in the choice of language by their proponents.

[15] Compare Okin (1979).

Donald Pfaff, for instance, speaks of biology as *limiting* us. The focus is on the constraining rather than on the enabling aspects of biology. In an essay entitled "The Neurobiological Origins of Human Values" Pfaff takes reciprocal cooperation to be paradigmatic of ethical action.[16] He argues that reciprocal cooperation can be analyzed into four modules, each of which can be accounted for in fairly straightforward neurophysiological terms: (1) representing an action, (2) remembering its consequences, (3) associating the consequences with oneself, and (4) evaluating the consequences. According to Pfaff, "except where motor acts which require neocortex for their very execution are involved, ethical behavior may consist of a series of relatively primitive steps, in which, especially in their association with positive or negative reward, neurologically primitive tissue in the limbic system and brainstem, play the crucial roles."[17] Ethical behavior is analogous to reproductive behavior in being susceptible to biological analysis if properly analyzed into its constituent steps.

I am not concerned with evaluating Pfaff's particular claims about the neurological mechanisms underlying each module but wish to draw attention to the reconceptualization of action that this analysis involves. An instance of reciprocal cooperation is the outcome of a sequence of physiological steps. It is classified as reciprocal cooperation because it is describable by a rule of cooperation, not because the behaving individual has followed such a rule. This classification procedure is similar to that which applies the name "altruism" to self-sacrificing behavior in ants. In Pfaff's description the idea of following a rule—the rule "do unto others as you would have done unto you" that he isolates as an ethical universal—is squeezed out of the account. A rule worth its salt as a rule, as Wittgenstein and others have taught us, is one that can be followed or not, which can be broken. There's no question here of the organism deciding whether or not it will follow the rule, or of deciding which rules apply in a given situation, or of sorting through conflicting moral demands. In fact, Pfaff supposes that the putting of self in place of the other—what we might in other contexts call imaginative empathy—could be a matter of failing to distinguish self and other, of forgetting whether the remembered consequences of previous instances of the proposed act occurred to one's self or to the/an other.

Pfaff thus reduces deliberation to relatively low-level processing, most of which can be carried out subcortically. It is subsumed within

[16] Pfaff (1983).
[17] Ibid., p. 149.

the paradigm of simple appetition realized in the limbic system. His procedure is analogous to that of many biologists concerned with the implications of their disciplines for ethics. Ethical behavior loses its status as behavior engaged in out of principle or in order to conform to notions of right and good. It becomes instead behavior that conforms to the writer's idea of what is right and good. The problem of understanding ethical behavior becomes the problem of producing it— of knowing what interventions are likely to increase its frequency. The implication for notions of autonomy and responsibility are clear. As traditionally understood, they no longer characterize human action. Decisions originate in the nervous system of the individual but not in those portions of the nervous system in which the higher cognitive processing involved in conscious inference, valuation, and deliberation is presumably realized. Decision making is thus not subject to conscious deliberation and reflection. These higher level cognitive phenomena become epiphenomenal relative to those neural processes that effectively cause behavior. Consequently, the specific human abilities that ground the claim to political liberty are eliminated by this theoretical treatment of action.

The other side of the undermining of this ideal is the positive support offered for various forms of intervention into individual decision making. The concept of action underlying the behavioral endocrinology program facilitates the medicalization of all sorts of human behavior. Even now rapists are, in some states, being treated with hormones to reduce their libido, as though rape were a matter of excess libido, an individual affliction to be individually cured. Homosexuality has only recently been removed from the American Psychiatric Association's list of personality disorders. And those uncomfortable with their homoeroticism can seek medical interventions in the form of hormone therapy. The point here is not whether such treatments would work but the conception of our own natures that we are encouraged to adopt. Human capacities for self-reflection and deliberation become idle epiphenomena—distractions from the real causal processes producing our behavior; processes at levels to which only the scientist or physician have access. Usually only deviations from acceptable behavior (whatever that may be) are medicalized. Criminality, always a favorite, is once again being given a biological treatment.[18] No one begins by asking for the biological determinants of heterosexuality or of acceptable social behavior, but the consequences of the medical model must be that these, too, are products of biological events early in our development. Although both the favorable and the critical reception of these

---

[18] Wilson and Herrnstein (1985).

ideas generally ignores this aspect, Pfaff's discussion of ethical decision making beautifully delineates this model's erosion of the idea of the person as a being capable of making and acting on intelligent decisions (whether right or wrong) about her or his own life.

Yet another impact on social ideals flows from the methodological atomism characterizing the research. The human activities studied must be described by externally measurable properties in order to develop their analogies to the animal behaviors whose physiological bases are more accessible to researchers. This behaviorist redescription of action situates it outside of the social context that gives it meaning. The full dimensions of what is decided upon, as well as the descriptions under which it is chosen, are lost from view. Not only is human behavior redescribed as analogous to animal behavior but both animal and human behavior are perceived in analogy to mechanistic systems. Such redescription supports a particular interpretation of political liberty— as the freedom to pursue one's own interest unhindered by external constraints. Social interactions are understood as enhancing or deflecting from one's pursuit of that interest rather as collisions between elastic bodies can change the direction and/or velocity of their motion. The claim of a right to liberty under this impoverished conception is easily given up in the face of biological research that purports to show that the motions constituting behavior are under the control of factors other than an agent's conscious deliberation.[19] Furthermore, the atomistic view of behavior encourages the individual who feels uncomfortable with her- or himself and those from whom she or he seeks help to see the problem as an individual rather than a social one.

Implications of the New Neurophysiology

The study of the biological bases of behavior need not be incompatible with the richer conception of liberty outlined above. I will support this point by briefly reviewing some of the implications of the group selective theory discussed in the previous chapter. Theorists focussing on higher brain function problematize human behaviors that as far as we know are unique to the species: the writing of symphonies, the construction of undecidable mathematical theorems. The questions are not couched in terms of understanding the physiological conditions sufficient to produce the kinds of behavior in question but in terms of understanding in a general way what kind of neurophysiological processes are necessary for intelligent, reflective, self-conscious, creative activity. By asking what the character of brain processes underlying complex human behavior must be the inquiry emphasizes the enabling

[19] See Winch (1958); also Taylor (1971).

rather than the limiting aspects of biology. Because the seat of cognition and intention is located in an organ that is common to all individuals of whatever category, this approach is compatible with assumptions of human equality in the capacities that matter to our status as persons. Because that organ develops its unique or individually differentiated qualities in interaction with experience, multipotentiality rather than limitation emerges as the character of the physiological contribution to behavior. The study of the role of higher brain processes embodying cognition and intention in mediating action returns both autonomy and responsibility to the person. The emphasis on the brain's plasticity and responsiveness to environment allows a role for processed social influence. The brain is an organ integrating inputs from physiology, environment, and, via phasic reentry, its own functions such as memory and self-awareness. Decisions are understood as the result of that integration, rather than as the summation of physiological, environmental, and memory vectors. This places control of action back in the individual consciousness without denying the biological nature of that consciousness or the role of social interactions in the formation of self.

The view of the brain that both guides and is emerging from these studies is thus, at this point, one that makes sense from the perspective of the political ideals outlined above and in light of which those ideals are realizable. The modern versions of these ideals have their origins in the Enlightenment illusion of the self's transparency to itself. The neurobiological work shows that we can reject this illusion without also having to reject the idea that we should strive for forms of political organization that assume individual autonomy and responsibility.

The secular character of contemporary culture means that ideas developed in a scientific context for purposes of research can have a profound impact on social values and ideals, just as social relations and cultural frameworks provide basic models of relationship to be elaborated in the research laboratory. The models in science and the social assumptions have ostensibly different functions, the generation of new knowledge and the guiding of action respectively. The incompleteness of both domains, however, means that each remains open to the other as a source of legitimation. Philosophical views about the nature of scientific knowledge direct us to contrasting assessments of this relationship.

IMPLICATIONS OF THE METASCIENTIFIC VIEWS

The account of scientific knowledge developed in the earlier sections of this book is a form of contextualism that understands knowledge as the historical product of interactions between contextual factors such as social needs, values, and traditions and practices of inquiry such as observation, experiment, and reasoning. This account was defended by appeal to certain features of the relation of evidence and hypothesis and certain features of the formative episodes of modern Western science. It is contrasted with the objectivism and scientism associated with logical empiricism and with the self-ratifying internalism of Kuhn (and of Laudan). These three approaches offer distinct perspectives on the relevance of scientific ideas to social, cultural, and political principles, practices, and ideals. In the preceding sections of this chapter I have detailed the alleged social, cultural, and political implications of certain research programs. These implications have either been explicitly endorsed by those pursuing these programs or represent a simple and, in some instances, naive extension of those programs to the social world. In this section I wish to spell out the implications of the metascientific accounts for our understanding of the extrascientific relevance of scientific theories and hypotheses.

Positivism and Realism

Positivism has different implications depending on which of its associated theses are emphasized. It can be understood as a form of epistemological reductionism. Under this aspect what is relevant to knowledge claims are experience and formal reasoning. If this means that empirical claims should be held to empirical criteria, there would be little to quarrel over. Positivists go even farther, of course, and claim that the very meaningfulness of a statement depends on there being experiential (observational) methods of verifying it. Only those things can be known which can be experienced or which have experiential consequences. Scientific knowledge is the systematically ordered set of accumulated observations expressed in sentences. This has well-known implications for the relation between facts and values. First of all, value claims, not being observationally verifiable, are cognitively meaningless. Values are not potential objects of knowledge but subjective preferences, and value claims are simply expressions of feeling. Secondly, scientific claims will always have priority over value-based claims in the question of what to believe. This follows a fortiori from the proposition that value claims are cognitively meaningless in contrast with scientific claims.

The second aspect of the positivist analysis that bears on this issue is what might be called its epistemological atomism. One implication of the positivist view is that research claims are independent of one another and can be analyzed in isolation. Thus, in assessing the consequences of a claim for social issues one need only examine the evidence for the claim and the particular social or value question under examination. The context in which the research is done is relevant to the assessment neither of the scientific claim nor of its alleged social implications.

One can see these implications deployed in certain of the media debates about science in society. A number of authors writing about research on sex differences assert that alleged findings of that research take precedence over feminist demands for sexual equality and over gay liberationist and feminist demands for an end to the idealization of masculinity and femininity. Thus Jo Durden-Smith and Diane deSimone, the authors of a book of popular journalism, *Sex and the Brain*, write: "[T]he constant scientific debate . . . threatens, in its spreading implications, the liberationist assumptions of feminists and homosexuals. And it undercuts the idea of absolute sexual equality for all."[20] They then go on to say:

> The differences between men and women—all the differences in brain and body and inheritance, in ability, fragility and immunity— are fundamental to our human biology. . . . This knowledge may not serve the turn of some of the entrenched institutions of our society, including big business. It may not suit the psychologized politics-for-self that is the current expression, all too often, of feminism and the other sexual liberation movements. . . . But it may lead to a greater understanding . . . of the essential integrity of the male and female body.[21]

Such overblown rhetoric confuses political equality with biological sameness. My point is that this conflation is encouraged by the positivist tenets.

In a similar vein, in a letter to the *New York Review of Books* psychologist Sandra Witelson attempts to discredit the idea that women have been unjustly turned away from scientific inquiry by appealing to cerebral asymmetry and other work on the biological bases of behavioral sex differences. "And what if natural differences are found to be partly responsible for sex differences in behavior? A physical basis of thought does imply scientific determinism of behavior. Unfortunately, this position is unpalatable to many because it is mistakenly thought to deprive human beings of free will."[22] As the authors of *Sex and the Brain* also insinuate, only wishful thinking prevents one from accept-

[20] Durden-Smith and deSimone (1983), p. 99.
[21] Ibid., p. 299.
[22] Witelson (1985), p. 53–54.

ing the truths of science. These sentiments echo B. F. Skinner's similar ridicule of those who objected to his behaviorist objectification of human action in *Beyond Freedom and Dignity*.[23]

Atomistic positivism supports the false impression that a research program, indeed the whole of scientific knowledge, is constructed additively by the joining of many independent research findings that turn out to be related. The theoretical claims and assumptions of a program are understood as following from the accumulated data rather than as playing any role in determining the collection of data and structuring their interpretation. Each supposed finding is presented in isolation without specification of its scientific context or of that context's larger sociocultural context. Each individual finding, no matter how close to insignificance, can be added to others to create the impression of an overwhelming case for some claim, for example, major structural and functional sex differences in the brain. The claim is not understood as developed in a social context of wild ideas about sex differences or in a research context whose primary purpose is the development of an account of behavior as determined as much as possible physiologically. In fact, Smith and deSimone present the work they discuss as conducted against the (mistaken) spirit of the age. Perhaps there was a moment in the 1970s when sexual egalitarianism seemed in the ascendancy. But this moment cannot have lasted long enough to be noticed by very many.

Another side of logical positivism, which it shares with the scientific realism that is its contemporary successor, is its implicit objectivism and scientism. This can be expressed as follows: there is a truth of matters, and the methods described by positivists and realists are adequate to the discovery of that truth. This assumes the capacity of the methods of empirical science, construed as guarantors of context independence, to fully reveal the actual character of things. This approach, applied to actual sciences, conceals the ambivalence noted in earlier chapters between the prescriptive and descriptive intentions of positivism. Prescriptive positivism provides criteria for the justification of belief and knowledge claims—hypothesis acceptance. Descriptive positivism claims that a particular field of inquiry satisfies these prescriptive requirements. Biologists who seek the biological foundation of value take value questions to admit of true (or false) answers. Those answers are obtainable by the methods of empirical science. Roger Sperry gives voice to this notion in his book *Science and Moral Priority*:

[23] Skinner (1971).

> Instead of separating science from values, the current [Sperry's] interpretation leads to a stand in which science—in its purest sense as a means of revealing an understanding of man and the natural order—becomes the best source, method, and authority for determining the ultimate criteria of moral values and those ultimate ethical axioms and guidelines to live and govern by.[24]

Granted, Sperry envisions an ontologically more permissive neuroscience than some might countenance, but this, too, he feels to be mandated by empirical methods. George Pugh describes his book *The Biological Origin of Human Values* as explaining " 'human values' as manifestations of a built-in *value system*, which is an essential part of evolution's basic 'design concept' for a biological 'decision system.' "[25] Pfaff's theory about the biological bases of morality is another example of the denial of independent meaning to ethical statements.

Thus one version of positivism involves the displacement of value-based claims by fact-based claims. Demands for equal treatment on the basis of fundamental sameness give way to proofs of difference. The second version treats value claims as themselves decidable on the basis of factual investigation. To reject the value implications requires showing that the scientific claim is false. History shows us that this is not effective, as new claims spring up to replace the old. In earlier chapters I've shown how inquiry is dependent upon assumptions establishing the relevance of data to hypotheses. I then showed that in a variety of research contexts those assumptions include value-based assumptions. The empiricistically inclined lay person, looking to scientific research for guidance in complex matters of social policy or cultural ideals, is as likely as not to provide the final conclusions of a circular argument.

There is a final expression of positivist views that should be noted. Biologist Helen Lambert has deplored the waste of intellectual and political energy spent on arguments regarding the biological basis of sex differences in behavior.[26] She seems inclined to accept on face value much of the research purporting to demonstrate such a basis. Contrary to many of the authors surveyed in this section, however, she attempted to separate the research findings from their commonly alleged implications for social action. The distribution of social benefits, she argued, should be independent of the outcome of sex differences research. We are not, as a society, bound to accept biologically based sex differences as immutable or as implying that individuals should be

[24] Sperry (1983), p. 113.
[25] Pugh (1977), p. 5.
[26] Lambert (1978).

tracked towards occupations suitable to their group's innate endowments or lack of them. Lambert seems to be insisting on the primacy of the commitment to equality and on a strong interpretation of that commitment, that is, to doing what is necessary to assure equal distribution of benefits. Biological differences (just like socially based differences) require that we compensate in the relevant ways.

While Lambert's approach turns aspects of the positivist view on their head, it suffers from two problems. One, of course, is the lack of political will. United States society, in spite of our rhetoric, does not have a primary commitment to equality. Decision making at many levels is governed by beliefs about differences and similarities, which are transmuted into beliefs about superiority and inferiority. Furthermore, the commitment to equal opportunity is a commitment to removing *socially* created obstacles, not "natural" ones. Secondly, even in engaging in compensatory measures, beliefs about the nature of the differences for which one wishes to compensate will determine the precise character of the compensatory action. Thus, research about their bases is relevant even if equal distribution of social benefits is preferred to distribution according to ability, contribution, or some other differentiated measure.[27] Overcoming biological differences in ability is likely to involve different sorts of interventions than changing the social conditions that result in different abilities.

Wholism

Wholism is the view that the meaning of any statement can only be understood in the context of the entire theory to which it belongs, that no part of a theory can stand independently of the whole. All meanings are theory-laden, and theories are thus incommensurable. The wholist position, too, can support two different stances regarding the relevance of scientific inquiry to norms, ideals, and values. Neither of these treats scientific research as an independent source of validation for such norms. It is not surprising, therefore, that we do not find expressions of these views among the scientists asserting the relevance of science to the solution of social problems and conflicts. I shall quickly sketch the two ways in which one can develop the wholist position.

If one holds that value-based assumptions are excluded from scientific theory, it might be argued that scientific claims are logically irrelevant to value claims because they are embedded in different theories. The meanings of any shared terms are different, and different valida-

[27] The recent EEOC case against Sears is an example of this. See Hall and Cooper (1986).

tional methods are appropriate to the two types of theory. For example, the term "natural" might occur in a scientific claim and in a moral claim. Suppose one claim is "The dominance of men over women is natural" and the other is "Neither the state nor individuals should attempt to alter natural relationships." If these statements are part of different theories, then "natural" is defined by each theory, and what is declared natural in one may not be so in the other. An emphasis on incommensurability, then, dictates the irrelevance of ideas developed and defended in the context of a scientific research program to cultural values and ideals.

For their part the scientists who invoke Kuhn to explain how particular social and cultural values have affected a body of research seem to make use of a different form of wholism. They seem to think that the political valence of scientific theorizing is inevitably a function of observational data laden with cultural assumptions and values. If we follow Hesse in saying that the theory/assumptions with which the observations are laden are not, or not necessarily, part of the theory whose support is in question, the account shades into the contextualist one discussed below. A strong wholism, by contrast, would hold those assumptions to be part of the theory purportedly supported by such data.

In this interpretation of wholism the ensemble of data, theory, and assumptions must be understood as a whole. Each element, including value-based assumptions, can only be understood in the context of the others. In this case value claims that are a part of a theory would be validated by the factual data of the theory as much or as little as any other claim is. Given the incommensurability of theories, however, value conflicts could not be settled independently of any theory. Thus, there would be no independent way of choosing between a theory that claims that some relationship is natural and one denying this, or between a theory prohibiting interference in natural relationships and one permitting it. If we are appraising theories in a scientific context and using Kuhnian criteria of evaluation such as problem-generating and problem-solving capacity, this is not a problem. If, however, we move outside the research context to that of social action and public policy, the resulting circularity becomes vicious and invalidating. On neither interpretation of wholism, then, can scientific inquiry be understood as independently relevant to the support of values or ideals.

Contextualism

The contextualist has greater flexibility than adherents of either of the internalist positions just discussed. The contextualist seeks not to eliminate but to understand the role of contextually based assumptions in scientific reasoning. Some background assumptions may involve conceptual, metaphysical, and normative dimensions that elude assessment by strict empirical criteria. Others may be subject to fairly straightforward empirical assessment. Arguments that use factual hypotheses to undermine or support claims about values provide good subjects for study. When the support for the relevant factual hypotheses is made explicit, it often turns out to include those same value claims or their presuppositions. The contextualist takes the presentation of arguments or positions such as those outlined above as an incentive to further investigation, not as an imperative for assent.

The work on mathematical ability, for example, rather than compelling the assent suggested in Witelson's letter quoted above, invites an exploration first of the assumptions and argumentative structure of the work and second of their relation to their social and cultural context. Several assumptions regarding the tests of ability were isolated earlier. These included: (A_1) there is only one form in which mathematical ability is expressed; (A_2) that form is expressed in performance on standardized tests such as the M-SAT; (A_3) the content of a problem has no bearing on the formal properties of a problem nor on an individual's grasp of those properties. A further assumption concerns the subjects taking the tests: (A_4) the appropriate measure of mathematical education is the amount of time spent in classes devoted to specific mathematical subjects.

These assumptions about what the tests measure and about the uniformity of preparation of the subjects tested facilitate the interpretation of variation in test performance as variation in innate mathematical ability. The contextualist must ask (1) what reasons can be offered for these assumptions and (2) what interests are served by the unchallenged persistence of these assumptions. What the tests test are mathematical performances and abilities of the sort that are used and expressed in the world in which the tests are devised. The fourth assumption, about the uniformity of preparation, has been persuasively rebutted by (1) the observation that male and female children are provided with toys and play experiences that encourage the development of quite different skills and (2) studies showing that girls and boys receive different treatment from the same teachers in the same classroom.[28] It is deficient on straightforward empirical grounds.

The first three assumptions are less straightforward and have not been investigated systematically. The first, in particular, might be

[28] Buerck (1985).

thought to mimic common sense: What is mathematical ability if it is not the ability to do what mathematicians do? That most mathematicians are male and thus are likely to have had different sorts of formative experiences than women of comparable class and race is salient only to those who have been excluded from careers in mathematics or whose abilities are impugned by the research in question, not to those whose position and success relative to others is justified by the research. The interests of the latter are served by not challenging the assumptions, indeed in not even seeing that they are assumptions. Certain developments in the study of mathematics education, particularly in the study of mathematics learning by groups hitherto excluded from scientific, mathematical, and technical subjects, do suggest that they may be problematic.[29] There is as yet, however, no conclusive reason to accept or reject them, but there is surely a certain amount of conventionality in deciding the boundaries of mathematics, a conventionality which leaves room for the play of various sorts of contextual interests and values.

Similarly, the persistence of research that implicitly eliminates autonomy and the basis of liberty and responsibility from our concepts of human nature can be understood as a function of the convergence of a number of contextual interests. The professional interests of biologists are surely served by research that brings as much of human behavior as is possible under biological control. The interests of sociomedical bureaucracies, however, are served by research that promises to reconceptualize human behavior as the product of discrete, measurable, and manipulable factors.[30] While the interventions sanctioned by the various theoretical directions currently being pursued are applied only to "deviants" and criminals as corrective (and thus "humane") approaches, the very idea of such intervention gives tremendous prescriptive power to the categories of normality and deviance. That one's behavior and dispositions could be medically corrected implies a norm worthy of such effort. This in itself is sufficient to create a degree of voluntary conformity to the norm, a self-regimentation that even further reinforces the rule's status as a norm.[31] The interests of a bureaucracy that requires a cooperative population to

[29] For the role of early play experience see Fennema and Sherman (1977). For classroom experience see Becker (1981) and Gore and Roumagoux (1983).

[30] Donna Haraway has documented the convergence of sociopolitical and scientific concerns in twentieth-century primatology. See Haraway (1978, 1985b).

[31] The work of Michel Foucault on knowledge and power brings out the basis in individual self-policing of order in the bureaucratic state. See Foucault (1977, 1978, 1980).

effectively exercise power are also served by the scientific legitimation of informal distinctions between normal and abnormal.

The components or auto parts conception of the bases of human personality (at least as it relates to sex and gender), moreover, reverberates in a troublesome way with the high tech aesthetic of late twentieth-century industrial societies. While robots and other instruments of machine intelligence can be understood as extending our manual and intellectual capacities, the auto parts view has a more reductive flavor. We become ourselves an integrated component system, plugged into the circuit like any other machine.[32]

As in all of the work discussed in this chapter, the point is not that these interests direct the research in any overt way. Rather, they create a climate in which the assumptions that shape the research are taken for granted, as a part of common sense, and are to that extent immune from scrutiny. Scientific knowledge, as I argued earlier, rests on a bed of presuppositions about what questions are important, what sorts of connections are meaningful, about the general direction of causal relations (or more precisely, about which causal relations are worth investigating or establishing). Research programs that apply the same models reinforce each other and their shared presuppositions without ever needing to subject them to direct examination. Those presuppositions that cohere with the interests of the (sub)culture of the researchers will not be seen as assumptions but, if seen at all, as self-evident truths.

As a view about scientific reasoning contextualism is quite consistent with a modified empiricism, understood as a prescriptive theory. Such a modified empiricism, cleansed of restrictions on meaningfulness and purged of assumptions about the absolute or fixed character of observations, would restrict instead those things we could be said to know. What we can know is what we can experience. The conclusions of inferences from experience that must use additional substantive assumptions as premises cannot be known absolutely. We give the name "knowledge" to the complex and more or less coherent sets of hypotheses, theories, and experimental-observational data accepted by a culture at a given time because this body of ideas functions as a public fund of justification and legitimation for new hypotheses as well as for action and policy.[33] This socially created knowledge which integrates experience and the needs and assumptions of a culture is true relative

[32] Haraway (1985a) alludes to the ambivalence inherent in our contemporary relationship to machines. The cyborg imagery aptly conveys its charged duality.

[33] The coherence referred to here is at best within fields or subfields and not across fields. Compare the discussion in the final section of Chapter Ten.

to those assumptions and, to the extent that those assumptions are context-dependent, is relative to that context. If scientific knowledge is social knowledge, to hold scientific claims to strict empirical criteria is to remain agnostic with respect to the context-independent truth or falsity of many of them. Unlike the empiricist-absolutist, the contextualist does not expect scientific claims to be capable of displacing value claims, nor are claims that are not experientially verifiable meaningless. Unlike the wholist, the contextualist can accept the primacy of experience as arbiter of knowledge claims. Certain claims, however, are not susceptible to direct empirical confirmation and so cannot be known to be true or false.

According to this view, shifts in theoretical orientation and in the relative centrality of observational data are comprehensible as the expression of complex interactions between what is known, what is assumed, and social-cognitive needs. While the official picture of a field presented in its textbooks is the picture of a uniform and consistent understanding, the background from which this understanding emerges/is selected contains alternative interpretations of the data included in the textbook picture as well as data inconsistent with it. The selection represents guesses about where a field is going, which itself is a function of what a society (those in a society with the power to effect their preferences and privilege their needs) thinks it should know or wants to know. Shifts in the official picture involve the saliency not necessarily of new facts and ideas but of facts and ideas, some accepted, some submerged, that in connection with social-cognitive needs assume sufficient coherence to constitute a uniform story.

In assessing claims about the social and ethical implications of some current research, therefore, the contextualist looks both to its larger scientific context *and* to its cultural context, to the framework of theory and assumptions within which it is embedded and to the needs and values they promise to satisfy.

CHAPTER NINE

Science and Ideology

SOME of the political critics of science have gone beyond a critique of particular research programs to argue that modern science, or the modern practice of science, is inherently oppressive. They have raised a corollary demand for a "new" science—a science that is liberatory rather than harnessed to the forces of domination and oppression. What can the analysis developed so far offer in response to such demands? In this chapter I shall consider the idea of a feminist science and use the ideas presented in Chapter Seven and Chapter Eight to provide an illustration of one possible type of feminist science. I shall then discuss the ideas of a group of contemporary thinkers who address the relations between politics, ideology, and science, and then focus on the convergences and divergences of my analysis with the views expressed by several neo-Marxist scientists, Jürgen Habermas, Michel Foucault, Evelyn Fox Keller, and Donna Haraway. Ideology may indeed operate globally in mainstream science, but counterideologies, if they are to be useful in changing science, must be brought to bear locally on specific research programs.

FEMINIST SCIENCE?

The hope for a feminist theoretical natural science has concealed an ambiguity between content and practice. In the content sense the idea of a feminist science involves a number of assumptions and calls a number of visions to mind. Some theorists have written as though a feminist science is one whose theories encode a particular world view, characterized by complexity, interaction, and wholism. Such a science is said to be feminist because it is the expression and valorization of a female sensibility or cognitive temperament. Alternatively it is claimed that women have certain traits (for example, dispositions to attend to particulars and interactive and cooperative social attitudes and behaviors rather than individualist and controlling ones) that enable them to understand the true character of natural processes (which are complex and interactive).[1] While proponents of this interactionist view see it as

---

[1] This seems to be suggested in Bleier (1983); Rose (1983); and in Sandra Harding's early work, for example, Harding (1980).

an improvement over most contemporary science, it has also been caricatured as soft—or antimathematical. Some women in the sciences who feel they are being asked to do not better science but inferior science have responded angrily to this characterization of feminist science, thinking that it is simply new clothing for the old idea that women can't do science. I think that the interactionist view can be defended against this response, although that requires rescuing it from some of its advocates as well. However, I also think that the characterization of feminist science as the expression of a distinctive female cognitive temperament has other drawbacks, the greatest being that it conflates feminine with feminist. While it is important to reject the traditional derogation of the virtues assigned to women, it is also important to remember that women are *constructed* to occupy positions of social subordinates. We should not uncritically embrace the feminine.

This characterization of feminist science is also a version of recently propounded notions of a "women's standpoint" or a "feminist standpoint" and suffers from the same suspect universalization that these ideas suffer from. If there is one such standpoint, there are many: as Maria Lugones and Elizabeth Spelman elucidate in their article "Have We Got a Theory for You!: Feminist Theory, Cultural Imperialism, and the Demand for 'The Woman's Voice,' " women are too diverse in our experiences to generate a single cognitive framework.[2] In addition, the sciences are themselves too diverse for me to think that they might be equally transformed by such a framework. The account of scientific knowledge defended here makes another conception of feminist science possible. By focussing on science as practice rather than content, as process rather than product, we can reach the idea of feminist science through that of doing science as a feminist.

Let me illustrate this point by talking about approaches to the biology of behavior. In chapters Six through Eight, I analyzed the logical structure and social implications of research on the biological bases of alleged gender difference and sex-related behavior. The behavioral endocrinology studies discussed in Chapter Six are vulnerable to criticisms of their data and of their observational methodologies. They also show clear evidence of androcentric bias—in the assumption that there are just two sexes and two genders (us and them), in the designation of appropriate and innappropriate behaviors for male and female children, in the caricatures of homosexuality, in the assumption of male mathematical superiority. While these sexist assumptions do affect the

[2] Lugones and Spelman (1983).

way the data are described, causal inferences from the alleged data are mediated by the linear-hormonal model that functions as a background assumption. To put it crudely, fetal gonadal hormones organize the brain at critical periods of development. The organism is thereby disposed as an adult to respond in a set series of ways to a range of environmental stimuli.

In Chapter Seven and Chapter Eight I contrasted this model with an alternative model of the role of the brain in behavior, drawn from the selectionist theory of brain development and function. Such a model allows not only for the interaction of physiological and environmental factors but also for the interaction of these with a continuously self-modifying, self-representational (and self-organizing) central processing system. While my preferences are undisguisable, I have tried to remain analytically neutral and have presented the constitutively based arguments that can be made for both approaches. In work with my colleague, Ruth Doell, however, we have been more partisan.[3] In particular, we have argued that a model of at least the degree of complexity characterizing the selectionist model is necessary to account for the human behaviors studied in the sex hormones and behavior research and that if gonadal hormones function at all at these levels, they will probably be found at most to facilitate or inhibit neural processing in general. The strategy we take is to argue that the degree of intentionality involved in the behaviors in question is greater than is presupposed by the hormonal influence researchers and to argue that that degree of intentionality implicates the higher brain processes.

Abandoning my polemical mood for a more reflective one, as I have done here, I want to say that in the final analysis commitment to one or another model is strongly influenced by values or other contextual features. The models themselves determine the relevance and interpretation of data. The linear or complex models are not in turn independently or conclusively supported by data. I doubt, therefore, that value-free inquiry could reveal the efficacy or inefficacy of intentional states or of physiological factors like hormone exposure in human action. I think instead that a research program in neuroscience that assumes the linear model and sex gender dualism will show the influence of hormone exposure on gender role behavior. And I think that a research program in neuroscience and psychology proceeding on the assumption that humans do possess the capacities for self-consciousness, self-reflection, and self-determination, and then asks how the structure of the human brain and nervous system enables the expression of these

[3] Doell and Longino (1988).

capacities, will reveal the efficacy of intentional states (understood as very complex sorts of brain states or processes).

While this latter assumption does not itself contain normative terms, I think that the decision to adopt it is motivated by value-laden considerations—by the desire to understand ourselves and others as self-determining (at least some of the time), that is, as capable of acting on the basis of concepts or representations of ourselves and the world in which we act. (Such representations are not necessarily correct and are surely mediated by our cultures; all I claim is that they are effective factors in human action.) I think further that that desire on Ruth Doell's and my part is, in several ways, an aspect of our feminism. Our preference for a neurobiological model that allows for agency, for the efficacy of intentionality, is partly a validation of our (and everyone's) subjective experience of thought, deliberation, and choice. One of the tenets of feminist research is the valorization of subjective experience, and so our preference in this regard conforms to feminist research patterns.

There is, however, a more direct way in which our feminism is expressed in this preference. Feminism is many things to many people, but it is at its core in part about the expansion of human potentiality. When feminists talk of breaking out and do break out of socially prescribed sex roles, when feminists criticize the institutions of domination, we are thereby insisting on the capacity of humans—male and female—to act on perceptions of self and society and to act to bring about changes in self and society on the basis of those perceptions. (Not overnight and not by a mere act of will. The point is that we act.) And so our criticism of theories of the hormonal influence or determination of so-called gender role behavior is not just a rejection of the sexist bias in the description of the phenomena—the behavior of the children studied, the sexual lives of lesbians, et cetera—but of the limitations on human capacity imposed by the explanatory model underlying such research.[4]

While the argument strategy we adopt against the linear model rests on a certain understanding of intention, the values motivating our adoption of that understanding remain hidden in that polemical context. Our political commitments, however, presuppose a certain understanding of human action, so that when faced with a conflict be-

---

[4] Ideological commitments other than feminist ones may lead to the same assumptions, and the variety of feminisms means that feminist commitments can lead to different and incompatible asssumptions.

tween these commitments and a particular model of brain-behavior relationships we allow the political commitments to guide the choice.

The relevance of my earlier arguments about value-free science to the issue of feminist science should be becoming clear. Feminists—in and out of science—often condemn masculine bias in the sciences from the vantage point of commitment to a value-free science. Androcentric bias, once identified, can then be seen as a violation of the rules—as "bad" science. Feminist science, by contrast, can eliminate that bias and produce "good," more true or gender-free science. From that perspective the process I've just described is anathema. But if scientific methods generated by constitutive values cannot guarantee independence from contextual values, then that approach to sexist science won't work. We cannot restrict ourselves simply to the elimination of bias but must expand our scope to include the detection of limiting interpretive frameworks and the finding or construction of more appropriate frameworks. We need not, indeed should not, wait for such a framework to emerge from the data. In waiting, if my argument is correct, we run the danger of working unconsciously with assumptions still laden with values from the context we seek to change. The idea of a value-free science presupposes that the object of inquiry is given in and by nature, whereas the contextual analysis shows that such objects are constituted in part by social needs and interests that become encoded in the assumptions of research programs. Instead of remaining passive with respect to the data and what the data suggest, we can, therefore, acknowledge our ability to affect the course of knowledge and fashion or favor research programs that are consistent with the values and commitments we express in the rest of our lives. From this perspective the idea of a value-free science is not just empty but pernicious.

Accepting the relevance of our political commitments to our scientific practice does not imply simple and crude impositions of those ideas onto the corner of the natural world under study. If we recognize, however, that knowledge is shaped by the assumptions, values, and interests of a culture and that, within limits, one can choose one's culture, then it's clear that as scientists/theorists we have a choice. We can continue to do establishment science, comfortably wrapped in the myths of scientific rhetoric or we can alter our intellectual allegiances. While remaining committed to an abstract goal of understanding, we can choose to whom, socially and politically, we are accountable in our pursuit of that goal. In particular we can choose between being accountable to the traditional establishment or to our political comrades.[5] The feminist scientist is responsive to the ideals of a political community as well as to some subset of the standards endorsed in her or his scientific community. These allegiances are themselves interactive, as the political ideals may indicate a priority ordering for the scientific standards and vice versa. One colleague has suggested that we can choose to be thus accountable to a world larger than both. I suppose this is so, as long as this world is a definable social community whose members can hold us accountable and not an imagined one or nature itself.

In focussing on accountability and choice this conception of feminist science differs from those that proceed from the assumption of a congruence between certain models of natural processes and women's inherent modes of understanding.[6] It also raises the question of what sort of choice is involved here. Let me address this issue first. To adopt a political framework is to adopt assumptions about human nature and potential. Radical and feminist scientists are poised at the center of tensions between the views embedded in certain scientific research programs and those embedded in their political allegiances. To the extent that they use one or the other in assessing research they are making a choice. Clearly the choice is not arbitrary, but neither is it dictated by data. Obviously model choice is also constrained by (what we know of) reality, that is, by the data. But reality (what we know of it) is, I have already argued, inadequate to uniquely determine model choice. The political choice involved may not be the simple choice of one set of assumptions over another but may be located at another level of thought and analysis. In examining the reasoning in support of some hypothesis in a contested area, however, there is some point at which one discovers political commitment. One may choose, for example, which of one's personae will be admitted to the laboratory. From the perspective of one persona, which includes a plethora of related values, beliefs, attitudes and practices, one assumption or model is clearly correct. From the perspective of another, it is not. In doing science we are, therefore, bringing other considerations to bear, implicitly or explicitly, in adopting one or another theoretical perspective.

The feminist theorists mentioned above have focussed on the relation between the content of a theory and female values or experiences, in particular on the perceived congruence between interactionist, wholist visions of nature and a form of understanding and set of values

---

[5] This description of the choice facing scientists presupposes that inquiry is always located in a political context. This follows from understanding knowledge as socially produced. Social processes always have political dimensions.

[6] Compare note 1, above.

widely attributed to women. In contrast, I am suggesting that a feminist scientific practice admits political considerations as relevant constraints on reasoning, which through their influence on reasoning and interpretation shape content. In this specific case those considerations in combination with the phenomena support an explanatory model that is highly interactionist, highly complex. This argument is so far, however, neutral on the issue of whether an interactionist and complex account of natural processes will always be the preferred one. If it is preferred, however, this will be because of explicitly political considerations and not because interactionism is the expression of "women's nature."

The accountability I describe does not demand a radical break with the science one has learned and practiced. The development of a "new" science involves a more dialectical evolution and more continuity with established science than the familiar language of scientific revolutions implies.[7] As I argued in Chapter Four, in order to survive and attract participants any new program of explanation or research must satisfy some of the standards/values characterizing the scientific community within which it is proposed. The gynecentric woman-the-gatherer model in human evolution studies is an example of a model that both expresses an alternative social vision and meets the standards set by the field in which it is proposed. In particular, only frameworks that make possible ordered interactions with a particular scientific subject matter will ever get serious attention.

These remarks about feminist science hold, *mutatis mutandem*, for oppositional or radical science generally. Social political values and interests are encoded differently in different fields and hence engage different oppositional commitments. In some areas, such as the complex of research programs having a bearing on the understanding of human behavior, certain moves, such as the one described above, seem quite obvious. In others it may not be clear how to express an alternate set of values in inquiry, or what values would be appropriate, nor even what the political dimensions of a field are. The first step, however, is to abandon the idea that scrutiny of the data yields a seamless web of knowledge. The second is to think through a particular field and try to understand just what its unstated and fundamental assumptions are and how they influence the course of inquiry. Knowing something of the history of a field is necessary to this process, as is continued conversation with other feminists.

The feminist interventions I imagine will be local, that is, specific to

---

[7] See Laudan (1985) for a gradualist model of scientific change.

a particular area of research; they may not be exclusive, that is, different feminist perspectives may be represented in theorizing; and they will be in some way continuous with existing scientific work. The accretion of such interventions, of science done by feminists as feminists and by members of other disenfranchised groups, has the potential, nevertheless, ultimately to transform the character of scientific discourse.

KNOWLEDGE AND POLITICS

A number of social theorists, as well as science scholars, have developed views about scientific knowledge that bear on the questions discussed here. These ideas have been alluded to or directly discussed in earlier chapters. In this section I will briefly discuss those views and examine how they converge with or diverge from the approach developed here. What will emerge most clearly from these discussions is (1) the tension between epistemological analysis and metaphysical views (in which I include certain social and political principles) and (2) the difficulty of simultaneously critiquing existing or establishment science and pointing towards a new liberatory science. Epistemology cannot be made the basis of a new world view, it can only open the way out of our current ones.

Neo-Marxism

Engels once took pains to argue for a scientific socialism. Marxism provided us, according to Engels, with a scientific analysis of economics and history. Engels and Marx presupposed a certain conception of science, and this sort of argument is not frequently heard these days. Science—as a real historical phenomenon—has become as problematic for Western Marxists as the disciplines of philosophy, economics, and history once were for Marx. A number of radical scientists have in fact mounted critiques of contemporary science that draw their inspiration from Marxist analysis.

These new or neo-Marxist accounts of scientific knowledge are characterized by three main themes. One is that the dystopic applications of modern science—the domination of political life by thermonuclear weapons, new particle beam weapons, and other monsters of annihilation; the control of human potentiality through genetic engineering; the proliferation of toxic wastes from science-based technologies; the displacement of human labor by automation—are not a misuse of socially neutral science but the inevitable result of bourgeois science. A second theme is the rejection of reductionism, which radical scientists take to be characteristic of bourgeois science and partly to blame for the inappropriate technologies. Reductionism reflects the bourgeois interest in centralized control. And a third theme is that a more adequate, even emancipatory, science is possible and that adoption of its methodology will reveal the truths of nature. Thus, contemporary, mainstream science is both morally and socially noxious and a misrepresentation of natural relations and processes.

Hilary Rose and Steven Rose have produced a number of anthologies of radical scientific writing as well as essays of their own calling for an emancipatory science.[8] Such a science, in their view, will have overcome the split between the object and the subject and the rational and the emotional and it will no longer be dominated by instrumental rationality. It will be characterized by democratic social relations, that is, the abandonment of elitism, and its theories will incorporate a dialectical view of nature.[9] Hilary Rose has used women's health clinics as examples of what an emancipatory science and its practice might look like.[10] In these settings work tends to be organized in a collective, egalitarian manner, and knowledge is produced through blending objective and subjective. A woman's own experience of her body is an integral element of the medical knowledge developed in these settings, and the capacity of staff to identify with, rather than detach from, their clients is essential to achieving such integration. Rose and Rose believe that scientific knowledge is progressive, that hypotheses can be confirmed or disconfirmed or, as they put it, can be more or less "in accord with the world's materiality." While they clearly believe that dialectical science will provide a more accurate picture of natural processes, they do not indicate how we might know this to be the case, or why we we should believe it. They seem, that is, to be urging the potential empirical superiority of the dialectical approach but do not offer empirical grounds for thinking it so.

Richard Levins and Richard Lewontin in their book *The Dialectical Biologist* also call for a science that incorporates a dialectical view of nature.[11] Their conception of dialectical science is both displayed in exemplars and explicitly outlined. Their dialectical world view is characterized by two basic ideas: (1) things are internally heterogeneous, so there is no least unit of analysis and (2) the correct division or decomposition of wholes into parts varies depending on what aspect of the whole is being investigated. Levins and Lewontin argue further that

[8] Rose and Rose, eds. (1976, 1979); Dialectics of Biology Group (1982).
[9] Rose and Rose (1982), pp. 50–59.
[10] Rose (1983).
[11] Levins and Lewontin (1985).

the internal heterogeneity of things means that change must be explained in terms of opposing processes united in an object. Evolutionary theory provides one illustration of dialectics in nature. Levins and Lewontin argue that traditional, reductive science sees organisms as produced by selective forces beyond their control—the environment. They propose instead that organisms both make and are made by their environments. Here the whole is a particular ecosystem. Their dialectical approach demands that no element be given sole causal efficacy. Rather these elements—organisms and their environments—are much more complexly related such that each acts upon the other. The changes in the ecosystem of which they are parts depend upon their interactions. The sense in which it is appropriate to speak of opposing processes here is the sense in which the direction of causal influence is reciprocal rather than unidirectional.

. Both of the approaches discussed have in common an unargued, bedrock commitment to a nonreductionist, dialectical view of nature. Not only is this view morally and politically preferable to mainstream and reductionist science but it is truer to nature. Since, however, the scientific methodology acceptable to these analysts is one that presupposes the truth of a dialectical world view, it is not clear that there is any way of finding out whether a reductionist or dialectical science really is truer to nature.

The spirit, therefore, of these analyses might be better served by seeing them as urging a reconception of objects of inquiry in particular fields—specifically as urging their colleagues to abandon questions presupposing unidirectional or linear causal relations and to understand objects as constituted partly of the parts of which they are wholes and partly of the wholes of which they are parts. If this shift could be accomplished on internalist grounds, there would be less struggle over its acceptance. I argued in Chapter Four that proponents of alternative theories must appeal to some standards held by the scientific community that they wish to persuade but that these standards are heterogeneous and can provide grounds for resistance to change as well as grounds for change. Internalist grounds would be drawn from these standards but would not be sufficient to decide the issue, or force the shift. This is particularly so if, for some, the standards include a commitment to a reductionist and linear mode of analysis; that is, if doing science just consists in the analysis of objects conceived atomistically and mechanistically. The relation of a dialectical method to a dialectical world view, then, is that adopting a dialectical world view requires adopting a dialectical method of inquiry. The latter will reveal the complexity of nature understood dialectically. But so will a reductionist methodology reveal the ultimate simplicity of nature conceived atomistically.[12]

According to this analysis, the neo-Marxists are understood as advocating an alternative vision of nature and natural processes largely on moral and sociopolitical grounds. Certain consequences of scientific inquiry on the mainstream model have been (and promise to continue to be) so horrific as to require an alternative. In this regard the neo-Marxists stand on the same ground as the feminist scientist. In order to practice science as a feminist, as a radical, or as a Marxist one must deliberately adopt a framework expressive of that political commitment. This does not mean ceasing to do science but doing science that reveals different relationships. The advocacy of the dialectical method is a call to those who espouse the political commitments of these authors: if you share our political beliefs, here is a way to do science that expresses those beliefs.

Jürgen Habermas

Political and social theorist Jürgen Habermas discusses scientific knowledge explicitly in his early work *Knowledge and Human Interests* and implicitly in his more recent work on communicative pragmatics, particularly in his account of truth.[13] In *Knowledge and Human Interests*, which presents in a formal way his thinking of the early and mid 1960s and which was published in Germany (as *Erkenntis und Interesse*) in 1968, Habermas was concerned with rolling back the claims of positivism. He rejected positivistic scientism on both external and internal grounds. From an external point of view positivism is judged mistaken in its extension of empiricism to the knowledge of persons and of social institutions whose understanding requires interpretation of meaning.[14] From an internal perspective positivism fails its own tests of meaningfulness.[15] Habermas's alternative proposal is that knowledge is constituted by fundamental cognitive human interests and that different kinds of knowledge are constituted by different kinds of interest. These interests are revealed by or discovered in what Habermas calls frames of reference, the ultimate frameworks of justification for knowledge claims. In the appendix to *Knowledge and Hu-*

---

[12] See Taylor (1986) for additional discussion of Levins' and Lewontin's dialectics.

[13] Habermas (1971). My reading of Habermas has benefited greatly from reading McCarthy (1978); Geuss (1981); and "Habermas and Postmodernism" in Jay (1988).

[14] Habermas (1971), pp. 301–308.

[15] Ibid., pp. 71–90.

man Interests the three types of knowledge-constitutive interests are identified as (1) technical, (2) practical, and (3) emancipatory.[16]

In particular, Habermas states that the "empirical-analytic sciences" (presumably mathematics and the natural sciences) are constituted by a technical cognitive interest, that is, an interest in "technical control over objectified processes." An ultimate ground of justification for any mathematical or natural science theory is that it promotes such control. In saying that such a frame of reference or interest establishes rules for the construction of theories and for their testing, Habermas's claims parallel my thesis that certain contextual values are integrated into inquiry as constitutive values.[17] Our examples are similar also— namely the interest in establishing control over and/or predictability of natural phenomena. Habermas seems, however, to suggest, at least in *Knowledge and Human Interests*, that this interest in combination with experience will generate acceptable theories and also that the pre-eminence of this interest is not itself historically constituted but constitutes some sort of transcendental ground of knowledge.[18] I have argued that inquiry is subordinated to human needs in the sense that the sorts of things we need to know about some aspect of phenomena/experience are projected onto the phenomena through the questions constituting our inquiry. The specific forms of these needs develop historically, as do our means of satisfying them. Thus, in the sixteenth and seventeenth centuries the need of Europeans to gain greater control over certain material processes gave rise to the mechanical philosophy, which characterized matter in a particular way. This characterization both permitted certain understandings of the mechanical workings of things to develop and gave moral license to certain heretofore forbidden interactions with the natural world. Habermas' knowledge-constitutive interests, by contrast, are described as transcendental limits that make objectivity (in the natural sciences) possible. If they are subject to historical change, Habermas does not explain how. Nor does he explain what the relation might be between the abstract cognitive interest in technical control or "feedback-monitored action" and particular interpretations of that interest.

Another point of partial convergence concerns the social character of knowledge. In *Knowledge and Human Interests* Habermas claims that the intersubjectivity of a community of investigators is the ground of clarification of metatheoretical problems of the natural sciences.[19]

[16] Ibid., p. 308.
[17] Ibid., p. 309.
[18] Ibid., pp. 307, 311.
[19] Ibid., p. 149.

Such intersubjectivity is possible only through interpretive knowledge, which is distinct from instrumental, technical knowledge, and incorporates a practical interest, that is, an interest in mutual understanding that can ground social action. I have argued, by contrast, for the necessary engagement of intersubjectivity and a multivocal community of scientists in the resolution of theoretical disputes and not just of metatheoretical ones. Habermas's purpose is to show that empirical knowledge (which is required for human, "purposive-rational," action) cannot ground itself and that there must, therefore, be forms of knowledge, defined by correlative cognitive interests, other than the technical-empirical. The ground of purposive action—that is, the knowledge-constitutive interest in technical control—is incomplete, and, argues Habermas, this incompleteness points to the interpretive-hermeneutic knowledge required for understanding others. It is not clear, however, whether this incompleteness as a ground of knowledge is a descriptive incompleteness, that is, a failure to encompass all forms of possible human knowledge, or an analytical incompleteness, that is, a failure to account fully for the instrumental knowledge required for purposive human action.

This ambiguity is not inconsequential, for it prevents us from seeing clearly what the Habermasian account would have us say about the two conflicting approaches to the biology of human behavior discussed in earlier chapters. Would Habermas argue that the hormonal account is an inappropriate (scientistic) attempt to extend the methods of the empirical sciences to an area belonging to the historical-hermeneutical sciences? That it is an instance of the illusion of the completeness of the interest in technical control as a ground of knowledge? Surely if it can be used to predict successfully (within an acceptable margin of error), it cannot be said to be illusory. Would he argue instead that the two approaches are both empirical accounts whose conflict generates a metatheoretical problem? According to this approach, the biology of human behavior remains within the framework of the empirical sciences, but the ground of these sciences, the interest in technical control, is inadequate to decide between competing models. Habermas does not explain how such decisions might be made. Presumably they and similar problems constitute the metatheoretical issues that the community of investigators (scientists) must decide through dialogue. Since one of the questions at issue is the type of control afforded by the two models, it would seem that the knowledge-constitutive interest in technical control is not a sufficient ground but must be given an interpretation in/by a given scientific context. Thus, the extent to which it can constitute what Habermas calls a transcendent ground of knowledge is unclear.

Another way to see this problem is as a challenge to Habermas's view that the domains of knowledge marked out by the several knowledge-constitutive, or cognitive, interests are independent. One could argue that the very possibility of hermeneutic understanding requires that one rather than another biological model be adopted, that is, the one within which it makes sense to ascribe intention and effective subjectivity to oneself and other human beings. This line of argument clearly dissolves the boundaries between technical and practical knowledge. The incursion, however, is not the familiar scientistic appropriation of the practical domain of human interaction but the reverse.

These neo-Kantian concerns with categorization and transcendence have given way in Habermas's later work to a more linguistically based investigation of human interaction.[20] The linguistic approach upon which Habermas builds is the pragmatic philosophy of language of John Austin and John Searle. This later work seems an elaboration of the claim in the earlier work that the intersubjectivity (dialogue) of a community of investigators is the necessary completion of the ground of empirical knowledge. His theory of communicative action includes a theory of truth that is similar to the account of objectivity developed in Chapter Four. This discussion of Habermas's theory is an opportunity, therefore, to reinforce the distinction between objectivity and truth. For Habermas those statements are true to which all participants in an ideal speech situation would agree. An ideal speech situation is one of completely free and uncoerced communication in which all have an equal chance to participate and equal power to impose their views (that is, the power of rational persuasion alone). A number of objections to this analysis of truth are well-known, and I shall mention only the most relevant for my purposes.

Devices similar to the ideal speech situation have been used by other contemporary political philosophers to describe the position from which one's interests as a human being rather than as a member of a particular social class could be identified.[21] However well such devices might work for the identification of real or legitimate interests, that is, for self-ascriptions of some kind, their relevance to other-ascriptions, which scientific assertions of necessity are, is not clear. What guarantees are there that the statements we would agree on in the ideal speech

[20] Habermas (1970a and 1970b).
[21] Rawls (1971) and Dworkin (1977) both use such devices.

situation would be accurate representations of reality? As Mary Hesse has argued, one needs some independent way to discover that those statements about which consensus is reached are indeed true before one can use consensus in an ideal speech situation as a criterion of truth.[22] Indeed one would also need some accounting of the connection between such consensus and truth before relying on consensus in those cases where the independent methods of verification are not in operation.

Matters are not improved by taking consensus to be a definition rather than a criterion of truth. What are we to say about changes in consensus over time? Has the truth of statements changed correspondingly? Just as problematic for a criterion or a definition is the possibility that there be no consensus regarding a particular question. Why should we suppose that we would all eventually come to agree that a particular theory is correct? And does it follow from a lack of consensus that there is no truth of a matter?

Both Habermas's truth and the scientific objectivity discussed above are socially achieved. Objectivity in the social account is, however, independent of truth. It refers not to the representational character of a thesis but to the conditions in which such a thesis becomes accepted. It may be accepted as true, but it does not follow, even in an ideal speech situation, that it really is true. If one understands Habermas not as offering a definition or criterion of truth but as analyzing the conditions under which consensus can be used as a criterion of truth, then it would be a necessary condition that consensus be achieved (or achievable) under the conditions of an ideal speech situation. What is not clear is that it could ever be a sufficient condition.

Habermas's conception of scientific inquiry is still, as Thomas McCarthy has noted, rooted in positivist conceptions of science.[23] Theories in natural science are described as collections of empirical generalizations rather than as attempts to use descriptions of one sort of process to explain other sorts. Habermas accepts a positivist account of natural science and is concerned only to restrict it to natural science. Because the Peircean embellishments, such as emphasis on the communitarian nature of inquiry, are attempts to resolve some of the dilemmas produced by positivism's overextension of empirical methods, they are not developed in a way that responds to epistemological problems arising within the sciences. The general rules of rational speech and inference that could operate in an ideal speech situation are not

[22] Hesse (1980), pp. 206–231.
[23] McCarthy (1978), pp. 60–68.

powerful enough to arbitrate between competing theories and their metaphysical-methodological contexts. Methodologies and rules of inference that permit the articulation of particular theories in relation to bodies of experience and data are specific to particular sociohistorical contexts and cannot be abstracted from those contexts. The alternative, oppositional frameworks discussed in the section on feminist science cannot be accommodated within Habermas's theory of natural science. In trying to clear a space for an autonomous social and critical theory, he has ceded nature to the positivists.

Michel Foucault

On the surface Foucault's writings on science seem not to address at all the concerns of this volume or traditional philosophical questions about the nature of scientific knowledge and understanding generally. His reluctance to theorize "in the grand style" means that we can find few general claims to hold on to or display as Foucault's theory. The implications of his work for the philosophical questions are considerable, however, if not transparently clear. I shall focus on the elimination of the knowing subject and the interconnections of power and knowledge.[24]

The Archeology of Knowledge is a theoretical volume that systematizes the analytic strategies deployed in *The Order of Things*.[25] Foucault develops a formidable armory of technical terms used to describe the emergence of a field of knowledge or scientific discipline. Several themes recur in the stages of his presentation and persist as well in his later work. Foucault is concerned with discourse, that is, with the characteristic ways of talking and writing about a subject matter. He attends to the rules of formation of a discourse, the coemergence of a discourse and its object, and the network of social, political, and economic relations within and upon which the discourse takes shape. This focus on ways of talking about something resembles the linguistic turn in twentieth-century analytic philosophy. It displaces the knowing (or believing) subject from the center of philosophical attention that it occupied from Descartes to Kant and makes questions about how an individual or group of individuals comes to believe or justifies a belief irrelevant. Just as beliefs or statements have no independent existence but are meaningful only in the context of a discursive practice, so the individual must be located in some network of authority and her/his

---

[24] This discussion of Foucault's ideas has benefited from my reading of Dreyfus and Rabinow (1983) and Sheridan (1980).
[25] Foucault (1970, 1972).

position in the network known in order that sense be made of her/his utterance.

Some discourses or "discursive formations" give rise to a science. This occurs when (informal) norms of verification are transformed into formal criteria. This way of seeing the emergence of a science of something requires that we abandon the idea that there is a unique one-to-one correspondence between descriptive sentences and the facts. Instead science, or scientificity, is to be seen as one stage of development of discursive formations: a stage in which norms of verification and coherence are incorporated into a fixed set of formal criteria. The discourse acquires a regimentation and organization such that only those statements that have been subjected to the rules are admissible as (1) worthy of discussion and (2) true or false. These rules, of course, are dependent on their historical context. For Foucault, therefore, the attainment of scientific status is not the shedding of ideology but the enshrinement of ideology in a science. Ideology enters a discursive formation in the rules of formation and norms of verification. Far from an accidental feature of a science, it is at the heart of a science.

The process Foucault describes here involves or can involve two processes discussed above. One is the inclusion of metaphysical—social, economic, political—assumptions among the background assumptions directing reasoning in a field, as the linear-hormonal model facilitating inferences about the causes of behavior incorporates assumptions embedded in what Foucault would call the discursive practices of the field of behavioral neuroendocrinology. The displacement from the center of analytic attention of the individual who knows or believes and its replacement with a focus on the discursive practices through which knowledge is created draws attention to the social character of knowledge production and to the residence of knowledge not in individuals but in their interactions and in the products of those interactions. The second process is the convergence of contextual and constitutive values in the constitution of a field of inquiry, as the social and political needs that require knowledge for their satisfaction direct the kind of knowledge sought and hence specify acceptable forms of solution to cognitive problems.

Our accounts differ in other respects, however. For example, Foucault in his later writings stressed the interaction of power and truth, suggesting, perhaps inadvertently, that inquiry is driven in a singular way by the requirements of power relations.[26] I say "inadvertently" because it may be Foucault's rhetoric and readers that suggest a

[26] Especially Foucault (1977, 1978, and 1980, pp. 78–133).

monolithic science rather than Foucault himself. Nevertheless, when Foucault states that knowledge is essential to power and that the direction in which power or ("biopower") pushes is toward totalizing normalization, he seems to suggest that knowledge and power produce each other in a univocal way.

Is there room in this scheme for other forms of knowledge? I have argued that oppositional science can be pursued at least to a limited extent and that there are areas of inquiry that may remain neutral with respect to power (in some of its forms). While the behavioral neuroendocrinology discussed in earlier chapters is clearly parallel to and coordinated with the bureaucratic drives towards the normalization of certain types, some neurophysiology is neutral with respect to what Foucault calls biopower and can be used in the creation of oppositional sciences. What remains problematic is the extent to which knowledge can successfully oppose or resist cooptive absorption by power. This question may be political and sociological rather than philosophical, however, depending on the possibility of contrary forms of power or, to use alternate terminology, depending on the extent to which alternative needs or interests can provide an organizing focus for alternative or oppositional knowledge. Foucault's forms of resistance seem mute rather than articulate, generated as they are in brute reaction to the physical experience of power. Thus the development of oppositional knowledge in Foucault's view may simply be a realignment of power and not an escape from the drive towards totalizing normalization.

Evelyn Fox Keller

Evelyn Keller has used object relations theory to explain how the natural sciences are permeated by an ideology of domination. Whereas Habermas sees the interest in technical mastery of an object theorized as other as constitutive of the empirical sciences, Keller suggests that it is a deformation of cognitive aims. In her view conceptions of what counts as scientific knowledge are informed by a (mis)understanding of objectivity that has its roots in infantile experience, which is itself shaped by social norms and structures.

Keller develops her argument in *Reflections on Gender and Science* on several different levels, which coexist in some tension with each other.[27] She is, first of all, making a claim that, historically, scientific inquiry is characterized by a plurality of contesting theories as well as contrasting visions of what inquiry should be. In spite of this plural-

[27] Keller (1985).

ism, however, one image of science and one kind of theory have tended to predominate, at least in the modern period. In the prevailing view the aim of science is to achieve objective knowledge, where the criteria of objectivity are emotional distance from and potential control of the object of knowledge. The search for objectivity is thus misidentified, in Keller's view, with the search for control over natural phenomena. As a consequence those theories are accepted which analyze their subject matter as objects or systems of control. Models of self-organization and strong forms of interaction may be proposed, but reductive and mechanistic explanations are consistently privileged by the scientific establishment.

A second strand of her argument has to do with the explanation for this state of affairs. Keller appeals to two convergent phenomena: the metaphoric genderization of scientific inquiry in the seventeenth century and the processes of individual psychological development. The seventeenth century saw a fierce struggle between two approaches to scientific inquiry, some aspects of which were described in Chapter Five. The conception of inquiry that ultimately triumphed was one that, among other things, envisioned the seeker after knowledge as male and the object of knowledge (nature) as female, and which described the activity of inquiry in language used to describe the male pursuit of females: rape and courtship. Keller sees the union (or collapse) of cognitive and affective models as having its origins in the Platonic identification of goodness and truth and hence of the highest form of love with the highest form of knowledge. The seventeenth-century adaptations of this identification appeal to *eros* rather than *phile* and reflect changing conceptions of gender as well. The successful version is a heterosexual fantasy of control and submission that makes science a properly masculine endeavor and made both women and nature appropriate objects of domination.

Because knowledge has thus been given an affective dimension, psychological accounts of emotional development can provide an insight into the absorption of social norms by the emotive structure of individual psyches and their consequent projection into nature as structures of knowledge. Feminist object relations theory provides the analytic tool Keller needs to demonstrate this relationship. Keller distinguishes two sorts of autonomy and, correlatively, of objectivity. Static autonomy is the condition of a self created in opposition to another (in particular, the mother). It is characterized by constant anxiety over the maintenance of the self's boundaries, an anxiety relieved by attempting to control all others who threaten those boundaries. Dynamic autonomy, on the other hand, is the condition of a self created through differentiation from but also relatedness with others. It is characterized by tolerance for ambiguous boundaries and a sense of agency exercised in a context of interacting agents.

These psychological orientations to the world produce corresponding cognitive ideals, expressed as interpretations of objectivity. Objectivity in general is defined by Keller as "the pursuit of a maximally authentic, and hence maximally reliable, understanding of the world around oneself."[28] Static objectivity is a search for knowledge that radically severs subject from object, just as the statically autonomous self is rigidly delineated from others. It is nonreflexive and keeps the self outside the realm of inquiry. Dynamic objectivity, by contrast, "aims at a form of knowledge that grants to the world around us its independent integrity but does so in a way that remains cognizant of, indeed, relies on, our connectivity with that world."[29] The psychological development of male children in this society in general tends to produce individuals characterized by static autonomy, who need to dominate others in order to maintain their own sense of self and identity and whose pursuit of knowledge is the attempt to understand a world of objects radically separate from and different from the self.[30] In Keller's language their pursuit of knowledge is an attempt to understand the natural world through a framework that relieves the (neurotic) anxiety about boundaries. The metaphoric identification of scientific inquiry with men's sexual relations to women, which makes both women and nature objects of domination, facilitates the recruitment into science of those whose ideal of knowledge is characterized by static rather than dynamic objectivity. Thus, scientific inquiry and the theories it produces are permeated by the ideology of domination: the relations among objects of study are typically described in the language of control and domination, and objects of study are characterized in such a way as to make of them proper targets of domination.

Keller's mode of explanation explains how it is that the sciences are, for the most part, directed towards the goal of controlling nature. It is because the persons who become scientists are psychologically ori-

[28] Ibid., p. 116.
[29] Keller (1985), p. 117.
[30] Keller's analysis here inherits a disabling universalism from object relations theory. The family structure within which this psychological profile develops is characteristic only of middle-class families in industrialized societies (and no longer many of them). If these phenomena are restricted to the middle class, then one cannot explain the social predominance of the cognitive ideals without a class-based or class sensitive analysis. If the cognitive ideals are not a class-restricted phenomenon, then the appeal to middle-class family structures is off the mark.

ented to such a goal.[31] But this is not the only point that Keller wishes to establish. She has herself a vision of what scientific inquiry could be. At this third, constructive level of her argument, however, her position becomes less clear. In the third section of *Reflections on Gender and Science* Keller seems to argue for two different, and not necessarily consistent, visions. One argument is a plea for pluralism, expressed most clearly in the Epilogue: "A healthy science is one that allows for the productive survival of diverse conceptions of mind and nature."[32] The contrary voice is the one heard in the chapter on dynamic objectivity and in the introduction to Part III. This voice urges a particular view of nature. Nature has its own integrity, is "orderly in its complexity, rather than lawful in its simplicity."[33] Interactionism, rather than control, is the watchword here. This philosophy of nature is vindicated in two of the case studies in Part III in which reductivist "master molecule" or "pacemaker" models are argued to be inferior to more complex and interactionist alternatives. The view of nature underlying these alternatives is made possible by dynamic rather than static objectivity. Dynamic objectivity provides more adequate and reliable representations of nature than are possible through static objectiviity.

There are two puzzles here. One is raised by the potential contradiction between the call for pluralism and the endorsement of interactionism. Keller's antipathy to relativism leads her to claim that the form of objectivity she endorses produces more reliable understandings of nature. Her respect for the achievements of modern science leads her to plead not for the replacement of current theories by these more reliable ones but for tolerance of diversity in the sciences. This apparent inconsistency could be resolved by saying that dynamic objectivity produces not one but several theoretical perspectives, that is, that there could be many interactionisms. While preserving a limited pluralism, however, this solution excludes mechanistic and reductionist theorizing, an exclusion that seems contrary to the spirit of pluralism and to the gradualism she endorses.

A second puzzle is related to her claims for interactionism and dynamic objectivity. How do we know that interactionist models are, other things equal, more reliable than reductivist or mechanical ones? Keller has given us reasons to think that dynamic objectivity is the cog-

---

[31] This mode of explanation seems to me, nevertheless, incomplete. In Chapter Five I mentioned research suggesting other factors—economic and political—that direct scientific inquiry towards control and mastery of natural processes. See also Longino (1988).

[32] Keller (1985), p. 178.

[33] Ibid., p. 136.

nitive goal of an emotionally undistorted and mature personal orientation to the world. What still requires explaining is the relation of that attitude to truth or reliability. Keller presents dynamic autonomy as an attitude that generates theories and models with certain characteristics. As she herself notes about Barbara McClintock's models of transposition and gene action, reductionistically inclined biologists claim that, in the end, the self-organizing and strongly interactive aspects of McClintock's models can be eliminated or understood in reductionist terms. These aspects of the theory, then, are neither self-evident nor generally viewed as compellingly supported by the data. The decisive reason for accepting them is their consistency with a particular philosophy of nature.

It is at this stage of the argument that Keller's position is most problematic. She has not yet provided the materials to show the inherent superiority of this philosophical approach over competing ones. If we look to *Reflections on Gender and Science*, the best support we could find for this philosophy of nature is that it is the cognitive outcome of a healthy psychological orientation to the world. Keller would undoubtedly reject this as a ground. For what justifies the claim that this orientation (that is, that of dynamic autonomy) is healthy? The answer that it is productive of less neurosis, or psychological pain, is vulnerable to the question raised above, namely what the relationship is between less psychological pain and truth. The answer that it is more conformable to reality begs the question.

One way to escape this dilemma is to detach psychological from epistemological and metaphysical virtues and to portray the interactionist philosophy of nature as an explicit component that is subject to rational criticism and evaluation. This procedure would treat interactionism generally (or, preferably, domain-specific articulations of interactionism or other nonreductionist views) as background assumptions establishing the relationship between certain sorts of observable or experimental phenomena and models and theories of natural processes. As I have argued, arguments about background assumptions are not definitive, and changes in prevailing background assumptions are brought about by changes in the goals of the sciences.

One of the great merits of Keller's discussion is to show how more general philosophical positions are expressed in particular scientific research programs. Her urge to comprehensiveness, however, prevents her from distinguishing between what one might say as a student of the sciences and what one might say as a scientist or philosopher of nature. In the first capacity one might argue for pluralism as the most reasonable position from an epistemological point of view. In the second capacity one must work within some framework, and a commitment to pluralism can only undermine one's implicit claim to correctness. A particular view put forward among others in a pluralistic context must be defended by arguments other than those supporting the context itself.

Donna Haraway

Historian of science Donna Haraway has been engaged in a very detailed study of twentieth-century primatology.[34] She situates her work in what she describes as a global oppositional movement to retell the Western origin stories that rationalize European economic and cultural imperialism. Primatology is the focus of her analysis because "the scientific practices and discourses of modern primatology participate in the preeminent political act in western [sic] history: the construction of Man."[35] As do other ideas belonging to political discourse, like freedom and equality, our ideas about what is just depend critically on our assumptions about human nature. The study of apes and monkeys, like the biology of behavior, is one attempt to define what is natural in that nature. Haraway establishes this thesis in two ways. One is to show the direct connection between the research programs of leaders in the field such as Robert Yerkes in the 1920s and Sherwood Washburn in the 1960s and 1970s and explicitly political agendas. Conference sponsorship, funding, and correspondence are all examined to demonstrate this connection. The other is through an analysis of primatological discourse. The texts of primatology reveal a recurrent obsession with otherness, boundaries, and origins and continually cast their subject matter in the language and categories of political economy. This second internal line of argument intersects more closely with the philosophical questions of knowledge and understanding, and in the following discussion I shall attend more closely to it than to the external argument.

Haraway's dissections of primatology are dense essays in politics and science that use the analytic techniques of deconstruction and narrative theory to support a reading of science as politics and science as culture. I will attempt to outline the view I read in this work in order to establish the points of connection with the philosophical issues discussed above.

Haraway, first of all, sees the sciences not only as a legitimator of

[34] This discussion draws on Haraway (1978, 1979, 1981–1982, 1985a, 1985b, 1988).

[35] Haraway (1985b), p. 489.

domination but as a resource for those who resist. The sciences, therefore, are neither univocal nor simplistic impositions of cultural mythology upon the natural world. Primatology in the twentieth century has in fact become increasingly sophisticated methodologically. Distinctions between the validity of observations made in the wild compared to those made of animals in captivity are only the beginning. A number of field workers, among them many women such as Jeanne Altmann, pioneered the development of protocols for the nontendentious (less anthropomorphic) description of primate behavior. Haraway presents primatology as governed by methodological (constitutive) rules that determine what counts as good science in primate studies—rules, however, that are negotiated and renegotiated in the actual practice of this field.

Good science is, however, not equivalent to objectivity. However rule-governed and technical the basic data gathering may be, the field's discourse is nevertheless characterized by metaphoric systems and what Haraway calls "core narratives" that both direct observations and serve to interpret them. The individual primate and the primate troop are constituted as objects of knowledge by these metaphoric systems, which mediate researchers' interactions with their objects of study. The effect of this metaphoric constitution is that, even though the apes and monkeys are the same organisms, as the conceptual system changes, so does the object of knowledge. What the researchers have "really" been investigating are systems of production characterized by internally generated principles of control. They use the data of primate behavior to work out how a natural system such as an individual organism or population of such organisms instantiates such principles. It is for this reason that it would be inappropriate to speak of a metaphor *simpliciter*. For the concepts from one domain are not simply transferred to the subject matter of another in order to explain the latter. Rather, the object of inquiry remains the first domain, whose scope has been extended to include the second.

Haraway's most dramatic demonstration of her claim about the "true" subject matter of primatology involves showing how the conceptual-metaphoric system of the discipline has changed. Organisms in the nineteenth and early twentieth century were described as systems of production and reproduction whose chief organizing principle was a hierarchical division of labor. Thus the concern with dominance in primate troops. The question is how dominance hierarchies are generated in a population or subpopulation—what sorts of interactions among the animals (aggression, competition) lead to their emergence. During and after World War II the study of organisms was partly absorbed by information science; organisms came to be studied as if they were information-generating and information-processing systems.[36] Organisms came to be described as systems of biotic components, and fields such as genetics and immunology, which are most concerned with coding, moved to the center of biology. Other fields, including, importantly, animal behavior, became recast in cybernetic language. The science is still about systems of production, but the kind of system has changed. The organism/population is no longer a factory but an information-processing system. The change, of course, has to do with changes in the political economy, in its transformation by electronic engineering into a massive electronic network. The major innovations in production, robotics, and genetic engineering are exercises of coding and decoding. As Haraway says in one of her articles, the artificial, counternatural character of the objects of knowledge in information science makes suspect the natural character of the familiar organismic categories they've replaced.[37] One is just as historically conditioned as the other. This is not to say that one or both are unnatural but that the natural is not an unconditioned given. Animal ethology never was about the animals directly, unmediated by conceptual or metaphoric structures that construct an object of knowledge, but about systems the animals were taken to instantiate.

Haraway is less concerned with the epistemological questions raised by her analysis, or with providing a method that could be applied elsewhere, than with decoding and deconstructing the specific texts of primatology—disclosing the ways in which they retell the story of male and white ("technologically advanced," "rational") development and superiority or, in some cases, tell a new story—of female activity and power, of cooperative societies conquered and coopted by aggressive ones, of resistance and sabotage, and so on. She herself describes her work as "about the social production of artifacts and meanings."[38] While her narratological analytic framework is superficially indifferent to the traditional questions of philosophers of science, Haraway's account of the subject matter of primatology should stimulate philosophers to new accounts of explanation and theories. In addition, the particular textual readings she offers suggest ways of analyzing the logic of those texts. It is possible, for instance, to bring the apparatus of theory-laden and "story-laden" observation and background assumption to bear on them to see with the help of Haraway's readings

36 Haraway (1979 and 1981–1982).
37 Haraway (1985a), pp. 80–81.
38 Haraway (personal communication).

where description and where reasoning are shaped by the political, economic, and cultural contexts within which these primatological inquiries take place. The approaches are complementary rather than contradictory.

Whatever the potential harmony of analytic methods, in some of her early work Haraway has expressed disdain, if not outright contempt, for the rhetoric of truth and objectivity that is the mark of scientific texts.[39] And indeed given the degree of dissent and variability that characterizes animal behavioral fields such as primatology, a suspicion of such rhetoric is highly appropriate. It does leave those who would try to draw epistemological lessons from her analysis either in a quandary or in the quagmire of relativism.[40] The quandary results, of course, from attending to her claims about the value of the sciences. One presumes it is different from the value of literature, but the extraction of meaning from scientific texts by the methods of literary analysis obscures what distinctive value the activities that produce such texts might have. Haraway seems to recognize this in a recent essay.[41] Only objectivity-as-transcendence or what Haraway calls "the God trick" is rejected now. She urges in its place a self-aware partiality.[42] Knowledge is always knowledge in a situation, from a certain point of view. It is, therefore, both incomplete and perspectival. Objectivity is recognition of the local, mediated, situated, and partial character of one's knowledge.

This position is, on the face of it, ambiguous. If the recognition is the recognition by an individual, then the knowledge characterized as objective could still be an individual's knowledge, or beliefs. Haraway urges another reading. The recognition of partiality is a recognition of the "historical location of discourses, tools, and 'subjects.' "[43] Subjects come into being in social fields of meaning, and discourses are themselves social. Partiality in this sense involves the potential of connection with other discourses to generate other partial and mutable systems of understanding. I have argued that scientific knowledge is the result of complex processes of criticism, modification, and incorpora-

[39] Haraway (1978), p. 59.

[40] Sandra Harding, for example, draws the following lesson from Haraway (1985a): "Haraway's argument would lead to an epistemology that justifies knowledge claims only insofar as they arise from enthusiastic violations of the founding taboos of Western humanism"; Harding (1986), p. 193. This seems to read Haraway as saying "anything goes, as long as it is in revolt against the dominant culture's founding principles."

[41] Haraway (1988).

[42] Ibid., p. 589.

[43] Haraway (personal communication).

tion, that is, of the transformative interrogation of ingredients that are themselves socially produced, if also individually claimed. It is not the individual recognition of partiality or, as used to be said, of one's subjectivity but the subjection of hypotheses and theories to multivocal criticism that makes objectivity possible. While the first reading is at variance with the position for which I have argued, the second is more compatible with it: reflexivity is communitywide, and the openness of partial knowledge facilitates transformation.

CONCLUSION

All the thinkers discussed in this chapter agree that human interests have played a crucial role in the construction of scientific knowledge to date. They differ about the kinds of interests and their exact mode of operation, and even more starkly about the possibility of a new science and the epistemological merits of such a science. Both Keller, in at least one of her voices, and the Marxists write as though the problem is method. Thus, adopting the right method—whether it be dialectical as for Levins and Lewontin or interactionist and attentive to difference as for Keller—will enable us to develop a better (more true?) account of natural phenomena. Natural phenomena are held to possess an intrinsic order whose understanding requires a proper key. Foucault's and Haraway's concerns with the mutual constitution of knowledge and power make them much more skeptical both of the prospect of a right method and of a new, epistemologically superior science or set of sciences. The creation of local and partial discourses responsive to alternative and oppositional values may produce something like knowledge, but they would deny the possibility of knowledge detached from particular points of view. There is in fact the whiff of an accusation of bad faith in Haraway's critical discussion of replacement projects. To seek a unified, if different, knowledge of the natural and social worlds is to seek power of the sort we reject when exerted over ourselves. The goals driving the search for such knowledge are unworthy of an emancipatory politics.

While I think it right to be suspicious of such projects, their rejection leaves unanswered the question of how the human species will or can address the global problems that require informed action. The various degradations of the environment, from the destruction of the world's rain forests to the evaporation of the ozone layer, pose technical and political problems. So does the need for clean and renewable energy sources. These are not problems from whose consideration we can excuse ourselves on political grounds, for we will all be affected by whatever actions (including inaction) are taken. Thus, while Habermas's analysis of the natural sciences is the least satisfactory, his insistence that some form of the traditional notion of knowledge must be retained seems responsive to the very real problems of how we as a species are to survive into the next centuries. So, too, is the insistence of the feminist scientist on developing a biology of thought and action consonant with a democratic politics in which women are full participants.

In thinking about the possibility of a feminist science I drew on elements of the analysis provided in earlier chapters to conclude that one could practice science as a feminist by (1) recognizing the ways in which the background assumptions of mainstream science facilitated certain conclusions and excluded others and (2) deliberately using background assumptions appropriately at variance with those of mainstream science. This kind of feminist science, or more generally of oppositional science, is always local and respectful of some of the standards of a specific scientific community. And it requires a mainstream or established tradition to which it is opposed and with which it is in some form of dialectical tension. Can oppositional science be transformed into successor or new science? Only a change in the social relations of the context in which science is done can effect such a transformation. Thus, which among any set of oppositional or muted scientific voices becomes the new science depends on what social relations and associated cognitive needs characterize a changed context. While eschewing the concept of a single truth or the hope of a singular epistemological blessing, we can nevertheless rank theories as to their acceptability, in particular their worthiness as bases for collective action to solve common problems. That theory which is the product of the most inclusive scientific community is better, other things being equal, than that which is the product of the most exclusive. It is better not as measured against some independently accessible reality but better as measured against the cognitive needs of a genuinely democratic community. This suggests that the problem of developing a new science is the problem of creating a new social and political reality.

CHAPTER 10

Conclusion: Social Knowledge

THE VIEW of scientific knowledge and reasoning that I have developed and applied in this book turns out to be an empiricist one. It is, however, a modest, pared down empiricism, one that shuns metaphysical meaning postulates and restricts itself to epistemology: what we can know is what we can experience. While modest, it is nevertheless a powerful tool for the analysis of the truth claims scientific inquiry. In this final chapter I will develop the implications of the analyses of the previous chapters, raise some of the broader questions regarding science and values, and indicate some of the directions for further research.

CONTEXTUAL EMPIRICISM

Overview

I have set out to address several related questions. Is there an account of scientific reasoning and knowledge that enables us to make sense of scientific debates involving both ideology and evidence? Is there a place for other than epistemic values in science? Can we make philosophical sense of the idea of socially constructed knowledge? To what extent can scientific research be a neutral arbiter of disputes about human nature? In particular, what can the biological sciences tell us about gender? Of current views about the relation between science and social values, neither the approach that ascribes value-laden science to methodological inadequacies nor the approach that admits all values by denying the power or relevance of methodologies provides satisfactory answers to these questions.

In developing an alternative answer I focus on the cognitive practices in science, particularly on reasoning between data and hypotheses, that is, evidential reasoning. Treating reasoning as a practice reminds us that it is not a disembodied computation but takes place in a particular context and is evaluated with respect to particular goals. I argued that evidential reasoning is always context-dependent, that data are evidence for a hypothesis only in light of background assumptions that assert a connection between the sorts of thing or event the data are and the processes or states of affairs described by the hypotheses. Background assumptions can also lead us to highlight certain aspects of a phenomenon over others, thus determining the way it is described and the kind of data it provides. Background assumptions are the means by which contextual values and ideology are incorporated into scientific inquiry. While not all such assumptions encode social values, their necessity to evidential reasoning means that the basic components of methodologies—logic and observation—are not sufficient to exclude values from proper inquiry. The role of background assumptions, however, poses a new problem. Scientific inquiry is not characterized by the expression of a multitude of individual subjective preferences. If scientific inquiry is to provide knowledge, rather than a random collection of opinions, there must be some way of minimizing the influence of subjective preferences and controlling the role of background assumptions.

The social account of objectivity solves this problem. The role of background assumptions in evidential reasoning is grounds for unbridled relativism only in the context of an individualist conception of scientific method and scientific knowledge. If our conception of the methods of knowledge construction in science is broadened to embrace the social activities of evidential and particularly conceptual criticism, we see how individual subjective preferences are minimized in the final products. The background assumptions that determine evidential reasoning are those that emerge from the transformative interrogation by the scientific community (or a sufficient part of it). This means that community values may well remain embedded in scientific reasoning and research programs. Social interactions determine what values remain encoded in inquiry and which are eliminated, and thus which values remain encoded in the theories and propositions taken as expressing scientific knowledge at any given time. Values are not incompatible with objectivity, but objectivity is analyzed as a function of community practices rather than as an attitude of individual researchers towards their material or a relation between representation and represented.

The social values that persist in science can influence research in a number of ways, as outlined in Chapter Five. Turning to the research on biological bases of human sex differences, we can see that both reasoning and observation (or data description) are affected. Many commentators have pointed out that the different value we place on masculinity and femininity results in the ascription of deficits to women, when what is at issue is simply difference. As I explain in Chapter Six, both the bivalent classification of gonadal hormones and the bivalent classification of behavior are influenced by the assumptions of sexual dimorphism and sexual essentialism.

While the classificatory labels used are context-dependent, the correlations of the phenomena so classified are a function of what happens: what the prenatal hormone exposures are and what behaviors characterize the child, adolescent, or adult. While there is not a perfect correlation between exposure and behavior, assuming the observations have been properly carried out, there is a statistically significant bipolar clustering. What are we entitled to infer from these correlations? I showed in Chapter Seven that a particular explanatory model functions as a background assumption in light of which correlations of prenatal hormone levels with later behavior serve as evidence for hypotheses about the causal influence of those hormones on that behavior via hormonal organization of the brain. The selectionist model of higher brain development and function provides an alternative account of the role of the brain in behavior and makes possible a quite different interpretation of the correlational data. First of all, the degree of individual variation becomes more important and the clustering around sexually dimorphic poles a more peripheral feature of the data. Secondly, the clustering itself can be explained by (and is evidentially relevant to) hypotheses about the role of ideals of personhood in the development of personality, behavior, and so on. Thus, only in light of some background assumption can we infer anything interesting from the correlations.

Two quite different pictures of human nature are embedded in these two biological approaches. In the research focussed on the role of hormones, the object of inquiry is a hormone-driven system, which comes in two basic (and complementary) types—male and female. The vision of human nature underlying this work is one of well-defined gender and sex role dimorphism and of personality, behavior, and cognitive capacities limited, even prescribed, by physiology. In the second model the object of inquiry is the brain as material enabler of complex cognitive processes and achievements. The vision of human nature underlying this work is one of multipotentiality, both in regard to those aspects of behavior and personality related to sex (and to reproduction) and in regard to other dimensions of thought and consciousness. The self emerges from the complex interactions of the human organism with its social and physical environment. In the first approach fundamental aspects of the self are the expression of patterns inscribed in the developing fetal brain. In the second the self is potentially more dynamic and active in its own construction. Many critics of the first approach have confined their critiques to the assumptions of gender and sex essentialism informing the work. The detailed comparison of the hormonal research program with the alternative program brings out the equally important role of linear and deterministic assumptions about human behavior and action, assumptions that must be made in order to apply the linear-hormonal model to humans.

The normative dimensions of these assumptions are spelled out in Chapter Eight. Many critics have condemned the sexism and androcentrism of the hormonal research. I believe that the research not only reflects the values, such as sexual essentialism, of its social context but that it strengthens them. The ideal of gender dimorphic personhood is reinforced and most varieties of sex and reproduction-related behaviors treated as pathological, as targets for suppression or "treatment." Bringing out the role of the linear explanatory model in this research demonstrates that the ideological implications of research on brain and behavior extend beyond gender ideology to concepts central to political democracy. Ideals like responsibility and liberty are subverted by the assumptions of the hormonal research. Pfaff's account of moral judgment as confusion of self and other vividly demonstrates this subversion. The more interactive account of brain development places control of action back in the individual's (in part socially formed) consciousness, thus making it possible to treat the varieties of sex-related behavior as aspects of human diversity. It also makes possible an account of human action within which it makes sense to speak of individual autonomy and responsibility. Neither the scientism of the positivists and scientific realists nor the relativism of the wholists provides a satisfactory understanding of the normative dimensions of this research. Only the contextualist approach enables us to pull the research apart to show the relation between its empirical and its assumptive foundations without denying the importance of either one.

The contextualist approach also makes it clear that the question of whether social values can play a positive role in the sciences is really the wrong question. Social and contextual values do play a role, and whether it is positive or negative depends on our orientation to the particular values in question. The feminist scientist, or the radical scientist, cannot simply try to be sensitive to the politically noxious values embedded in some research programs or try to avoid ideology by sticking to the data. "Letting the data suggest" is a recipe for replicating the mainstream values and ideology that feminist and radical scientists reject. The contextualist approach indicates that it is counterproductive to try to split oneself into different selves, doing different tasks—a scientist here, a political actor there, perhaps an aesthete over there. Scientific inquiry is not detached in the requisite manner from the social, political, and cultural contexts that support it.

To express this in terms of the questions posed in the first chapter, science is not a culturally autonomous activity. Furthermore, the question of the integrity of science is misconceived. The intellectual practices of observation and reason do not exist in a purified form. When purged of assumptions carrying social and cultural values, they are too impoverished to produce scientific theories of the beauty and power that characterize even the theories we do have. If we understand integrity not as purity but as wholeness, the integrity of the scientist is honored when she permits her values to play a role in her scientific work. This role is not to overwhelm the observational and experimental data but to guide interpretations and suggest models within which the data can be ordered and organized. A greater recognition of the role of social processes (for example, of criticism) in knowledge construction as well as of the role of background assumptions in mainstream science might encourage the individual researcher to take more risks in her interpretations. This, of course, requires a communitywide acknowledgment of these aspects of knowledge construction with a consequent loosening of the pressure for individual conformity. One further outcome of such a process may be, of course, the development of new classifications of and relations among observational data as well as the production of new observational and experimental data.

I call this view of scientific knowledge contextual empiricism. It is empiricist in treating experience as the basis of knowledge claims in the sciences. It is contextual in its insistence on the relevance of context—both the context of assumptions that supports reasoning and the social and cultural context that supports scientific inquiry—to the construction of knowledge. This form of empiricism is further distinguished from positivist forms of empiricism in that it is a thesis about knowledge only, not about meaning. Thus observational and experimental terms do not provide a semantic foundation for theoretical language. Nor does theoretical language do the same for observational language. Thus, while contextual empiricism insists upon the relevance of background assumptions in reasoning and the analysis of observational data, it does not collapse into wholism. Theory and experience are inferentially, not semantically, related.

Contextual empiricism does distinguish the empirical—observational and experimental—dimension of science from the theoretical dimension, particularly insofar as our access to truth is concerned. Because evidential reasoning is context dependent, the hypotheses that are supported by a given body of data will change as the context of assumptions changes. As we have no other access to the purported entities, processes, and relations, there is no possibility of our knowing in any absolute sense whether they are true. On the other hand, contrary to the claims of relativists it does not follow that all claims are similarly context relative, or that their context dependence has the same epistemic consequences. In particular, our observational judgments (about data) will change in different ways. We may adjust the meanings of terms by introducing new subcategories where before there was one, or by redefining terms. After such changes new or different observational claims will be made, but because meanings have changed, earlier judgments are not so much contradicted as set aside. The same judgments would be made were the earlier meanings to be retained. Our observational judgments may also shift in centrality. In the context of assumptions of sexual dimorphism the clustering of individuals around sexually dimorphic poles is a significant aspect of the data. In the context of assumptions about the intentional character of behavior and the role of complexly interacting cognitive, environmental, and physiological factors in the development of gender and sex role behavior, the degree of individual variation in the data becomes more central than the degree of bipolar clustering.

Knowledge and Experience

The distinction between observation and theory, between observational language and statements and theoretical language and statements is not drawn over a fixed boundary. Observational and theoretical terms acquire and retain their meanings just like other nonscientific terms do. Thus neither category serves as the semantic foundation for the other. Moreover, the role particular experiences or observations serve in the epistemic foundation for hypotheses and theories depends on the context within which evidential assessments are made. The boundary between the description of our experience and the cognitive structures we develop to explain and systematize that experience shifts over time. It may best be drawn in a communicative context. A group of particle theorists speaking among themselves may describe the squiggles on a sheet of photographic paper as the bombardment and disintegration of a certain particle. When speaking in a context that includes members of other scientific and intellectual disciplines or the "lay public," they will more precisely describe the squiggles as photographic representations of the (ionized) traces left in a gas (presumably) by disintegrating particles. What is observational and what is theoretical changes depending on what can be contested or what can be taken for granted. It must be remembered, however, that the use of language from theory to describe experimental results is an achievement of interpretation and not a simple reading from nature; an interpretation, moreover, that could conceivably change with suitable changes of theory.

Experience itself must be rethought as an interactive rather than a passive process. The classical empiricist view of mutually independent sense data presenting themselves to a receptive mind that responds to the resemblances among them has been in disrepute for some time. Our experience is a product of the interaction of our senses, our conceptual apparatus, and "the world out there." It is also a function of what aspects of "the world out there" we choose or are directed by intellectual or other commitments to interact with. There is always much more going on about us than we are aware of, not just because some of it is beyond our sensory thresholds or behind our backs but because in giving coherence to our experience we by necessity select out some facts and ignore others. In addition, as I argued in Chapter Three, any of the reality experienced at a given time is susceptible to a variety of descriptions. Philosophers have developed persuasive arguments to the effect that the search for a privileged level of description is futile, and I shall not repeat them. The point to be stressed here is that what constitutes "our world" is not a given but a product of the interaction between the external material reality that is "the world" and our own pragmatic and intellectual needs.

The subject of experience, the individual, is a nexus of interpretation coming into existence at the boundary of nature and culture. What we contribute to the structure of experience can change over time, as the cultures in which our sensory capacities develop and are educated change. These capacities seem to be transparent transmitters of information from the external world until juxtaposition with another version of the same state of affairs reveals their opacity—their role in the formation of experience. The existence of dominance structures in primate troops seems obvious until a different way of describing the interactions reveals that dominance is an interpretation of social interactions facilitated by the researchers' assumptions and expectations about social behavior.

Loosening up the experiential/theoretical boundary need not, however, and should not lead us to unbridled relativism. We are not forced to admit that anything goes. What we experience at a given time and place can be described and measured in conventionally fixed ways. Once we say of a mark on a gauge that it represents 10 units of a measure, we cannot read it as 7 or 13 without the consent of those with whom we need to communicate about the gauge and without changing other descriptions related to those of the gauge. It is neither our desires, nor beliefs, nor values, nor social conventions that make a gauge register a 10 when employed in measurement but processes independent of those cultural phenomena. That we describe what has happened as attaining degree 10 rather than being intense, or having a certain density or color, or any of the other things we might say *is* a social matter: a function of the language and instruments available and the kind of information we deem it important to have.

Whether we are reading an instrument or observing a troop of baboons, there is always some minimal level of description of the common world to which we can retreat when our initial descriptions of what is the same state of affairs differs. By retreating to that level (or attempting to) we discover where our inferences differ and where our experiences (structured by culture, social position, et cetera) differ. This level may vary from context to context, but without such a minimum level of commonality to which participants in a communicative context can commit themselves, the differences whose discovery may push us to relativism cannot even be discovered. What Aristotle said of Protagoras still holds. As in the distinction between observational and theoretical, however, no absolute or privileged level can be identified as that to which all rational, or human, or effectively communicative beings must subscribe.

This view of experience and the constraints it places on justifiable belief leads to a minimalist form of realism. There is a world independent of our senses with which those senses interact to produce our sensations and the regularities of our experience. There is "something out there" that imposes limits on what we can say about it. Once we have decided on a system for measuring movement, the speed of an object is not arbitrary. The sorts of things we measure, however, will change as our needs, interests, and understanding change. The processes that occur in the world will continue regardless of changes in our descriptive systems. Indeed, it is that very constancy that enables us to develop a descriptive system at all, let alone one with the precision and detail to which we are accustomed. The reliability of such systems lies not in their ability to transparently represent the natural world as it is "in itself" but in the fact that the gradations and changes in parameters of a system match gradations and changes in the natural world. The fact that not all changes and gradations can be encompassed by any given system and that the changes and gradations that are important to us change over time is one of the phenomena driving scientific change.

Knowledge and Values

The notion of the intrinsic value neutrality of the sciences is, therefore, built on inadequate notions of experience, of inference, and of the inquiring subject. As I argued in Chapter Four, however, it doesn't follow that the sciences are completely determined by contextual values. Constitutive values provide a check on the role of contextual values and cultural assumptions. These constraints include empirical and conceptual evaluation of assumptions. What I have argued is that the practices of observation and inference cannot be structured so as to eliminate contextual values without severely truncating the explanatory ambitions of the sciences. Indeed, our needs and desires for certain kinds of knowledge structure the objects about which we seek knowledge.

The processes that are available to minimize the influence of values, such as intersubjective criticism, are only partially effective barriers. While they can make visible and available for consideration (and adoption or rejection) some value-laden assumptions, those shared by all members of the scientific community will remain hidden. Such assumptions build commonly held values into the accepted background in the context of which data are evaluated and inferences are made and thus hide those values from scrutiny. Struggles to exclude would-be scientists from the professional scientific community, represented, for example, by the conflict of mechanicists against seventeenth-century hermeticists, of experimentalists against proponents of *Naturphilosophie* in the nineteenth century, and of biological mechanicists against organicists in the twentieth century, are, among other things, battles to reduce the number of formative assumptions, thus stabilizing the object of inquiry and enabling the development of theory under a unifying or unified and eventually transparent set of values.

Philosophical methodology of science is less influential on scientific practice than on how scientists and the rest of us think about that practice and its products. It licenses certain kinds of argumentative moves and not others, and it can blind us to certain features of scientific inquiry while highlighting others. Some aspects of inquiry are such that general awareness of them can hinder scientific development. Methodologies that hide these aspects may from some points of view, therefore, serve a useful function.

In particular, the knowledge-extending mission of science requires that its critical mission be blocked. Were the critical dimension of science not controlled, inquiry would consist in endless testing; endless new proposals and new ideas would be subjected to critical scrutiny and rejected. However, pragmatic-epistemic needs, that is, what we need to know the truth about, and metaphysical assumptions derived from such needs as well as from social experience and aspiration provide stabilizing frameworks for the selection and interpretation of data. They provide a characterization of the objects under study that is reflected in the questions asked about those objects. Thus explanations can be developed and systematic accounts of phenomena can bring them under the umbrella of a few unifying concepts. These acounts are not any wholesale imposition of theory on data. Rather they represent the outcome of a complex and intricate interaction between framework and experience. While the selection and highlighting of some observational and experimental data over others is framework or context dependent, the hypotheses generated must fit that data to be acceptable. The modification and adjustment of hypotheses is accomplished through the social interactions among scientists described in Chapter Four. What emerges from this process is knowledge as it is represented in textbooks and the claims taken as proved in a given community. The transformation of an idea into scientific knowledge has the effect of purging it of idiosyncratic features of its initial proponents. This gives it an impersonalism often misinterpreted as objectivity. It is not the impersonality, however, but the collaborative social process of transformative interrogation that makes it objective. And while the marks of individuals may be eliminated by this process, the marks of the culture are not.

The systematic and unifying treatment of phenomena enables us to interact with the natural world with reliable expectations. A methodology that legitimates the stabilization of inquiry thus serves some constitutive ends of knowledge seeking. It must also, however, subordinate science's critical function in order to avoid the endless testing and constant generation of new explanatory frameworks that would subvert knowledge extension, and it must disguise that subordination to deflect the accusation that the sciences are not after all concerned with truth. One way to achieve this disguise is through the adoption of an account that minimizes the need for and role of criticism beyond hypothesis testing, that is, by an account that can render invisible the role of background assumptions. The methodologies associated with logical positivism did render them invisible, which is, I suspect, one reason they remain persuasive among scientists even after being abandoned by philosophers. If there are no background assumptions, there is no need to examine, criticize, or replace them. If there are such assumptions and we deny their existence, they become enshrined and all the more powerful for being invisible. Ironically, therefore, a conception of knowledge and inquiry developed in part to overcome the weight of tradition in favor of facts has become identified with a conservative tendency within the sciences.

The myth of scientific value neutrality that is a consequence of the more general view that scientific inquiry is independent of its social context is, thus, a functional myth. It clears the way, conceptually, for the elaboration of a particular approach to a set of phenomena once that approach has attracted the consensus of a significant portion of the relevant scientific community. This makes it possible to adjust a framework or the theories and hypotheses generated under its aegis to the brute facts. Viewed from another angle, however, the myth is clearly dysfunctional. By concealing the reliance of inquiry on a background of assumptions of very mixed character, it discourages the investigation of alternative frameworks. Those who might otherwise be inclined to do so, in the spirit of free inquiry, are dissuaded by a combination of related phenomena: from the desire to be a "good," effectively orthodox scientist to the lack of attention accorded nonmainstream ideas. As Feyerabend might say, we are deprived of the new insights and new knowledge that can only come from bucking the trend. What I argued in particular for feminist science in the previous chapter can be made more general: if the assumptions shaping our inferences are hidden, we will not see the level at which we might entertain and seriously develop new ideas.

In addition, the myth of value neutrality seriously disempowers the lay consumer of science. Because science-based technologies play an ever increasing role in our lives, whether in our homes and workplaces, or as "neighbors" in the form of toxic disposal sites or nuclear power stations, we are increasingly dependent on sophisticated methods of inquiry to know certain seemingly elementary facts: whether the contraceptives, pesticides, and other chemicals we use will have or have had deleterious effects on our health. It is crucial to understand the technical—biological, chemical, statistical—dimensions of such inquiry, but unless we also understand the ways in which contextual interests can shape inquiry, we will be unable to be properly critical of studies purporting to blame or exonerate these concomitants of modern industrial life.

REDUCTIONISM AND ANTIREDUCTIONISM IN BIOLOGY AND EPISTEMOLOGY

Historians and philosophers of science have noted the continual tension between reductive and nonreductive explanatory strategies and consequent metaphysics. The reductive strategy has been dominant in the more visible fields of science and in our conception of the sciences. This has not, however, meant the elimination of but rather the muffling of dissenting voices. Radical scientists in particular have made a variety of stands against reductionism in the sciences. Such a position is not unique to them, however, making crucial the kind of antireductionist argument that one adopts.

The arguments developed in this book run counter to several reductionist tendencies in the sciences and their philosophies. In arguing that the linear-hormonal model is not the only way to interpret the biological and behavioral data, I am blocking two related reductionist moves in biology. One is a metaphysical reductionism, the other a theoretical reductionism. In arguing for the social character of scientific knowledge and for the necessary involvement of social interests in the construction of that knowledge, I am rejecting epistemological reductionism. Not all antireductionisms are alike, and I wish to close the book with some brief remarks on the implication of the preceeding arguments for the reductionism debate.

Reductionism in the Sciences

Reductionism is both a methodological practice and a metaphysical view. Methodologically, reductionism is the practice of characterizing a system or process in terms of its smallest functional units. Metaphysical or ontological reductionism argues that those smallest functional units are what is real and that all causal processes can ultimately be understood as a function of interactions among these least bits. Methodological reductionism is often very useful in guiding researchers to the mechanisms or material constituents of a process. The biochemical analysis of metabolic processes is certainly a positive result of methodological reductionism. Metaphysical reductionism, however, conflates the pragmatic successes of local applications of methodological reductionism with both a guarantor of truth and the promise of universal reducibility.

In Chapter Seven I described the selectionist model of higher brain function as strongly interactive in contrast with the at best weakly interactive character of the linear-hormonal model. The hormonal model exemplifies reductionist theorizing in at least two ways. Human action is understood as mechanical reactions that can be described and classified independently of an agents' intentions or beliefs about the world or of a social network in which actions receive meaning. This descriptive reductionism facilitates an explanatory reductionism that treats the behavior ultimately as a straightforward outcome of fetal physiological processes, processes involving simple constituents of the organism. The kind of causality involved is a simple mechanistic causality that permits only additive interactions with other (environmental) phenomena. Intentional and social dimensions of action and behavior are eliminated. This permits a metaphysical reductionism that locates all causally significant processes in the simplest constituents of the organism.

In the less complex animals behavioral dispositions are thought to be produced simply by hormones acting on the developing brain. We are, therefore, considering a system driven by prenatal physiological factors only—external or social factors act merely as stimuli. Biological theories of human behavior and behavioral dispositions (at least those related to sex and gender) are to be shaped by that template. What is highlighted as the salient biological factor is the prenatal hormonal organization of the brain.

But even the animal model that grounds the linear-hormonal model is achieved by reductionist simplification. Goldfoot and Neff, in the paper cited earlier, have noted the importance of such social factors as birth order and maternal behavior in the expression of rough and tumble play by young rhesus monkeys. But even our trusty rodents offer only equivocal support for the hormonal determination of the laboratory behaviors studied, both of so-called fighting behavior as well as of the more stereotyped reproductive behaviors of mounting and lordosis. The most marked behavioral effects are usually observed in the first trial.[1] Repeated trials with the same animal within a relatively short amount of time tend to show a diminution of the effect. In addition, both the housing conditions of hormonally altered test animals and their prior fighting experience have significant effects in fighting tests.[2] Thus environment and learning are significant even for the less complex rodent species, and the idea that perinatal hormones are the only significant factors in the expression of aggressive behavior is a useful, but false, simplification. Environment and learning are stuffed into the *ceteris paribus* clause that is always a component of a lawlike statement.[3]

The linear-hormonal model must, therefore, always allow for environmental influences on the behaviors studied. When such complexity is admitted, however, biology-environment interactions introduced to account for this greater complexity are of the weak, additive sort. The hormonally programmed animal responds in an environment that, one might say, selects one among the range of responses in the program. I indicated some of the problems with this model of interactionism above. Here I wish to focus on the contrast with the strong interaction-

[1] Clemens, Heroi, and Gorski (1969).
[2] Edwards and Rowe (1975); Bevan et al. (1960).
[3] Cartwright (1983), pp. 44–73, discusses *ceteris paribus* laws.

ism characteristic of the selectionist model. First, as outlined in Chapter Seven, in the selectionist model social experience is involved in the very development of the biological structures implicated in behavior, and these structures can continue to change throughout the individual's lifetime. Neither biology nor environment are fixed but are themselves altered by the very actions they can, from one point of view, be said to bring about. Secondly, in the selectionist view the brain is understood as self-ordering and not solely as the product of independent causal factors such as genes or hormones. Causality, therefore, is not unidirectional, nor can causal relations be understood as determined by the structure of the least bits of the organs and organisms in question.

While there is still room for reductionist claims in further development of the selectionist theory, the strongly interactive and self-ordering character of the system as described place it in the camp of complexity rather than simplicity. Earlier in the century a similar tension was expressed in the debates between adherents of mechanistic and organismic conceptions of living systems. Mechanists urged the analogy to machines that are the sum of their parts and organicists urged the dominance of the parts by a whole that was greater than their sum. In recent decades this tension is exemplified both by the triumph of molecular biology, with its mapping of DNA and resultant promise of genetic engineering, but also by its rejection of views like those of Barbara McClintock who sought to understand gene and chromosomal action in the context of the entire organism.[4] To argue for multiple levels of causality, including interaction among levels, is not, however, to argue for vitalism or for organicism. Nor does thinking of the brain as self-ordering (subject of course to relevant internal constraints and in response to environmental conditions) imply such a commitment. As Evelyn Keller said of McClintock's work, "The capacity of organisms to reprogram themselves . . . merely confirms the existence of forms of order more complex than we have, at least thus far, been able to account for."[5] Secondly, the theoretical antireductionism implicitly defended in the early chapters of this book, and which I shall address shortly, undermines the possibility of any such global alternative.

Keller writes of her own attempts to develop, with fellow researcher Lee Segel, a model of slime mold aggregation that avoided what she has called the "master molecule" approach to biological analysis.[6]

[4] McClintock (1980). An excellent account of McClintock's work is provided in Keller (1983a).

[5] Keller (1985), p. 171.

[6] Keller and Segel (1970); Keller (1983b).

Dictyostelium discoideum can exist as single cells or as a multicellular organism formed by aggregation of the single cells under conditions of starvation. What triggers the transition from one form to another? The Keller-Segel model used some mathematical ideas of Alan Turing's to describe aggregation as a self-organizing phenomenon among the initially undifferentiated cells. The cells aggregate in response to the release of c-AMP among them. Those cells in a patch of slime mold furthest from the periphery and, thus, from nourishment release the chemical whose diffusion through the patch is followed by the cells coming together to form the new organism. The competing form of explanation appeals instead to the notion of a founder or pacemaker cell, genetically different from the majority of slime mold cells, that alone has the capacity to release the c-AMP. The pacemaker cells are perceived as directing the activity of the other cells as they aggregate. Though this example is in many ways different from the contrasted models in the accounts of the neurobiological substrates of behavior, there are some gross similarities, particularly in the distinction between a model requiring a differentiated initiator (gonadal hormone exposure inducing sex-differentiated brain organization) and one postulating a form of self-organization in response to environmental conditions (the formation of secondary repertoires by selective processes in response to experience). Contemporary ecological science is a site of similar contests between a simplifying reductionist approach and a more complex and interactive one.[7]

Clearly, a reductionist methodology holds out the promise of greater tractability of the subject matter to which it is applied. If we can understand a phenomenon as the product of mechanistic interactions among a discrete set of independent variables, we are much more likely to be able to intervene and thus exercise some form of control over the sequence. We are also in a better position to initiate, imitate, or create a variant of the sequence, as when synthetically produced hormones are introduced into the female reproductive system to control fertility. The assumptions associated with reductive methodologies, however, not only support certain metaphysical conceptions of natural systems but have also provided conceptual support for, in retrospect inappropriate, interventions, such as the use of lobotomies and hysterectomies to correct behavioral disorders.

Hormonal interventions could well have the effect, in a particular social environment, of suppressing or promoting certain behaviors. This would most likely be seen as the "working" of the hormonal the-

---

[7] See the essays in Saarinen (1982). See also Taylor (1986).

ory. However, (1) there is no reason to think that the behavioral effects are produced through hormonal brain programming as distinct from other physiological avenues of influence, and (2) it is at least as likely, on the evidence of past experience, that the effects of hormone administration would not be limited to those intended but would be more far-reaching. Hormones are part of a powerful but delicately balanced regulatory system. Humans act as whole animals, and endocrine balance surely makes a difference. The selectionist theory of brain function gives us alternative ways to understand that difference. The account of human action it makes possible envisions quite different forms of interactions directed to altering or influencing such action. In particular, it mandates engaging the cognitive and intentional bases of action, with all the potential for resistance and reciprocity such engagement carries.

Reductionism in Philosophy

The analytically neutral stance reflects my commitment to theoretical pluralism. Several philosophers in recent years have argued that the sciences cannot be unified, either by arguing against the translation across disciplinary boundaries that would be required or by arguing that there is disunity even where we most presuppose unity. Such arguments address both horizontal and vertical integration. Geoffrey Joseph, for example, has argued that theories of the four fundamental physical forces are not consistent with one another, even though physicists work with and are committed to the existence of all four forces as described in those theories.[8] This argument undermines claims about horizontal integration. Patrick Suppes has argued that the insolubility of the N-body problem in physics should discount all talk of the reducibility of the other sciences to physics.[9] And a number of philosophers and biologists have argued against the reducibility of Mendelian principles of heredity to the molecular theory of the gene,[10] against the reducibility of all cases of species evolution to selection operating on individual organisms,[11] against the reducibility of individual organismic development to the expression of a genetic program.[12]

Theoretical pluralism accepts a variety of theories on a given subject matter. Which theory we use to guide our interactions with or interventions in natural processes, which we appeal to in providing expla-

---

[8] Joseph (1980).
[9] Suppes (1984), pp. 125–130.
[10] Hull (1973), pp. 8–43.
[11] Wilson (1983); Wade (1977).
[12] Lewontin (1982, 1983). See also Burian (1981–1982).

nations depends on our interests at a particular time. The endocrinologist who wants to explore the effects of hormones, including their effects on behavior, has different questions and different explanatory interests than the neurophysiologist or the developmental and social psychologist. Where we err is in thinking that since they (may) have inconsistent theories only one can be right and we must know which in order to make public policy. Except in the case of using empirical findings to challenge theoretical assumptions, the science is only relevant to the policy making that accepts the assumptive framework of the research. It cannot help us make the metaphysical, moral, and political decisions about human nature that provide the most basic kinds of foundation for policy.

Finally, in advocating a social analysis of knowledge I am rejecting the epistemological reductionism that characterizes much mainstream Anglo-American philosophy. There are several respects in which our epistemological tradition is reductionist. In the first place, the tendency toward foundationalism is reductionistic to the degree that a certain core, for example, sense data, is identified as what we really know and everything else treated as an elaboration reducible to elements of the foundation. Secondly, theories of knowledge tend to be theories about an individual's knowledge. They address questions about the criteria that an individual's belief that p must satisfy in order to count as knowledge that p. The criteria are themselves individualistic, making no essential reference to an individual's social context. The assumption is that once we have settled the problem of what counts as an individual's knowing, there is no further philosophical problem of knowledge. Any other form of knowledge is just some form of individual knowledge or additive collections of individual knowledges. In this regard our theories of knowledge have followed the path set by our social theories that traditionally understand societies as collections of individuals and treat social processes and properties as explicable in terms of individual processes and properties.

I have argued, in contrast, that scientific knowledge is social knowledge, that is, that it is constructed through interactions among individuals. Those interactions are themselves shaped by social relations existing among those individuals. The account I have defended is antireductionist in two related respects. Scientific knowledge cannot be reduced to the knowledge of an individual and cannot be understood in terms of processes in principle individualistic, such as the simple additive accumulation of individuals' knowledges. Secondly, an individual's scientific knowledge is made possible by that individual's social and cultural context, that is, it rests on the work of others as well as on social conventions of interpretation and it requires participation in practices of transformative criticism.[13] A consequence of embracing the social character of knowledge is the abandonment of the ideals of certainty and of the permanence of knowledge. Since no epistemological theory has been able to guarantee the attainment of those ideals, this seems a minor loss.

The more complex and interactive visions to which I have drawn attention in this chapter encode different attitudes towards nature and natural processes than are represented in mainstream science. Will these alternative visions survive to generate both theoretical understanding and a basis for concrete interactions with natural phenomena? Such survival depends on whether we want to know the world under those more complex descriptions.

[13] The selectionist account of brain development implies that all knowledge, and not just scientific knowledge, is social. The gap between the first glimmerings of cognition in brain development and scientific knowledge is quite dramatic, however. The prospect of developing a more encompassing social analysis of knowledge presents a tantalizing challenge for future research.

Achinstein, Peter. 1968. *Concepts of Science*. Baltimore, MD: The Johns Hopkins University Press.

————. 1971. *Law and Explanation*. Oxford: Oxford University Press.

Addelson, Kathryn Pyne. 1983. "The Man of Professional Wisdom." In *Discovering Reality: Feminist Perspectives on Epistemology, Metaphysics, Methodology, and Philosophy of Science*, ed. Sandra Harding and Merrill Hintikka, pp. 165–186. Dordrecht: D. Reidel.

Adkins, Elizabeth. 1980. "Genes, Hormones, Sex and Gender." In *Sociobiology: Beyond Nature/Nurture?* ed. George Barlow and J. Silverberg, pp. 385–415. Washington: American Association for the Advancement of Science.

Ann Arbor Science for the People Collective. 1977. *Biology as a Social Weapon*. Minneapolis, MN: Burgess Publishing Co.

Bacon, Francis. 1960. *The New Organon*. Edited by F. Anderson. Indianapolis: Bobbs Merrill.

Baker, Susan. 1980. "Biological Influences on Sex and Gender." *Signs: Journal of Women in Culture and Society*. 6, no. 1:80–96.

Bardin, C. Wayne, and James F. Catterall. 1981. "Testosterone: A Major Determinant of Extragenital Sexual Dimorphism." *Science* 211:1285–1294.

Barnes, Barry, and David Bloor. 1982. "Relativism, Rationalism and the Sociology of Knowledge." In *Rationality and Relativism*, ed. Martin Hollis and Steven Lukes, pp. 21–47. Cambridge, MA: MIT Press.

Barnes, Barry, and David Edge, eds. 1982. *Science in Context*. Cambridge, MA: MIT Press.

Beardsley, Elizabeth. 1982. "On Curing Conceptual Confusion: Response to Mary Anne Warren." In *"Femininity," "Masculinity," and "Androgyny,"* ed. Mary Vetterling-Braggin, pp. 197–200. Totowa, NJ: Littlefield Adams.

Beatty, John. 1985. "Pluralism and Panselectionism." In *PSA 1984*, ed. Peter Asquith and Philip Kitcher, pp. 25–83. East Lansing, MI: Philosophy of Science Association.

Becker, J. R. 1981. "Differential Treatment of Females and Males in Mathematics Classes." *Journal for Research in Mathematics Education* 12:40–53.

Bem, Sandra. 1985. "Androgyny and Gender Schema Theory: A Conceptual and Empirical Integration." In *Nebraska Symposium on Motivation*, vol. 34, *Psychology and Gender*, ed. Theo Sonderegger, pp. 179–226. Lincoln, NB: University of Nebraska Press.

Benbow, Camilla, and Julian Stanley. 1980. "Sex Differences in Math Ability: Fact or Artifact?" *Science* 210:1262–1264.

Benbow, Camilla, and Julian Stanley. 1983. "Sex Differences in Mathematical Reasoning Ability: More Facts." *Science* 222:1029–1031.

Benbow, Camilla, and Robert Benbow. 1984. "Biological Correlates of High Mathematical Reasoning Ability." In *Progress in Brain Research*, vol. 61, *Sex Differences in the Brain*, ed. G. J. DeVries, J.P.C. De Bruin, H.B.M. Uylings, and M. A. Corner, pp. 469–490. Amsterdam: Elsevier Press.

Benowitz, S. I. 1984. "Interferon May Reduce MS Attacks." *Science News* 126:231.

Benveniste, Jacques. 1988. "Reply to Maddox, Randi and Stewart." *Nature* 334:291.

Bermant, Gordon, and Julian Davidson. 1974. *Biological Bases of Sexual Behavior*. New York: Harper and Row.

Bernstein, Jeremy. 1973. *Einstein*. Bungay: William Collins and Son, Ltd.

Bevan, William, Walter F. Daves, and Girard W. Levy. 1960. "The Relation of Castration, Androgen Therapy, and Pre-Test Fighting Experience to Competitive Aggression in Male C% 7BL/10 Mice." *Animal Behavior* 8, no. 1:6–12.

Blackwood, Evelyn. 1984. "Sexuality and Gender in Certain Native American Tribes: The Case of Cross-Gender Females." *Signs: Journal of Women in Culture and Society* 10, no. 1:27–42.

Bleier, Ruth. 1983. *Science and Gender*. Elmsford, NY: Pergamon.

Bloor, David. 1982. "Durkheim and Mauss Revisited: Classification and the Sociology of Knowledge." *Studies in History and Philosophy of Science* 13:267–297.

Boyd, Richard. 1973. "Realism, Underdetermination, and a Causal Theory of Evidence." *Nous* 7:1–12.

———. 1984. "The Current Status of Scientific Realism." In *Scientific Realism*, ed. Jarrett Leplin, pp. 41–82. Berkeley, CA: University of California Press.

Broad, William. 1981. "Fraud and the Structure of Science." *Science* 212:137–141.

Bronson, F. H., and C. Desjardins. 1976. "Steroid Hormones and Aggressive Behavior in Mammals." In *The Physiology of Aggression*, ed. Kenneth Moyer, pp. 100–105. New York: Raven Press.

Broverman, I. K., D. M. Broverman, F. E. Clarkson, P. S. Rosenkrantz, and S. R. Vogel. 1970. "Sex Role Stereotypes and Clinical Judgments of Mental Health." *Journal of Consulting and Clinical Psychology* 34:1–7.

Buchdahl, Gerd. 1970. "History of Science and Criteria of Choice." In *Minnesota Studies in the Philosophy of Science*, ed. Roger Steuwer, 5:204–230. Minneapolis, MN: University of Minnesota Press.

Buerck, Dorothy. 1985. "The Voices of Women Making Meaning in Mathematics." *Journal of Education* 167, no. 3:59–70.

Burian, Richard. 1981–1982. "Human Sociobiology and Genetic Determinism." *Philosophical Forum* 13:43–66.

Burtt, E. A. 1927. *The Metaphysical Foundations of Modern Science*. New York: Harcourt Brace.

Caplan, Paula, Gael MacPherson, and Patricia Tobin. 1985. "Do Sex Differences in Spatial Ability Really Exist?" *American Psychologist* 40, no. 7:786–798.

Cartwright, Nancy. 1983. *How the Laws of Physics Lie*. New York: Oxford University Press.

Changeux, Jean-Pierre. 1985. *Neuronal Man*. Translated by Laurence Garey. New York: Pantheon.

Chodorow, Nancy. 1978. *The Reproduction of Mothering*. Berkeley, CA: University of California Press.

Clemens, L. G., M. Heroi, and R. Gorski. 1969. "Induction and Facilitation of Female Mating Behavior in Rats Treated Neonatally with Low Doses of Testosterone Propionate." *Endocrinology* 84:1430–1438.

Cole, Stephen, Leonard Rubin, and Jonathan R. Cole. 1977. "Peer Review and the Support of Science." *Scientific American* 237, no. 4:34–41.

Cole, Stephen, Jonathan R. Cole, and Gary Simons. 1981. "Chance and Consensus in Peer Review." *Science* 214:881–886.

Conant, J. B. 1957. "The Overthrow of the Phlogiston Theory." In *Harvard Case Studies in Experimental Science*, ed. J. B. Conant, 1:65–115. Cambridge, MA: Harvard University Press.

Dialectics of Biology Group. 1982. *Against Biological Determinism*. London: Alison and Busby.

Dickson, David. 1984. *The New Politics of Science*. New York: Pantheon.

Dijksterhuis, E. J. 1961. *The Mechanization of the World Picture*. London: Oxford University Press.

Dinnerstein, Dorothy. 1977. *The Mermaid and the Minotaur*. New York: Harper and Row.

Djerassi, Carl. 1981. "Birth Control in the Year 2001." *Bulletin of the Atomic Scientists* 37 (March):24–28.

Doell, Ruth, and Helen E. Longino. 1988. "Sex Hormones and Human Behavior: A Critique of the Linear Model." *Journal of Homosexuality* 15, no. 3/4:55–79.

Dörner, Gunter. 1976. *Hormones and Brain Differentiation*. Amsterdam: Elsevier Press.

Dreyfus, Hubert L., and Paul Rabinow. 1983. *Michel Foucault: Beyond Structuralism and Hermeneutics*. 2d ed. Chicago, IL: University of Chicago Press.

Durden-Smith, Jo. 1980. "Interview with Roger Gorski." *Quest/80* 1:96.

———, and Diane deSimone. 1983. *Sex and the Brain*. New York: Arbor House.

Dworkin, Ronald. 1977. *Taking Rights Seriously*. Cambridge, MA: Harvard University Press.

Eccles, Jacquelynne S., and Janis E. Jacobs. 1986. "Social Forces Shape Math

Attitudes and Performance." *Signs: Journal of Women in Culture and Society* 11:367–389.

Edelman, Gerald. 1981. "Group Selection as the Basis for Higher Brain Function." In *The Organization of the Cerebral Cortex*, ed. F. O. Schmitt, F. G. Worden, G. Adelman, and S. G. Dennis, pp. 535–563. Cambridge, MA: MIT Press.

———. 1983. "Cell Adhesion Molecules." *Science* 219:450–457.

———. 1985. "Molecular Regulation of Neural Morphogenesis." In *Molecular Bases of Neural Development*, ed. Gerald M. Edelman, W. E. Gall, and W. M. Cowan, pp. 35–59. New York: Wiley.

———. 1987. *Neural Darwinism*. New York: Basic Books.

———, and Vernon Mountcastle. 1978. *The Mindful Brain*. Cambridge, MA: MIT Press.

Edwards, D. A. 1976. "Early Androgen Stimulation and Aggressive Behavior in Male and Female Mice." In *The Physiology of Aggression*, ed. Kenneth Moyer, pp. 69–75. New York: Raven Press.

———, and R. Rowe. 1975. "Neural Factors in Aggression." In *Hormonal Correlates of Behavior*, ed. Basil Eleftheriou and R. L. Sprott, pp. 275–303. New York: Plenum Press.

Ehrhardt, Anke. 1979. "The Interactional Model of Sex Hormones and Behavior." In *Human Sexuality*, ed. Herant Katchadourian, pp. 150–160. Berkeley, CA: University of California Press.

———. 1985. "Gender Differences: A Biosocial Perspective." In *Nebraska Symposium on Motivation*, vol. 34, *Psychology and Gender*, ed. Theo Sonderegger, pp. 37–57. Lincoln, NB: University of Nebraska Press.

———, S. E. Ince, and Heino Meyer-Bahlburg. 1981. "Career Aspiration and Gender Role Development in Young Girls." *Archives of Sexual Behavior* 10:281–299.

Ehrhardt, Anke, and Heino Meyer-Bahlburg. 1979. "Prenatal Sex Hormones and the Developing Brain." *Annual Review of Medicine*. Palo Alto, CA: W.P. Creger Annual Reviews, Inc.

———. 1981. "Effects of Prenatal Sex Hormones on Gender-Related Behavior." *Science* 211:1312–1318.

Ehrhardt, Anke, Heino Meyer-Bahlburg, L. R. Rosen, J. F. Feldman, N. P. Veridiano, I. Zimmerman, and B. McEwen. 1985. "Sexual Orientation after Prenatal Exposure to Exogenous Estrogen." *Archives of Sexual Behavior* 14:57–77.

Eldredge, Niles, and Stephen J. Gould. 1972. "Punctuated Equilibria: An Alternative to Phyletic Gradualism." In *Models in Paleobiology*, ed. T.J.M. Schopf, pp. 82–115. San Francisco, CA: Freeman, Cooper and Co.

Eleftheriou, Basil, and R. L. Sprott, eds. 1975. *Hormonal Correlates of Behavior*. New York: Plenum Press.

Ember, Carol. 1973. "Feminine Task Assignment and the Social Behavior of Boys." *Ethos* 1, no. 4:424–439.

Fairweather, Hugh. 1980. "Sex Differences: Still Being Dressed in the Emperor's New Clothes." *Behavioral and Brain Sciences* 3:235.

Fausto-Sterling, Anne. 1985. *Myths of Gender*. New York: Basic Books.

———. 1988. "Trends in Developmental Biology: A Feminist Perspective." In *Programs, Papers and Abstracts for the Joint Conference of the British Society for the History of Science and the History of Science Society, Manchester, England, 11–15 July, 1988*, pp. 316–325. Madison, WI: Omnipress.

Feinberg, Gerald. 1978. *What is the World Made of?* New York: Anchor Press.

Fennema, Elizabeth, and Julia Sherman. 1977. "Sex-Related Differences in Mathematics Achievement, Spatial Visualization and Affective Factors." *American Educational Research Journal* 14:51–71.

Feyerabend, Paul K. 1962. "Explanation, Reduction, and Empiricism." In *Minnesota Studies in the Philosophy of Science*, ed. Herbert Feigl and Grover Maxwell, 3:28–97. Minneapolis, MN: University of Minnesota Press.

———. 1970a. "Against Method." In *Minnesota Studies in the Philosophy of Science*, ed. Michael Radner and Stephen Winokur, 4:17–130. Minneapolis, MN: University of Minnesota Press.

———. 1970b. "Consolations for the Specialist." In *Criticism and Growth of Knowledge*, ed. Imre Lakatos and Alan Musgrave, pp. 197–230. Cambridge: Cambridge University Press.

———. 1974. "Zahar on Einstein." *British Journal for the Philosophy of Science* 25:25–28.

———. 1975. *Against Method*. London: Verso.

Fine, Arthur. 1984. "The Natural Ontological Attitude." In *Scientific Realism*, ed. Jarrett Leplin, pp. 83–107. Berkeley, CA: University of California Press.

Fischette, Christine, Anat Bigon, and Bruce McEwen. 1983. "Sex Differences in Serotonin 1 Receptor Binding in Rat Brain." *Science* 222:333–335.

Foss, G. L. 1951. "The Influence of Androgens on Sexuality in Women." *Lancet* 1:667–669.

Foucault, Michel. 1970. *The Order of Things*. Translated by Alan Sheridan. New York: Pantheon.

———. 1977. *Discipline and Punish: The Birth of the Prison*. Translated by Alan Sheridan. New York: Random House.

———. 1978. *The History of Sexuality. Volume I: An Introduction*. Trans. Robert Hurley. New York: Random House.

———. 1980. *Power/Knowledge*. Edited by Colin Gordon. New York: Pantheon.

———. 1982. *The Archeology of Knowledge*. Translated by Alan M. Sheridan. New York: Pantheon. (First published 1972. London: Tavistock.)

Freeman, Derek. 1983. *Margaret Mead and Samoa: The Making and Unmaking of an Anthropological Myth*. Cambridge, MA: Harvard University Press.

Freeman, L. G. 1968. "A Theoretical Framework for Interpreting Archeological Materials." In *Man the Hunter*, ed. R. B. Lee and Irven DeVore, pp. 262–267. Chicago: Aldine Publishing.

Fried, Barbara. 1979. "Boys Will Be Boys Will Be Boys." In *Women Look at Biology Looking at Women*, ed. Ruth Hubbard, Mary Sue Henifin, and Barbara Fried, p. 37. Cambridge, MA: Schenkman Publishing Co.

Geschwind, Norman, and Peter Behan. 1984. "Laterality, Hormones and Immunity." In *Cerebral Dominance: The Biological Foundations*, ed. Norman Geschwind and Albert Galaburda, pp. 211–224. Cambridge, MA: Harvard University Press.

Geschwind, Norman, and Albert Galaburda. 1985. "Cerebral Lateralization." *Archives of Neurology* 42:428–459.

Geuss, Raymond. 1981. *The Idea of a Critical Theory*. Cambridge: Cambridge University Press.

Gladue, Brian, Richard Green, and Ronald Hellman. 1984. "Neuroendocrine Response to Estrogen and Sexual Orientation." *Science* 225:1496–1499.

Glazer, Sarah. 1988. "Combating Science Fraud." *Editorial Research Reports* 2:390–399.

Glymour, Clark. 1980. *Theory and Evidence*. Princeton, NJ: Princeton University Press.

Goldberg, Stephen. 1973. *The Inevitability of Patriarchy*. New York: Morrow.

Goldfoot, David, and Deborah Neff. 1985. "On Measuring Behavioral Sex Differences in Social Contexts." In *Handbook of Behavioral Neurobiology*, vol. 7, *Reproduction*, ed. N. Adler, D. Pfaff, and R. W. Goy, pp. 767–783. New York: Plenum Press.

Goleman, Daniel. 1987. "Failing to Recognize Bias in Science." *Technology Review* 90 (November–December):26–27.

Gore, D. A., and D. V. Roumagoux. 1983. "Wait-Time as a Variable in Sex-Related Difference during Fourth-Grade Mathematics Instruction." *Journal of Educational Research* 76:273–275.

Gould, Stephen J. 1980. "Sociobiology and the Theory of Natural Selection." In *Sociobiology: Beyond Nature/Nurture?* ed. George Barlow and James Silverberg, pp. 257–269. Boulder, CO: Westview Press.

———. 1981. *The Mismeasure of Man*. New York: W.W. Norton and Co.

———, and Eldredge Niles. 1977. "Punctuated Equilibria: The Tempo and Mode of Evolution Reconsidered." *Paleobiology* 3:115–151.

Goy, Robert, and D. Goldfoot. 1975. "Neuroendocrinology: Animal Models and Problems of Human Sexuality." In *New Directions in Sex Research*, ed. Eli Rubinstein and Richard Green, pp. 83–98. New York: Plenum Press.

Goy, Robert, and Bruce McEwen. 1980. *Sexual Differentiation of the Brain*. Cambridge, MA: MIT Press.

Graf, Richard, and Jeanne Riddell. 1972. "Sex Differences in Problem-Solving as a Function of Problem Content." *Journal of Educational Research* 65:451.

Graham, Loren. 1981. *Between Science and Values*. New York: Columbia University Press.

Grene, Marjorie. 1966. *The Knower and the Known*. New York: Basic Books.

———. 1985. "Perception, Interpretation and the Sciences." In *Evolution at a Crossroads*, ed. David Depew and Bruce Weber, pp. 1–20. Cambridge, MA: MIT Press.

Grünbaum, Adolf. 1963. *Philosophical Problems of Space and Time*. New York: Alfred Knopf.

Gurin, Joel, and Nancy Pfund. 1980. "Bonanza in the Biolab." *The Nation*, 22 November, pp. 529–548.

Haas, Violet, and Carolyn Perruci, eds. 1984. *Women in Scientific and Engineering Professions*. Ann Arbor, MI: University of Michigan Press.

Habermas, Jürgen. 1970a. "On Systematically Distorted Communication." *Inquiry* 13:205–218.

———. 1970b. "Towards a Theory of Communicative Competence." *Inquiry* 13:360–376.

———. 1971. *Knowledge and Human Interests*. Translated by Jeremy Shapiro. Boston, MA: Beacon Press.

Hall, Jacquelynne Dowd, and Sandi Cooper. 1986. "Women's History Goes to Trial." *Signs: Journal of Women in Culture and Society* 11, no. 4:751–779.

Hanson, Norwood Russell. 1958. *Patterns of Discovery*. Cambridge: Cambridge University Press.

Haraway, Donna. 1978. "Animal Sociology and the Body Politic." *Signs: Journal of Women in Culture and Society* 4, no. 1:21–60.

———. 1979. "The Biological Enterprise: Sex, Mind and Profit from Human Engineering to Sociobiology." *Radical History Review* 20:206–237.

———. 1981. "In the Beginning Was the Word: The Genesis of Biological Theory." *Signs: Journal of Women in Culture and Society* 6, no. 3:469–482.

———. 1981–1982. "The High Cost of Information in Post-World War II Evolutionary Biology." *Philosophical Forum* 13:244–278.

———. 1985a. "A Manifesto for Cyborgs." *Socialist Review* no. 80, pp. 65–107.

———. 1985b. "Primatology is Politics by Other Means." In *PSA 1984*, ed. Peter Asquith and Philip Kitcher, pp. 489–524. East Lansing, MI: Philosophy of Science Association.

———. 1988. "Situated Knowledges: The Science Question in Feminism and the Privilege of Partial Perspective." *Feminist Studies* 14, no. 3:575–599.

Hardin, Garrett. 1968. "The Tragedy of the Commons." *Science* 162:1243–1248.

Harding, Sandra. 1978. "Four Contributions Values Can Make to the Objectivity of the Social Sciences." In *Proceedings of the 1978 Biennial Meeting of the Philosophy of Science Association*, ed. Peter Asquith and Ian Hacking, pp. 199–209. East Lansing, MI: Philosophy of Science Association.

Harding, Sandra. 1980. "The Norms of Inquiry and Masculine Experience." In *PSA 1980*, ed. Peter Asquith and Ronald Giere, 2:305–324. East Lansing, MI: Philosophy of Science Association.

———. 1986. *The Science Question in Feminism*. Ithaca, NY: Cornell University Press.

Harman, Gilbert. 1965. "The Inference to the Best Explanation." *Philosophical Review* 74:88–95.

———. 1968. "Enumerative Induction as Inference to the Best Explanation." *Journal of Philosophy* 65:529–533.

Harnad, Stevan. 1983. *Peer Commentary on Peer Review: A Case Study in Scientific Quality Control*. Ann Arbor, MI: Books on Demand UMI.

Hartsock, Nancy. 1983. "The Feminist Standpoint: Developing the Ground for a Specifically Feminist Historical Materialism." In *Discovering Reality: Feminist Perspectives on Epistemology, Metaphysics, Methodology and Philosophy of Science*, ed. Sandra Harding and Merrill Hintikka, pp. 283–310. Dordrecht: D. Reidel.

Hempel, Carl Gustav. 1960. "Science and Human Values." In *Social Control in a Free Society*, ed. R. E. Spiller, pp. 39–64. Philadelphia, PA: University of Pennsylvania Press.

———. 1965. "Studies in the Logic of Confirmation." In *Aspects of Scientific Explanation*, pp. 3–51. New York: The Free Press.

———. 1966. *Philosophy of Natural Science*. Englewood Cliffs, NJ: Prentice Hall.

Hesse, Mary. 1965. *Forces and Fields*. Totowa, NJ: Littlefield Adams.

———. 1980. *Revolutions and Reconstructions in the Philosophy of Science*. Bloomington, IN: Indiana University Press.

Hier, Daniel, and William Crowley. 1982. "Spatial Ability in Androgen-Deficient Men." *The New England Journal of Medicine* 306, no. 20:1202–1205.

Holton, Gerald. 1973. *Thematic Origins of Scientific Thought*. Cambridge, MA: Harvard University Press.

———. 1978. "Subelectrons and Presuppositions and the Millikan-Ehrenhaft Dispute." In *The Scientific Imagination*, pp. 25–83. Cambridge: Cambridge University Press.

Hubbard, Ruth, Mary Sue Henifin, and Barbara Fried, eds. 1979. *Women Look at Biology Looking at Women*. Cambridge, MA: Schenkman Publishing Co.

Hubbard, Ruth, and Marian Lowe, eds. 1979. *Genes and Gender II*: New York: Gordian Press.

Hubel, D., and T. N. Wiesel. 1977. "Functional Architecture of Macaque Monkey Visual Cortex." *Proceedings of the Royal Society* 198:1–59.

Hull, David. 1973. *Philosophy of Biological Science*. Englewood Cliffs, NJ: Prentice Hall.

Imperato-McGinley, Julianne, Ralph E. Peterson, Teofilo Gautier, and Erasmo Sturla. 1979. "Androgens and the Evolution of Male-Gender Identity among Male Pseudohermaphrodites with 5-α Reductase Deficiency." *New England Journal of Medicine* 300, no. 22:1233–1237.

Jacob, James, and Margaret Jacob. 1980. "The Anglican Origins of Modern Science." *Isis* 71, no 257:251–267.

Jaffe, Bernard. 1960. *Michelson and the Speed of Light*. Garden City, NY: Doubleday and Co.

Jaggar, Alison. 1985. *Feminist Politics and Human Nature*. Totowa, NJ: Rowman and Allanheld.

Jay, Martin. 1988. *Fin de Siècle Socialism and Other Essays*. New York: Routledge.

Jensen, Arthur. 1969. "How Much Can We Boost I.Q. and Scholastic Achievement?" *Harvard Educational Review* 33:1–123.

Jolly, Clifford, ed. 1978. *Early Hominids of Africa*. London: Gerald Duckworth and Co., Ltd.

Joseph, Geoffrey. 1980. "The Many Sciences and the One World." *Journal of Philosophy* 77:773–790.

Karsch, F. J., D. J. Dierschke, and E. Knobil. 1972. "Sexual Differentiation of Pituitary Function." *Science* 179:484–486.

Keller, Evelyn F. 1983a. *A Feeling for the Organism*. San Francisco, CA: W. H. Freeman and Co.

———. 1983b. "The Force of the Pacemaker Concept in Theories of Aggregation of Cellular Slime Mold." *Perspectives in Biology and Medicine* 26:515–521.

———. 1985. *Reflections on Gender and Science*. New Haven, CT: Yale University Press.

———, and Lee Segel. 1970. "Initiation of Slime Mold Aggregation Viewed as an Instability." *Journal of Theoretical Biology* 26:399–415.

Kessler, Suzanne J., and Wendy McKenna. 1985. *Gender*. Chicago, IL: University of Chicago Press.

Knorr-Cetina, Karin, and Michael Mulkay, eds. 1983. *Science Observed*. London: Sage Publications.

Korenbrot, Carol. 1979. "Experiences with Systemic Contraceptives." *Toxic Substances: Decisions and Values, Conference II: Information Flow*. Washington, DC: Technical Information Project.

Kuhn, Thomas. 1957. *The Copernican Revolution*. New York: Random House.

———. 1970a. "Reflections on my Critics." In *Criticism and the Growth of Knowledge*, ed. Imre Lakatos and Alan Musgrave, pp. 231–278. Cambridge: Cambridge University Press.

———. 1970b. *The Structure of Scientific Revolutions*. 2d ed. Chicago: University of Chicago Press.

———. 1977a. *The Essential Tension*. Chicago, IL: University of Chicago Press.

———. 1977b. "Theory Change as Structure Change: Comments on the Sneed Formalism." In *Historical and Philosophical Dimensions of Logic,*

Methodology, and Philosophy of Science, ed. Robert Butts and Jaako Hintikka, pp. 289–309. Dordrecht: D. Reidel.

Lambert, Helen. 1978. "Biology and Equality: A Perspective on Sex Differences." *Signs: Journal of Women in Culture and Society* 4, no. 1:97–117.

Latour, Bruno. 1987. *Science in Action*. Cambridge, MA: Harvard University Press.

Laudan, Larry. 1977. *Progress and Its Problems*. Berkeley, CA: University of California Press.

———. 1981. "A Confutation of Convergent Realism." *Philosophy of Science* 48, no.1:19–49.

———. 1985. *Science and Values*. Berkeley, CA: University of California Press.

Laughlin, William. 1968. "Hunting: An Integrating Biobehavior System and Its Evolutionary Importance." In *Man the Hunter*, ed. R. B. Lee and Irven DeVore, pp. 304–320. Chicago: Aldine Publishing Co.

Lavoisier, Antoine. 1952. *Elements of Chemistry*. Translated by Robert Kerry. Chicago: Encyclopedia Britannica, Inc.

Leakey, L.S.B. 1968. "An Early Miocene Member of Hominidae." In *Perspectives on Human Evolution*, ed. Sherwood Washburn and Phyllis Jay, pp. 61–84. New York: Holt Rinehart and Winston.

Leakey, Mary D. 1979. "Footprints in the Ashes of Time." *National Geographic* 155, no. 4:446–457.

———, and R. L. Hay. 1979. "Pliocene Footprints in the Laetolil Beds at Laetoli, Northern Tanzania." *Nature* 278:317–332.

Leibowitz, Lila. 1979. "Universals and Male Dominance among Primates: A Critical Examination." In *Genes and Gender II*, ed. Ruth Hubbard and Marian Lowe, pp. 35–48. New York: Gordian Press.

Leplin, Jarrett. 1984. "Truth and Scientific Progress." In *Scientific Realism*, ed. Jarrett Leplin, pp. 193–217. Berkeley, CA: University of California Press.

Levins, Richard, and Richard Lewontin. 1985. *The Dialectical Biologist*. Cambridge, MA: Harvard University Press.

Lewontin, Richard. 1970. "Race and Intelligence." *Bulletin of the Atomic Scientists* 26 (March):2–8.

———. 1974. "The Analysis of Variance and the Analysis of Causes." *American Journal of Human Genetics* 26:400–411.

———. 1982. "Organism and Environment." In *Learning, Development and Culture*, ed. H. C. Plotkin, pp. 151–170. New York: John Wiley.

———. 1983. "The Organism as Subject and Object of Evolution." *Scientia* 118:63–82.

———, Steven Rose, and Leon Kamin. 1984. *Not in Our Genes: Biology, Ideology and Human Nature*. New York: Pantheon Books.

Linn, Marcia C., and Anne Peterson. 1985. "Emergence and Characterization of Sex Differences in Spatial Ability: A Meta-Analysis." *Child Development* 56:1479–1498.

Locke, Don. 1968. *Myself and Others*. London: Oxford University Press.

Longino, Helen E. 1983. "Beyond 'Bad Science': Skeptical Reflections on the Value Freedom of Scientific Inquiry." In *Science, Technology, and Human Values* 8, no 1:7–17.

———. 1986. "Science Overrun: Limits to Freedom from External Control." In *Science and Technology in a Democracy: Who Shall Govern?* ed. Malcolm Goggin, pp. 57–74. Chattanooga, TN: University of Tennessee Press.

———. 1987. "What's Really Wrong with Quantitative Risk Assessment?" In *PSA 1986*, ed. Arthur Fine and Peter Machamer, pp. 376–383. East Lansing, MI: Philosophy of Science Association.

———. 1988. "Science, Objectivity, and Feminist Values." *Feminist Studies* 14, no. 31:561–574.

———, and Ruth Doell. 1983. "Body, Bias and Behavior: A Comparative Analysis of Reasoning in Two Areas of Biological Science." *Signs: Journal of Women in Culture and Society* 9, no. 2:206–227.

Lovejoy, C. Owen. 1981. "The Origin of Man." *Science* 211:341–350.

Lugones, Maria, and Elizabeth V. Spelman. 1983. "Have We Got a Theory for You!: Feminist Theory, Cultural Imperialism, and the Demand for 'The Woman's Voice.' " *Women's Studies International Forum* 6, no. 6:573–581.

McCarthy, Thomas. 1978. *The Critical Theory of Jürgen Habermas.* Cambridge, MA: MIT Press.

McClintock, Barbara. 1980. "Modified Gene Expressions Induced by Transposable Elements." In *Mobilization and Reassembly of Genetic Information*, W. A. Scott et al., pp. 11–19. New York: Academic Press.

Maccoby, Eleanor, and Carol Jacklin. 1974. *The Psychology of Sex Differences.* Stanford, CA: Stanford University Press.

McEwen, Bruce. 1981. "Neural Gonadal Steroid Actions." *Science* 211:1303–1311.

MacIntyre, Alasdair. 1981. *After Virtue.* Notre Dame, IN: University of Notre Dame Press.

MacLusky, Neil J., and Frederick Naftolin. 1981. "Sexual Differentiation of the Central Nervous System." *Science* 211:1294–1303.

Maddox, John, James Randi, and Walter W. Stewart. 1988. "High Dilution Experiments a Delusion." *Nature* 334:287–290.

Marr, David. 1982. *Vision.* New York: W.H. Freeman, Inc.

Martin, M. Kay, and Barbara Voorhies. 1975. *The Female of the Species.* New York: Columbia University Press.

Maxwell, Grover. 1962. "The Ontological Status of Theoretical Entities." In *Minnesota Studies in the Philosophy of Science*, ed. H. Feigl and G. Maxwell, pp. 3–27. Minneapolis, MN: University of Minnesota Press.

Maxwell, Nicholas. 1980. "Science, Reason, Knowledge and Wisdom: A Critique of Specialism." *Inquiry* 23, no. 1:19–81.

Mead, Margaret. 1935. *Sex and Temperament in Three Primitive Societies.* New York: William Morrow.

Merchant, Carolyn. 1980. *The Death of Nature*. San Francisco, CA: Harper and Row.

Merton, Robert K. 1938. "Science, Technology and Society in Seventeenth-Century England." *Osiris* 4:360–632.

Meyer-Bahlburg, Heino. 1982. "Hormones and Psychosexual Differentiation: Implications for the Management of Intersexuality, Homosexuality and Transexuality." *Clinics in Endocrinology and Metabolism* 11, no. 3:681–701.

Miller, Arthur. 1974. "On Lorentz's Methodology." *British Journal for the Philosophy of Science* 25:29–45.

Minuchin, P. 1965. "Sex-Role Concepts and Sex-Typing in Children as a Function of School and Home Environments." *Child Development* 36:1033–1048.

Money, John, and Anke Ehrhardt. 1972. *Man and Woman, Boy and Girl*. Baltimore, MD: The Johns Hopkins University Press.

Moyer, Kenneth, ed. 1976. *The Physiology of Aggression*. New York: Raven Press.

Mulkay, Michael. 1977. "Sociology of the Scientific Research Community." In *Science, Technology and Society: A Cross-Disciplinary Perspective*, ed. Ina Spiegel-Rosing and Derek deSolla Price, pp. 93–148. Beverly Hills, CA: Sage Publications.

Musgrave, Alan. 1974. "Logical versus Historical Theories of Confirmation." *British Journal for the Philosophy of Science* 25:1–23.

Nagata, Shigekazu, Hideharu Taira, Alan Hall, Lorraine Johnsrud, Michael Streuli, Josef Ecsödi, Werner Boll, Kari Cantell, and Charles Weissman. 1980. "Synthesis of E. Coli of a Polypeptide with Human Leukocyte Interferon Activity." *Nature* 284:316–320.

Nature. 1980. Vol. 283: 24 January; vol. 284: 13 March, 17 April; vol. 285: 1 May.

Nelkin, Dorothy. 1987. *Selling Science*. San Francisco, CA: W.H. Freeman and Co.

Newton, Isaac. 1953. "Rules of Reasoning in Philosophy." In *Newton's Philosophy of Nature*, ed. H. S. Thayer, pp. 3–5. New York: Hafner.

Newton-Smith, W. H. 1981. *The Rationality of Science*. Cambridge: Cambridge University Press.

Okin, Susan Moller. 1979. *Women in Western Political Thought*. Princeton, NJ: Princeton University Press.

Pascal, Blaise. 1937. *Physical Treatises*. Translated by I.H.B. and A.G.H. Spiers; Introduction and Notes by Frederick Barry. New York: Columbia University Press.

———. 1952. *The Provincial Letters, Pensées, Scientific Treatises*. Translated by Thomas M'Crie, W. F. Trotter, Richard Scofield. In *Great Books of the Western World*. Vol. 33. Chicago, IL: Encyclopedia Britannica.

Perkins, M. W. 1981. "Female Homosexuality and Body Build." *Archives of Sexual Behavior* 10:337–345.

Peters, Donald, and Stephen Ceci. 1982. "Peer Review Practices of Psycholog-ical Journals: The Fate of Published Articles Submitted Again." *Behav-ioral and Brain Sciences* 5:187–195.

———. 1985. "Beauty Is in the Eye of the Beholder." *Behavioral and Brain Sciences* 8, no. 4:747–749.

Pfaff, Donald. 1980. *Estrogens and Brain Function*. New York: Springer-Ver-lag.

———. 1983. "The Neurobiological Origins of Human Values." In *Ethical Questions in Brain and Behavior: Problems and Opportunities*, ed. Don-ald Pfaff, pp. 141–151. New York: Springer-Verlag.

Pilbeam, David. 1984. "The Descent of Hominoids and Hominids." *Scientific American* 250, no. 3:84–96.

———, Grant E. Meyer, Catherine Badgley, M. D. Rose, M.H.L. Picksford, A. K. Behrensmeyer, S. M. Ibrahim Shah. 1977. "New Hominoid Pri-mates from the Siwaliks of Pakistan and their Bearing on Hominoid Evo-lution." *Nature* 270:689–695.

Pincus, Gregory. 1965. *The Control of Fertility*. New York: Academic Press.

Popper, Karl. 1959. *The Logic of Scientific Discovery*. London: Hutchinson.

———. 1962. *Conjectures and Refutations*. New York: Basic Books.

Pugh, George. 1977. *The Biological Origin of Human Values*. New York: Ba-sic Books.

Putnam, Hilary. 1974. "The 'Corroboration' of Theories." In *The Philosophy of Karl Popper*, ed. Paul Arthur Schilpp, 1:221–240. LaSalle, IL: Open Court Publishing Co.

———. 1975. "What Theories Are Not." *Mathematics, Matter and Method*. Cambridge: Cambridge University Press.

———. 1978. *Meaning and the Moral Sciences*. London: Routledge and Ke-gan Paul.

Rawls, John. 1971. *A Theory of Justice*. Cambridge, MA: Harvard University Press.

Reinisch, June M. 1981. "Prenatal Exposure to Synthetic Progestins Increases Potential for Aggression in Humans." *Science* 211:1171–1173.

———, and Stephanie Sanders. 1984. "Prenatal Gonadal Steroidal Influences on Gender-Related Behavior." In *Progress in Brain Research*, vol. 61, *Sex Differences in the Brain*, ed. G. J. De Vries, J.P.C. De Bruin, H.B.M. Uyl-ings, and M. A. Corner, pp. 402–416. Amsterdam: Elsevier Press.

Richardson, Robert C. 1984. "Biology and Ideology: The Interpenetration of Science and Values." *Philosophy of Science* 51, no. 2:396–420.

Rosaldo, Michelle, and Louise Lamphere, eds. 1974. *Woman, Culture and Society*. Stanford, CA: Stanford University Press.

Rose, Hilary. 1983. "Hand, Brain, and Heart: A Feminist Epistemology for the Natural Sciences." *Signs: Journal of Women in Culture and Society* 9, no. 1:73–90.

———, and Steven Rose. 1982. "On Oppositions to Reductionism." In

Against Biological Determinism, ed. Dialectics of Biology Group, pp. 50–59. London: Alison and Busby.

Rose, Hilary, and Steven Rose, eds. 1976. *The Radicalization of Science*. London: The MacMillan Press, Ltd.

———, eds. 1979. *Ideology of/in the Natural Sciences*. Cambridge, MA: Schenkman Publishing Co.

Rossi, Alice. 1975. "A Biosocial Perspective on Parenting." *Daedelus* 106:1–31.

———. 1978. "The Biosocial Side of Parenting." *Human Nature* 1, no. 6:72–79.

Rowell, Thelma. 1974. "The Concept of Dominance." *Behavioral Biology* 11:131–154.

Rubin, Robert, June Reinisch, and Roger Haskell. 1981. "Postnatal Gonadal Steroid Effects on Human Behavior." *Science* 211:1318–1324.

Rumelhart, David, James L. McClelland, and the PDP Research Group. 1986. *Parallel Distributed Processing: Explorations in the Microstructure of Cognition*. Vols. 1 and 2. Cambridge, MA: MIT Press.

Saarinen, Esa. 1982. *Conceptual Issues in Ecology*. Boston, MA: David Reidel Publishing Co.

Saghir, M. T., and E. Robins. 1973. *Male and Female Homosexuality*. New York: Williams and Wilkins.

Sayre, Nora. 1975. *Rosalind Franklin and DNA*. New York: W. W. Norton.

Schafer, Alice T., and Mary W. Gray. 1981. "Sex and Mathematics." *Science* 211:231.

Schaffner, Kenneth. 1974. "Einstein versus Lorentz: Research Programmes and the Logic of Theory Evaluation." *British Journal for the Philosophy of Science* 25:45–78.

Schmitt, F. O., F. G. Worden, G. Adelman, and S. G. Dennis, eds. 1981. *The Organization of the Cerebral Cortex*. Cambridge, MA: MIT Press.

Science. 1980. "News and Comment." Vol. 207:1 February, 21 March; vol. 208:16 May.

Science News. 1980. Vol. 117:26 January, 15 March, 7 June.

Scriven, Michael. 1958. "Definitions, Explanations and Theories." In *Minnesota Studies in the Philosophy of Science*, ed. Herbert Feigl, Grover Maxwell, and Michael Scriven, pp. 99–196. Minneapolis, MN: University of Minnesota Press.

Seavey, C., P. Katz, and S. Rosenberg Zalk. 1975. "Baby X: The Effect of Gender Labels on Adult Response to Infants." *Sex Roles* 1, no. 2:103–109.

Shapere, Dudley. 1964. "The Structure of Scientific Revolutions." *Philosophical Review* 73:393–394.

Sheridan, Alan. 1980. *Michel Foucault: The Will to Truth*. London: Tavistock.

Simons, Elwyn. 1968a. "New Fossil Primates: A Review." In *Persepctives on Human Evolution*, ed. Sherwood Washburn and Phyllis Jay, pp. 41–60. New York: Holt Rinehart and Winston.

————. 1968b. "Some Fallacies in the Study of Human Phylogeny." In *Perspectives on Human Evolution*, ed. Sherwood Washburn and Phyllis Jay, pp. 18–40. New York: Holt Rinehart and Winston.

Skinner, B. F. 1971. *Beyond Freedom and Dignity*. New York: Knopf.

Slijper, Froukje. 1984. "Androgens and Gender Role Behavior in Girls with Congenital Adrenal Hyperplasia (CAH)." In *Progress in Brain Research*, vol. 61, *Sex Differences in the Brain*, ed. G. J. De Vries, J.P.C. De Bruin, H.B.M. Uylings, and M. A. Corner, pp. 417–422. Amsterdam: Elsevier Press.

Slocum, Sally. 1975. "Woman the Gatherer: Male Bias in Anthropology." In *Toward an Anthropology of Women*, ed. Rayna R. Reiter, pp. 36–50. New York: Monthly Review Press.

Sobran, Joseph. 1984. "Girls and Boys." *National Review* 36:46–48.

Spelman, Elizabeth V. 1989. *Innessential Woman: Problems of Exclusion in Feminist Thought*. Boston, MA: Beacon Press.

Sperry, Roger. 1983. *Science and Moral Priority*. New York: Columbia University Press.

Stein, Sarah Bennett. 1984. *Girls and Boys: The Limits of Nonsexist Childrearing*. New York: Scribner's.

Stimpson, Catharine. 1974. "The Androgyne and the Homosexual." *Women's Studies* 2, no. 2:237–248.

Suppes, Patrick. 1984. *Probabilistic Metaphysics*. Oxford, UK: Basil Blackwell.

Tanner, Nancy. 1981. *On Becoming Human*. Cambridge: Cambridge University Press.

————. and Adrienne Zihlman. 1976. "Women in Evolution, Part I." *Signs: Journal of Women in Culture and Society* 1, no. 3:585–608.

Taylor, Charles. 1971. "Interpretation and the Sciences of Man." *Review of Metaphysics* 75:3–51.

Taylor, Peter. 1986. "Dialectical Biology as Political Practice: Looking for More than Contradictions." In *Science as Politics*, ed. Les Davidow, pp. 81–111. London: Free Association Books.

Thomas, Keith. 1980. *Witch-Hunting, Magic and the New Philosophy*. Brighton, Sussex: Harvester Press.

van Fraassen, Bas. 1980. *The Scientific Image*. Oxford: Oxford University Press.

van Gelder, R. 1978. "The Voice of the Missing Link." In *Early Hominids of Africa*, ed. Clifford Jolly, pp. 431–449. London: Gerald Duckworth and Co., Ltd.

Van Wyck, P. H., and C. S. Geist. 1984. "Psychosocial Development of Heterosexual, Bisexual and Homosexual Behavior." *Archives of Sexual Behavior* 13, no. 6:505–544.

Wade, Michael. 1977. "An Experimental Study of Group Selection." *Evolution*. 31:134–153.

Warren, Mary Anne. 1982. "Is Androgyny the Answer to Sexual Stereotyping?" In *"Femininity," "Masculinity," and "Androgyny."* ed. Mary Vetterling-Braggin, pp. 170–186. Totowa, NJ: Littlefield Adams.

Washburn, Sherwood. 1978. "The Evolution of Man." *Scientific American* 239, no. 3:195–208.

———, and C. S. Lancaster. 1968. "The Evolution of Hunting." In *Man the Hunter*, ed. R. B. Lee and Irven DeVore, pp. 293–303. Chicago: Aldine Publishing Co.

Watson, James. 1968. *The Double Helix*. New York: Atheneum.

Weinberg, Stephen. 1977. *The First Three Minutes*. New York: Basic Books.

Weisstein, Naomi. 1971. "Psychology Constructs the Female." In *Woman in Sexist Society*, ed. Vivian Gornick and Barbara Moran, pp. 133–146. New York: Basic Books.

Weizenbaum, Joseph. 1976. *Computer Power and Human Reason*. San Francisco, CA: W. H. Freeman and Co.

Westfall, Richard. 1977. *The Construction of Modern Science*. Cambridge: Cambridge University Press.

Whalen, Richard. 1984. "Multiple Actions of Steroids and their Antagonists." *Archives of Sexual Behavior* 13, no. 5:497–502.

Whiting, B., and C. Pope-Edwards. 1973. "A Cross-Cultural Analysis of Sex Differences in the Behavior of Children Aged Three to Eleven." *Journal of Social Psychology* 91:171–188.

Williams, L. Pearce. 1966. *The Origins of Field Theory*. New York: Random House.

Williams, Walter. 1986. *The Spirit and the Flesh: Sexual Diversity in American Indian Culture*. Boston, MA: Beacon Press.

Wilson, David Sloan. 1983. "The Group Selection Controversy: History and Current Status." *Annual Review of Ecology and Systematics* 14:159–187.

Wilson, Edward O. 1975. *Sociobiology: The New Synthesis*. Cambridge, MA: Harvard University Press.

———. 1978. *On Human Nature*. Cambridge, MA: Harvard University Press; Bantam Press ed.

Wilson, James Q., and Richard Herrnstein. 1985. *Crime and Human Nature*. New York: Simon and Schuster.

Wilson, Jean D., Frederick W. George, and James E. Griffin. 1981. "The Hormonal Control of Sexual Development." *Science* 211:1278–1284.

Winch, Peter. 1958. *The Idea of a Social Science*. London: Routledge and Kegan Paul.

Witelson, Sandra. 1985. "An Exchange on 'Gender.'" *New York Review of Books* 32, no. 16:53–54.

Yoxen, Edward. 1986. *The Gene Business*. New York: Oxford University Press.

Zahar, Elie. 1973. "Why Did Einstein's Programme Supersede Lorentz's?" *British Journal for the Philosophy of Science* 24:95–123; 223–262.

Zihlman, Adrienne. 1978. "Women in Evolution, Part II." *Signs: Journal of Women in Culture and Society* 4, no. 1:4–20.

———. 1981. "Women as Shapers of the Human Adaptation." In *Woman the Gatherer*, ed. Frances Dahlberg, pp. 75–120. New Haven, CT: Yale University Press.

———. 1982. *The Human Evolution Coloring Book*. New York: Harper and Row.